MARXISM

This introductory text is a critical theory .
use of Karl Marx's ideas in media, communication, and cultural studies.

Karl Marx's ideas remain of crucial relevance, and in this short, student-friendly book, leading expert Christian Fuchs introduces Marx to the reader by discussing 15 of his key concepts and showing how they matter for understanding the digital and communicative capitalism that shapes human life in twenty-first century society. Key concepts covered include: the dialectic, materialism, commodities, capital, capitalism, labour, surplus-value, the working class, alienation, means of communication, the general intellect, ideology, socialism, communism, and class struggles.

Students taking courses in Media, Culture, and Society; Communication Theory; Media Economics; Political Communication; and Cultural Studies will find Fuchs's concise introduction an essential guide to Marx.

Christian Fuchs is a professor of media and communication studies and a critical theorist of communication and society. He is co-editor of the journal *tripleC: Communication, Capitalism & Critique* (www.triple-c.at) and author of many books, including *Communication and Capitalism: A Critical Theory*, *Rereading Marx in the Age of Digital Capitalism*, *Nationalism on the Internet: Critical Theory and Ideology in the Age of Social Media and Fake News*, *Social Media: A Critical Introduction*, *Digital Demagogue: Authoritarian Capitalism in the Age of Trump and Twitter*, *Digital Labour and Karl Marx*, and *Internet and Society: Social Theory in the Information Age*.

KEY IDEAS IN MEDIA AND CULTURAL STUDIES

The *Key Ideas in Media and Cultural Studies* series covers the main concepts, issues, debates, and controversies in contemporary media and cultural studies. Titles in the series constitute authoritative, original essays rather than literary surveys, but are also written explicitly to support undergraduate teaching. The series provides students and teachers with lively and original treatments of key topics in the field.

Cultural Policy
David Bell and Kate Oakley

Reality TV
Annette Hill

Culture
Ben Highmore

Representation
Jenny Kidd

Celebrity
Sean Redmond

Global Cultural Economy
Christiaan De Beukelaer and Kim-Marie Spence

Marxism
Christian Fuchs

For more information about this series, please visit: www.routledge.com/Key-Ideas-in-Media–Cultural-Studies/book-series/KEYIDEA

MARXISM

Karl Marx's Fifteen Key Concepts for Cultural and Communication Studies

Christian Fuchs

NEW YORK AND LONDON

First published 2020
by Routledge
52 Vanderbilt Avenue, New York, NY 10017

and by Routledge
2 Park Square, Milton Park, Abingdon, Oxon, OX14 4RN

Routledge is an imprint of the Taylor & Francis Group, an informa business

Library of Congress Cataloging-in-Publication Data
Names: Fuchs, Christian, 1976- author.
Title: Marxism : Karl Marx's fifteen key concepts for cultural and communication studies / Christian Fuchs.
Description: 1st Edition. | New York : Routledge, 2019. | Series: Key ideas in media & cultural studies | Includes bibliographical references and index.
Identifiers: LCCN 2019033746 (print) | LCCN 2019033747 (ebook) | ISBN 9780367418786 (hardback) | ISBN 9780367418779 (paperback) | ISBN 9780367816759 (ebook) | ISBN 9781000744118 (adobe pdf) | ISBN 9781000750492 (epub) | ISBN 9781000747300 (mobi)
Subjects: LCSH: Marxian economics. | Dialectical materialism. | Social conflict. | Alienation (Philosophy)
Classification: LCC HB97.5 .F823 2019 (print) | LCC HB97.5 (ebook) | DDC 335.4–dc23
LC record available at https://lccn.loc.gov/2019033746
LC ebook record available at https://lccn.loc.gov/2019033747

ISBN: 978-0-367-41878-6 (hbk)
ISBN: 978-0-367-41877-9 (pbk)
ISBN: 978-0-367-81675-9 (ebk)

Typeset in Garamond
by Swales & Willis, Exeter, Devon, UK

Contents

Figures

Tables

1

INTRODUCTION

This book is an introductory text that shows how to make use of Karl Marx's ideas in media, communication and cultural studies. Karl Marx was the key thinker of 19th-century critical theory. He influenced all critical thought that exists today. Marx analysed how capitalism and class society work and what their problems are. Given that we today live in a capitalist society, in which communication technologies have become more important, a fresh look at Marx's ideas helps us to critically understand the digital and communicative capitalism that shapes human life in 21st-century society.

This book introduces Marx to the reader by discussing 15 of his key concepts and showing how they matter for understanding communication, culture, digital technologies, the Internet, and the media. These key concepts are: the dialectic, materialism, commodities, capital, capitalism, labour, surplus-value, the working class, alienation, means of communication, the general intellect, ideology, socialism, communism, and class struggles. The introduction of these key ideas and their application to the Marxian study of communication is organised into ten chapters:

- The Dialectic (Chapter 2)
- Materialism: The Base/Superstructure Problem (Chapter 3)
- Commodities, Capital, Capitalism (Chapter 4)
- Labour and Surplus-Value (Chapter 5)
- The Working Class (Chapter 6)
- Alienation (Chapter 7)
- Means of Communication and the General Intellect (Chapter 8)
- Ideology (Chapter 9)
- Socialism and Communism (Chapter 10)
- Class Struggles (Chapter 11)

Each chapter provides key quotes by Karl Marx and discusses Marx's ideas in the context of communication, culture, and the media. This book is a critical theory toolkit on how to think critically about communication, culture, digital technologies, the Internet, and the media with the help of Karl Marx's key ideas.

At the end of each chapter, there is a list of recommended readings. I also briefly introduce each reading. For work in the classroom and seminars, I recommend that students first read and discuss my chapters. As a second step, it is feasible that students read the recommended texts. And as a third step of learning, it helps to discuss these texts in small groups of three to four students followed by a plenary discussion.

Most of this work was newly written in 2019. Some paragraphs in chapters of this volume are based on material from my 2015 Routledge book *Reading Marx in the Information Age: A Media and Communication Studies Perspective on "Capital Volume 1"* that provides a chapter-by-chapter introduction to Marx's opus magnum *Capital*.

Quotes from Marx are taken from *Marx & Engels Collected Works* (abbreviated as *MECW*), a 50-volume edition of Karl Marx and Friedrich Engels's works. Some of these writings were originally in English, but most were written in German, which is why this edition contains many translations. For some key books, there are better English translations available than those in *MECW*. Therefore, quotes from *Capital Volume 1*, *Capital Volume 2*, *Capital Volume 3* as well as *Grundrisse: Foundations of the Critique of Political Economy* are taken from the Penguin editions. The sources of quotes are indicated in footnotes. In some cases, I go back to Marx's original German writings using the *Marx Engels Werke* (abbreviated as *MEW*), a 44-volume German edition.

2

THE DIALECTIC

2.1 INTRODUCTION

Marx's approach to the analysis of society uses the dialectic as a way of thinking and a method of analysis. The dialectic in the form that Marx uses it goes back to Georg Wilhelm Friedrich Hegel's dialectical philosophy. Marx developed this approach and applied it to the analysis in capitalism.

This chapter introduces dialectical thinking (Section 2.2) and outlines some aspects of its relevance for the analysis of communication, culture, and the media (Section 2.3).

2.2 THE NOTION OF THE DIALECTIC

Hegel

Georg Wilhelm Friedrich Hegel was a German philosopher who lived from 1770 until 1831. Karl Marx was born in 1818 and was heavily influenced by Hegel's philosophy. Marx applied Hegel's ideas to the analysis of capitalism and as an intellectual tool of critique in struggles for a communist society, where humans control the economy and the political system in common. Because they had left-wing political goals, some followers of Hegel, including Marx and Ludwig Feuerbach (1804–1872), were called Left Hegelians.

Hegel's most important concept is the dialectic. In his book *The Encyclopaedia Logic*,[1] Hegel gives a systematic overview of the foundations of dialectical philosophy. By the dialectic he means that the world is contradictory: Phenomena are not isolated, but stand in contradiction to each other. Hegel also says that they "negate" each other or that two contradictory phenomena attract and repulse each other.

The dialectic involves several dimensions:

- *Relations*: The world and its phenomena are relational.
- *Contradiction*: Two phenomena contradict each other. They are at the same time identical and different.
- *Movement*: The tension between phenomena results in changes of the world or what Hegel calls "movement".
- *Points of change*: At certain points of time, the contradictions between two phenomena might be "sublated", which means that something new emerges from the contradiction.
- *Sublation*: "Sublation" is the English translation of the German term *Aufhebung* that has three meanings: To eliminate, to preserve, to lift something up. For Hegel, sublation means that a contradiction is eliminated, but at the same time preserved at a new level of organisation and in a new phenomenon. The old status is lifted to a new level, where new qualities are present.
- *Dynamics*: A new phenomenon again stands in contradiction to another phenomenon so that one contradiction leads through sublation to new contradictions. The world develops through contradictions. For Hegel, the world is dynamic, relational, and holds potentials for change that are realised through sublation processes. Hegel expresses this endless change of the world in the following words: "Something becomes an other, but the other is itself a something, so it likewise becomes an other, and so on ad infinitum".[2]

An example of the dialectic is the relationship of the individual and groups: No human being can live alone. If we were completely isolated, we would not be able to survive and would either die from lonesomeness and depression or from not mastering complexities of life such as organising food and shelter, etc. Each individual depends on other individuals, such as friends and family members. But each individual is also a separate human being with its own identity. Humans depend on and are different from each other. The dialectical contradiction of humanity is one between individuals that form groups. The individual is part of the group, the group consists of individuals. Each individual is more than the sum of the groups it belongs to. Each group is more than the sum of its individuals. The dialectic of humanity means that humans live in and through social relations. But such relations are not fixed. From time to time, they are sublated, which means that old relations and groups vanish and new ones emerge. An example is that a child is born, which creates a new relation between the family members and the child.

Marx

Karl Marx employs a materialist interpretation of Hegel's dialectical method for the analysis of capitalism. Dialectical analysis identifies and studies how contradictions between two dimensions of reality work, how two phenomena are identical and different at the same time, how they exclude and require each other mutually, how such contradictions result in crisis and struggles, and how contradictions are sublated, and so give rise to new systems. According to Marx, the dialectic

> includes in its positive understanding of what exists a simultaneous recognition of its negation, its inevitable destruction; because it regards every historically developed form as being in a fluid state, in motion, and therefore grasps its transient aspects as well; and because it does not let itself be impressed by anything, being in its very essence critical and revolutionary.[3]

The dialectic has for Marx an objective-structural dimension and an aspect of subjective agency/class struggle. Marx identifies structural contradictions of capitalism, capitalism's objectivity, that result in crisis: "The fact that the movement of capitalist society is full of contradictions impresses itself most strikingly on the practical bourgeois in the changes of the periodic cycle through which modern industry passes, the summit of which is the general crisis".[4] For Marx, crises of capitalism and class struggle are two important dialectical phenomena of the class society we live in. Crises are an expression of capitalism's objective dialectic. Class struggles are manifestations of capitalism's subjective dialectic or what Marx also terms praxis, being the collective action of humans that is directed against exploitation and domination.

The dialectic's subjective side has for Marx to do with class struggles that question capitalist interests. He points out that his work is not just an analysis of how capitalism works and of its objective contradictions, but also a revolutionary theory that sides with the interests of the working class and wants to provide intellectual means of class struggle against capitalism: "In so far as such a critique represents a class, it can only represent the class whose historical task is the overthrow of the capitalist mode of production and the final abolition of all classes – the proletariat".[5]

For Marx, the dialectic of capitalism is one between the ruling capitalist class that owns capital and the means of production, and the working class that does not own significant wealth. The working class is compelled to work for the capitalist class and produce goods that the latter owns. If its members do not work, then they will starve. The class antagonism is one between the wealth of the ruling class and the poverty of the exploited class. Marx formulates this dialectic of capitalists' ownership of capital and workers' non-ownership most powerfully in his work *Grundrisse* as the concept of the working class' poverty:

> Separation of property from labour appears as the necessary law of this exchange between capital and labour. Labour posited as not-capital as such is: (1) not-objectified labour [*nicht-vergegenständlichte Arbeit*], conceived negatively (itself still objective; the not-objective itself in objective form). As such it is not-raw material, not-instrument of labour, not-raw-

> product: labour separated from all means and objects of labour, from its entire objectivity. This living labour, existing as an abstraction from these moments of its actual reality (also, not-value); this complete denudation, purely subjective existence of labour, stripped of all objectivity. Labour as absolute poverty: poverty not as shortage, but as total exclusion of objective wealth. Or also as the existing not-value, and hence purely objective use value, existing without mediation, this objectivity can only be an objectivity not separated from the person: only an objectivity coinciding with his immediate bodily existence. Since the objectivity is purely immediate, it is just as much direct not-objectivity. In other words, not an objectivity which falls outside the immediate presence [*Dasein*] of the individual himself. (2) Not-objectified labour, not-value, conceived positively, or as a negativity in relation to itself, is the not-objectified, hence non-objective, i.e. subjective existence of labour itself. Labour not as an object, but as activity; not as itself value, but as the living source of value. [Namely, it is] general wealth (in contrast to capital in which it exists objectively, as reality) as the general possibility of the same, which proves itself as such in action. Thus, it is not at all contradictory, or, rather, the in-every-way mutually contradictory statements that labour is absolute poverty as object, on one side, and is, on the other side, the general possibility of wealth as subject and as activity, are reciprocally determined and follow from the essence of labour, such as it is presupposed by capital as its contradiction and as its contradictory being, and such as it, in turn, presupposes capital.[6]

For Marx, "absolute poverty" = "total exclusion of objective wealth"[7] (Marx 1857/1858, 296). The working class is excluded from wealth: It does not own the goods that it produces. These commodities are capital and therefore the private property of capitalists. But at the same time, Marx points out that this poverty of the working class's labour is not just "absolute poverty as object", but also "the general possibility of wealth as subject and as activity".[8] Capital's wealth is the working class's poverty. Every capital accumulation process deepens the working class's absolute poverty, but also constitutes its power to overthrow capital because capital is dependent on exploiting labour and labour can in collective action refuse its exploitation and bring accumulation to a standstill.

2.3 THE DIALECTIC IN MEDIA/COMMUNICATION STUDIES AND CULTURAL ANALYSIS

The Communication Process as the Dialectic of Subject and Object

The world can, based on dialectical philosophy, be explained as a dialectic of subject and object. In any system, there is a subject that interacts with another subject that is an object for it. For the object, the subject is an object. This dialectic constitutes a contradiction between subject and object from which new qualities (a subject-object) or new systems can emerge when the contradiction is sublated. Take the example of human communication: A human subject S_1 communicates information to another human being S_2. S_2 is S_1's object because the symbols communicated by S_1 result in some interpretation of it by S_2. S_2 gives meaning to it, which means that the cognitive patterns in his/her brain change. S_1's information has been objectified in S_2. If S_2 responds to S_1, then S_2 is the subject and S_1 the object who interprets the communicated information. The subject is at the same time an object and the object a subject. New qualities and systems can emerge from this contradictory relation. If two people communicate long enough, they may find out that they have joint interests and so a new social system such as a friendship or a hobby group or a professional organisation may emerge. Conversely, they may find out they really hate each other; that they compete and want to harm each other. Such a competitive relationship is also an emergent quality, albeit a negative one, in which that which emerges may be the destruction of existing qualities. If two nations go to war, they interact as subjects and objects. Their bombings result in the emergence of something – this something is, however, a destruction of what exists. The emergence then is an immergence, a disappearance of that which exists.

Figure 2.1 visualises the communication process as a dialectic of subject and object. In communication, humans produce and reproduce social relations, social structures, social systems, and society. Communication is the production process of human

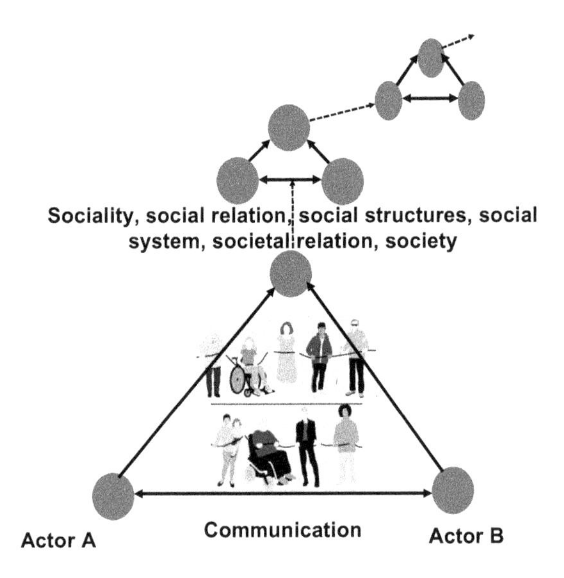

Figure 2.1 Communication as the dialectic of subject and object in society

sociality. In communication, humans relate to each other via symbols that their bodies and minds create and that signify certain phenomena. Communication is the mutual symbolic interaction process between at least two human beings through which sociality is produced and reproduced. Without communication there can be no society just like there can be no society without food, shelter, friendship, and co-operative work, etc.

The Dialectic as Critical Mode of Thinking

The dialectic is a helpful tool for thinking critically about media, culture, and communication. Whenever we are confronted with a communication or cultural phenomenon, we can, based on the dialectic, ask a series of critical questions in order to better understand the role these phenomena play in society:

- *Relations*: What social relations between humans are we confronted with in a certain communication or cultural phenomenon?
- *Contradiction*: Can we observe a power relationship between humans, a relationship in which one group exploits, coerces, or dominates another one? What are the causes of this power relationship? Who benefits from it? Who has disadvantages from it? How is this power relationship communicated or not communicated?
- *Movement*: What changes and crises in society have conditioned the emergence of the power relationship? How are the causes of the power relationships that frame the studied phenomenon communicated in public? If there is silence about it (no public communication), why is this the case?
- *Points of change*: What has to happen so that social struggles emerge that sublate the power relationship and the injustices it causes? How can the need for change best be communicated to the public?
- *Sublation*: What could a sublation of the power relationship and its communicative dimension look like? What alternatives are there that benefit all affected humans? How can these alternatives best be reached?
- *Dynamics*: Is there the danger, if an old power relationship disappears, that new power relations and inequalities emerge? What are the communicative dimensions of these power relations? How can the turn from one inequality into another be prevented?

Let us discuss a concrete example. On 23 August 2016, the largest British tabloid *The Sun* ran the following story in its online version (excerpt):

> 16 EVERY DAY: 18,000 illegal immigrants caught working in Britain in just three years ... but only A THIRD are kicked out
>
> The shocking stats equate to 16 immigrants entering Britain every day with only one in three eventually being deported.
>
> NEARLY 18,000 illegal immigrants have been caught working in Britain over the past three years – equivalent to 16 every day. In the

> latest sign of Britain's woeful border controls, The Sun can reveal immigration officers discovered 4,863 alone last year. [...] A Home Office spokesman said: 'Illegal working cheats the taxpayer, undercuts honest employers and means legitimate job seekers are denied employment opportunities'.[9]

Let us analyse this story in a dialectical manner:

- *Relations*: *The Sun* is known as a right-wing newspaper. The story constructs a nationalist stereotype by implying there is a problematic relationship between British citizens and immigrants.
- *Contradiction*: The story claims there is a contradiction between British workers and illegal migrants. The latter are said to harm "honest employers" and to be the cause of unemployment ("legitimate job seekers are denied employment opportunities"). The part of the story that is missing is that migrant workers are often very low-paid and often more exploited than British workers. Capital exploits both British and immigrant workers by all means possible.
- *Movement*: The causes of xenophobia and nationalism are ideological. Both are ideologies that distract attention from the real power relations that underpin society's problems. Tabloid media and right-wing politicians who scapegoat migrants for society's problems conceal society's class and power structures.
- *Points of change*: Xenophobic news stories can only disappear if xenophobia disappears. We require anti-racist and anti-capitalist struggles for overcoming this ideology. News stories that scapegoat need to be publicly called out as being xenophobic.
- *Sublation*: Alternatives are news media that report about the benefits that migration has brought to society. Alternative media are ways of challenging biased mainstream media.
- *Dynamics*: If we manage to create a society without or with low levels of xenophobia, then there is no guarantee that at certain points in time new forms of xenophobia will not emerge and be publicly communicated.

The Dialectic as Dialectic of Communication Technology and Society

Technological determinism is a logic of argumentation that claims that technology is the sole or main cause of certain changes in society. It is an undialectical, instrumental logic because it leaves out how society's antagonisms, i.e. its power and class relations, shape the way technology operates in society. Technological optimism is a form of technological determinism that claims that technology only has positive consequences in society. Technological pessimism is a form of determinism that argues that technology's consequences are only positive.

Here are some examples of technological determinism:

- "Television is making us stupid".
- "The Internet is the cause of unemployment and precarious labour".
- "The rise of the mobile phone has created a society where humans no longer talk to each other, but just stare at their screens".
- "The Internet has resulted in economic growth through entrepreneurial spirit".
- "The Internet will renew democracy".

The first three claims are forms of technological pessimism, the latter two are examples of technological optimism. The problem with all of these claims is that technologies as such do not act and cause something. They are designed and used by human beings, which means that contemporary society's power and class structures shape technologies. In an antagonistic society, technologies often have antagonistic potential. They do not just mediate one type of action, but potentially have multiple, contradictory effects. Technologies do not necessarily or automatically result in stupidity, unemployment, isolation, economic growth, or democracy. If, when, and to what degree such social phenomena emerge depends on social relations and society's contradictions, not on technologies. Technological determinism "dehumanises" society by claiming that technologies are actors that are independent and operate autonomously from social relations.

The dialectic of technology and society is an alternative logic that challenges technological determinism. It is based on the following assumptions:

- Mutual shaping: Society shapes and influences technology, technology shapes and influences technology.
- Technology stands in the context of society: In class societies, technologies have antagonistic potentials. They can have both positive and negative consequences. What consequences prevail depends on the result of social struggles that shape the design, use and political regulation (policies) of technology.
- Contradictions of society, contradictions of technology: There are often multiple, contradictory potential or actual effects of technologies in society. And there are often multiple contradictions that shape the character of technologies.
- Social struggles over technologies: Struggles over technologies (including communication technologies) are part of society's power struggles. They are part of struggles over the question of whether only a class of humans benefits at the expense of others or whether all humans benefit and lead good lives.

Here are some examples of dialectical statements about technology:

- "What programmes are broadcast on television is a question of economic, political, and cultural power. What intellectual implications television has for its viewers depends on the structure of society".
- "The Internet is embedded into the class contradiction between capital and labour. Capital uses it as a means for establishing new forms of exploitation. The Internet can also be designed and used in socialist manners so that it advances the co-operative ownership of resources and means of production".
- "Communication technologies such as phone apps can be designed in different ways that increasingly advance or limit human communication over the phone".

- "Class struggles over the question of who controls wealth are today also manifested on the Internet".
- "The Internet as such does not automatically harm or automatically strengthen democracy. The status of politics and democracy depends on power structures that in contemporary society also shape the structure and use of the Internet in political life".

In media/communication studies and cultural analysis, one is again and again confronted with technological determinism. It is the task of critical media, communication and cultural studies to challenge and question such claims. Let us consider three examples from media and communication theory:

- Marshall McLuhan writes that "print causes nationalism".[10] He also says that print technologies "created individualism and nationalism".[11] In contrast, he sees electronic technologies such as television as having very positive effects: "But certainly the electro-magnetic discoveries have recreated the simultaneous 'field' in all human affairs so that the human family now exists under conditions of a 'global village'".[12]
- Friedrich Kittler: "Media determine our situation".[13]
- Martin Heidegger: Newspapers and magazines "set public opinion to swallowing what is printed, so that a set configuration of opinion becomes available on demand".[14] "But we do not yet hear, we whose hearing and seeing are perishing through radio and film under the rule of technology".[15]

Marshall McLuhan (1911–1980) was a Canadian media theorist. Friedrich Kittler (1943–2011) was a literary and media theorist from Germany. Martin Heidegger (1889–1976) was a German philosopher. All three were conservative thinkers. The example quotes show that these three thinkers' writings about media and technology contain elements of technological determinism.

Technology is said to do something: "print causes", "print created", electronic media "have recreated", "media determine", newspapers and magazines "set public opinion", "hearing and seeing are perishing through radio and film". Technology is presented as the source of certain social phenomena. The Heidegger quotes are examples of technological pessimism. The first McLuhan quote is a form of technological pessimism, the second one a form of technological optimism. All of these claims abstract from how capitalism, class, class struggles, domination, and inequalities frame technologies, their design and use.

Raymond Williams (1921–1988) was a Marxist cultural, literary, media, and social theorist. He was critical of technological determinists. For example, in his book *Television* he criticises Marshall McLuhan's media theory:

> Here, characteristically – and as explicit ratification of particular uses – there is an apparent sophistication in just the critical area of cause and effect which we have been discussing. It is an apparently sophisticated technological determinism which has the significant effect of indicating a social and cultural determinism: a determinism, that is to say, which ratifies the society and culture we now have, and especially its most powerful internal directions. For if the medium – whether print or television – is the cause, all other causes, all that men ordinarily see as history, are at once reduced to effects. Similarly, what are elsewhere seen as effects, and as such subject to social, cultural, psychological and moral questioning, are excluded as irrelevant by comparison with the direct physiological and therefore "psychic" effects of the media as such. The initial formulation – "the medium is the message" – was a simple formalism. The subsequent formulation – "the medium is the massage" – is a direct and functioning ideology. [...] But it is then interesting that from this wholly unhistorical and asocial base McLuhan projects certain images of society: "retribalisation" by the "electronic age"; the "global village". As descriptions of any observable social state or tendency, in the period in which electronic media have been dominant, these are so ludicrous as to raise a further question. The physical fact of instant transmission, as a technical possibility, has been uncritically raised to a social fact, without any pause to notice that virtually all such transmission is at once selected and controlled by existing social authorities. [...] The particular rhetoric of McLuhan's theory of communications is unlikely to last long. But it is significant mainly as an example of an ideological representation of technology as a cause, and in this sense it will have

successors, as particular formulations lose their force. What has to be seen, by contrast, is the radically different position in which technology, including communication technology, and specifically television, is at once an intention and an effect of a particular social order.[16]

2.4 CONCLUSION

Marx's dialectical analysis is an application of Hegel's theory for the critique of capitalism and class society. The dialectic allows a complex, relational, dynamic analysis of the world.

In media and communication studies and cultural analysis, the dialectic allows us to understand communication as a subject/object dialectic, to ask critical questions about and conduct critical analyses of communication, culture and the media; and to challenge technological determinism by the dialectic of technology and society.

Recommended Further Readings about The Dialectic

Herbert Marcuse. 1941/2000. *Reason and Revolution: Hegel and the Rise of Social Theory*. London: Routlege.

This book is a well-written introduction to Hegel's philosophy. Chapters I.4, I.5, I.6 and I.7 in Part II introduce how Marx makes use of Hegel (I.4: Marx: Alienated Labor, I.5: The Abolition of Labor, I.6: The Analysis of the Labor Process, I.7: The Marxian Dialectic).

Bertell Ollman. 2003. *Dance of the Dialectic. Steps in Marx's Method.* Urbana, IL: University of Illinois Press.

In this book, Bertell Ollman provides a comprehensive introduction to Marx's dialectical method. Ollman uses the metaphor of a dance for the dialectic.

Christian Fuchs. 2014. The Dialectic: Not just the Absolute Recoil, but the World's Living Fire that Extinguishes and Kindles Itself. Reflections on Slavoj Žižek's Version of Dialectical Philosophy in "Absolute Recoil: Towards a New Foundation of Dialectical Materialism". *tripleC: Communication, Capitalism & Critique* 12(2): 848–875.

In his book *Absolute Recoil: Towards a New Foundation of Dialectical Materialism* (2014, London: Verso), Slavoj Žižek updates dialectical materialism. This article is a comment on Žižek's approach and introduces some key aspects of Marxist dialectical philosophy.

Notes

1 Georg Wilhelm Friedrich Hegel. 1830/1991. *The Encyclopaedia Logic (with the Zusätze). Part I of the Encyclopaedia of the Philosophical Sciences with the Zusätze.* Indianapolis, IN: Hackett.
2 Ibid., §93.
3 Karl Marx. 1867. *Capital Volume* 1. London: Penguin. p. 103.
4 Ibid., p. 103.
5 Ibid., p. 98.
6 Karl Marx. 1857/1858. *Grundrisse: Foundations of the Critique of Political Economy.* London: Penguin. pp. 295–296.
7 Ibid., p. 296.
8 Ibid., p. 296.
9 The Sun Online, available on www.thesun.co.uk/news/1661782/18000-illegal-immigrants-caught-working-in-britain-in-just-three-years-but-only-a-third-are-kicked-out
10 Marshall McLuhan. 1997. The Gutenberg Galaxy. In *Essential McLuhan*, ed. Eric McLuhan and Frank Zingrone. London: Routledge. p. 141.
11 Ibid., p. 157.
12 Marshall McLuhan. 1962. *The Gutenberg Galaxy: The Making of Typographic Man.* Toronto: University of Toronto Press. p. 31.
13 Friedrich Kittler. 1999. *Gramophone, Film, Typewriter.* Stanford, CA: Stanford University Press. p. xxxix.
14 Martin Heidegger. 1977. *The Question Concernign Technology and Other Essays.* New York & London: Garland Publishing. p. 18.
15 Ibid., p. 48.
16 Raymond Williams. 1974/2003. *Television: Technology and Cultural Form.* London: Routledge. pp. 130, 131, 132.

3

MATERIALISM

THE BASE/SUPERSTRUCTURE PROBLEM

3.1 INTRODUCTION

Dialectical materialism is Marx's way of looking at the world, society, and class societies. Materialism stresses the importance of material factors in the world. Culture, communication, and the media have to do with the production, distribution, and consumption of ideas, meanings, and symbols. The question therefore arises: what role do they play in society? Materialism is a way of answering the question of what role culture and consciousness play in society. In Marxism, this question is also known as the base/superstructure problem.

This chapter introduces the foundations of materialism (Section 3.2), discusses structuralist Marxism's base/superstructure model (Section 3.3), and outlines the foundations of the approach of communicative and cultural materialism (Section 3.4).

3.2 FOUNDATIONS OF MATERIALISM

Idealism

Materialism is a philosophical worldview that is distinct from idealism. Idealism is an approach to philosophy and the world that sees spirit as the decisive aspect of the world. Aspects of spirit that idealists stress include belief, faith, religion, and the human mind on the one hand, and God(s), ghosts, angels, and other supernatural beings on the other. This means that esotericism and forms of religion that argue that the fate of humanity, individuals, and society is determined by mystical, supernatural forces that are beyond human control are forms of idealism. Marx's understanding of the world challenges such assumptions. He is critical of the claim that humans cannot change the world and therefore stresses: Humans "make their own history, but they do not make it just as they please; they do not make it under circumstances chosen by themselves, but under circumstances directly encountered, given and transmitted from the past".[1]

Marx's Materialism

For Marx, materialism means in general that it is not supernatural forces but forces that are immanent in the world itself that shape the world. In society, this means that human beings and their social relations shape how society develops. Collective human action is a power that has the potential to change society. Given that Marx is both a dialectical and a materialist thinker, he stresses that contradictions are forces of potential change in the world. In society this means that social antagonisms such as the ones between the ruling and the ruled class, the rich and the poor, or the powerful and the powerless are the sources of social change. Societies that are based on social antagonisms are societies that are shaped by domination and exploitation. From these antagonisms, again and again, social struggles erupt.

When the dominant groups win these struggles, then the dominant order is reproduced. When they lose, then the interests of the dominated groups are strengthened, which results either in compromises or in phases of revolutionary transition to a different type of society. For example, the French Revolution was a revolutionary phase through which France was transformed from a feudal society, where the aristocracy and emperors ruled, to a capitalist society, where the capitalist class rules. Marx therefore stresses that social struggles are a decisive factor in how societies and their histories develop. In *The Manifesto of the Communist Party*, Marx and Engels therefore write: "The history of all hitherto existing society is the history of class struggles".[2] In their first joint work, *The Holy Family*, Marx and Engels stress that history is no actor and does not develop in an automatic manner. History depends on human activity. Social struggles are relations between human beings, from which the history of society emerges:

> *History* does *nothing*, it 'possesses *no* immense wealth', it 'wages *no* battles'. It is *man*, real, living man who does all that, who possesses and fights; 'history' is not, as it were, a person apart, using man as a means to achieve *its own* aims; history is *nothing but* the activity of man pursuing his aims.[3]

The Foundation of Materialist Philosophy

Marx formulates the foundation of materialist philosophy in the following manner:

> "The mode of production of material life conditions the general process of social, political and intellectual life. It is not the consciousness of men that determines their existence, but their social existence that determines their consciousness".[4]
>
> Humans, "developing their material production and their material intercourse, alter, along with this their real existence, their thinking and the products of their thinking. Life is not determined by consciousness, but consciousness by life. In the first method of approach the starting-point is consciousness taken as the living

> individual; in the second method, which conforms to real life, it is the real living individuals themselves, and consciousness is considered solely as their consciousness".[5]

Marx argues that, in society, humans' social existence and life shapes their ways of thought. These formulations are primarily directed against idealist worldviews that assume that religious belief or supernatural forces determine the life of humans. Marx reminds us that it is we humans and our social relations that determine what our lives look like. Marx says explicitly that we should understand the formulations that "life is not determined by consciousness" and that consciousness does not determine human existence as meaning that "consciousness" is not "the living individual", but rather "real living individuals themselves" make "real life". What also becomes evident from these quotes is that Marx sees humans' social production processes as key factors in the development of society, which is why he stresses the role of the "mode of production", "material production" and "material intercourse" in society. In the preface to his book *Origins of the Family, Private Property, and the State*, Friedrich Engels points out the importance of social production in society:

> According to the materialist conception, the determining factor in history is, in the last resort, the production and reproduction of immediate life. But this itself is again of a twofold character. On the one hand, the production of the means of subsistence, of food, clothing and shelter and the implements required for this; on the other, the production of human beings themselves, the propagation of the species.[6]

The interesting aspect of this quote is that Engels speaks of "production and reproduction". He does not limit social production to the creation of "food, clothing and shelter", but also stresses "the production of human beings themselves", which includes housework, education, communication, sexuality, and procreation, etc. Marxist feminism speaks in this context of reproductive work, work that reproduces the human being and human work capacity.[7]

In *Feminism for the 99 Percent: A Manifesto*, Cinzia Arruzza, Tithi Bhattacharya, and Nancy Fraser argue that capitalism's "*key move was to separate the making of people from the making of profit, to assign the first job to women, and to subordinate it to the second*".[8] The three authors describe reproductive labour as the "work of people-making".[9] The sphere of social reproduction "encompasses activities that sustain human beings as embodied social beings who must not only eat and sleep but also raise their children, care for their families, and maintain their communities".[10] The realm of reproduction exists in all societies. In capitalism, the spheres of production and reproduction are split apart[11] and not just production but also reproduction is subsumed under capital. Struggles such as the ones "for universal health care and free education, for environmental justice and access to clean energy, and for housing and public transportation"[12] are struggles about the conditions of the social reproduction of humans and should therefore be practised as anti-capitalist struggles directed against capitalism.

There are two major interpretations of what it means for social production to be society's key factor. The first one goes back to Marx's *Preface to A Contribution to the Critique of Political Economy*,[13] a short text that Marx published in 1859 to a book that was an early draft of *Capital*. The second one is based on Marx's chapter "Feuerbach: Opposition of the Materialist and Idealist Outlooks"[14] in *The German Ideology*, a long manuscript that Marx and Engels wrote in 1845/1846 to clarify their own understanding of materialist philosophy.

3.3 BASE AND SUPERSTRUCTURE IN STRUCTURALIST MARXISM

Preface to a Contribution to the Critique of Political Economy

Let us first have a look at the first interpretation, the one that is based on an often-cited passage in the *Preface to A Contribution to the Critique of Political Economy*. Marx argues that "material interests" have to do with "economic questions".[15] The relevant passage reads as follows:

> In the social production of their existence, men inevitably enter into definite relations, which are independent of their will, namely relations of production appropriate to a given stage in the development of their material forces of production. The totality of these relations of production constitutes the economic structure of society, the real foundation, on which arises a legal and political superstructure and to which correspond definite forms of social consciousness. [...] The changes in the economic foundation lead sooner or later to the transformation of the whole immense superstructure. In studying such transformations it is always necessary to distinguish between the material transformation of the economic conditions of production, which can be determined with the precision of natural science, and the legal, political, religious, artistic or philosophic – in short, ideological forms in which men become conscious of this conflict and fight it out. Just as one does not judge an individual by what he thinks about himself, so one cannot judge such a period of transformation by its consciousness, but, on the contrary, this consciousness must be explained from the contradictions of material life, from the conflict existing between the social forces of production and the relations of production.[16]

The first interpretation of what social production and materialism mean is that production and social matter are the content of the economic system and that the realm of politics, culture, ideas, legal matters, belief, religion, art, philosophy – what some call social consciousness – is located as a "superstructure" outside and on top of the economic system ("the base"). This is the structuralist interpretation of Marx. It distinguishes between two separate realms, the economic structure ("the base") and the cultural and political "superstructure". The problem of this interpretation is that it has in certain forms of theory resulted in the reductionist assumption that when one knows what the economy looks like (what and how humans produce), one can deduce what the political and cultural systems look like. In such an approach, thought, communication, and consciousness are mere echoes and reflexes of the economy. Such arguments constitute a reductive, mechanistic materialism.

Louis Althusser

The French structuralist Marxist Louis Althusser (1918–1990) advanced the approach of mechanistic materialism. For Althusser, the mode of production consists of the forces and relations of production[17] that form contradictions and are the social formation's "*conditions of existence*".[18] The superstructure includes "the State, the dominant ideology, religion, politically organized movements, and so on".[19] He goes on to write: "So in every society we can posit, in forms which are sometimes very paradoxical, the existence of an economic activity as the base, a political organization and 'ideological' forms (religion, ethics, philosophy, etc.)".[20] For Althusser, the base consists of forces and relations of production[21] whereas the superstructure is made up by "the State and all the legal, political and ideological forms".[22] Althusser employs the metaphor of an edifice that has different floors for society.[23] For him, society is an edifice where the economy is the ground floor and the political and cultural systems form the upper floors. In this approach, the economy determines thinking and the products of thought. For Althusser, it is "the base which in the last instance determines the whole edifice".[24] Superstructures are in this approach "instances which derive from" the economic mode of production.[25]

The problem of Althusser's theory is that it portrays society as static. Edifices do not really change but, like buildings, they remain unchanged for a long time. Althusser overestimates and underestimates the part played by the economy in society. Separating society into a base and a superstructure ignores that the economy exists in all realms of society and all social systems in the form of human production. In Althusser's approach, human beings disappear behind structures. They do not have an active role as producers of society. Rules, political power, and ideologies need to be created and reproduced by humans. The economy operates inside of the political and the cultural system that at the same time has qualities that go beyond the economy. The political and the cultural systems have economic and non-economic aspects. And the political and the cultural also operate inside the economy in the form of economic rules and organisational philosophies. Althusser does not take into account the operation of the economic in the non-economic and of the non-economic in the economy. An example of how the non-economic operates in the economy is that of the neoliberal ideology of constant self-development, loving your job and being responsible for failures, which shapes contemporary labour. The culture industry is an example of how the economy was in the 20th century, extended to cultural aspects of society that had not taken on the form of commodities in earlier times. In the culture industry, entertainment, news, music, films, software, art, and other forms of culture take on the form of commodities. Althusser's static base/superstructure model fails to explain the complex dialectics of the economic sphere and the non-economic spheres.

In a letter written in 1890, Engels draws a clear, dualistic separation between the economic "base" and the political and cultural "superstructure". He argues that there is "the interaction of all these factors".[26] But he nonetheless relegates "political forms of the class struggle, [...] forms of law and the reflections of all these real struggles in the minds of the participants, i.e. political, philosophical and legal theories, religious views"[27] to a non-economic superstructure, which overlooks the fact that culture and politics are produced and reproduced by bureaucrats, administrators, white-collar workers, politicians, theorists, intellectuals, academics, artists, and cultural workers, etc. To speak of an interaction leaves the economic and the non-economic separate and is not dialectical enough. In a dialectic, two poles interpenetrate, overgrasp in each other, and are at the same time identical and non-identical.

3.4 COMMUNICATIVE AND CULTURAL MATERIALISM

The German Ideology's *Chapter on Feuerbach*

Communicative and cultural materialism is a second interpretation of what social production is and what dialectical materialism means for society. It takes Marx's concept of materialism as outlined in *The German Ideology*'s Feuerbach section as its starting point.

Marx argues that social production and materialism in society means that humans produce means of subsistence in social relations: Humans "begin to distinguish themselves from animals as soon as they begin to produce their means of subsistence [...] By producing their means of subsistence men are indirectly producing their actual material life".[28] In order to subsist, humans need to produce and use physical products and phenomena such as food, beverages, sleep, rest, social products such as friendships and love, individual goals such as self-fulfilment, and cultural products such as education, skills, creativity, knowledge, and communication. The implication is that culture and communication do not stand outside of material production but are material products of humans and society.

Marx writes in this context: "As individuals express their life, so they are. What they are, therefore, coincides with their production, both with *what* they produce and with *how* they produce".[29] The original German of the first sentence reads as follows: "Wie die Individuen ihr Leben äußern, so sind sie".[30] The German original of the phrase "to express" is *äußern*, the verb form of the noun *Äußerung*. *Äußerung* means both externalisation and utterance. Humans externalise ideas through communicative utterance. And they externalise bodily energy in work processes. The externalisation of bodily and mental activities always interact in each human activity. In knowledge work, mental externalisation interacts with bodily externalisation in such a way that knowledge products are created.

For Marx, consciousness emerges from social production, which means it is a social product. The mind relates to the social and natural environment with which humans interact through work and communication:

> For the animal, its relation to others does not exist as a relation. Consciousness is, therefore, from the very beginning a social product, and remains so as long as men exist at all. Consciousness is at first, of course, merely consciousness concerning the immediate sensuous environment and consciousness of the limited connection with other persons and things outside the individual who is growing self-conscious. At the same time it is consciousness of nature.[31]

That ideas and consciousness are social products means that they are part of material production:

> The production of ideas, of conceptions, of consciousness, is at first directly interwoven with the material activity and the material intercourse of men, the language of real life. Conceiving, thinking, the mental intercourse of men, appear at this stage as the direct efflux of their material behaviour. The same applies to mental production as expressed in the language of politics, laws, morality, religion, metaphysics, etc., of a people. Men are the producers of their conceptions, ideas, etc. – real, active men, as they are conditioned by a definite development of their productive forces and of the intercourse corresponding to these, up to its furthest forms.[32]

The implication of these arguments is that, for Marx, in the *The German Ideology* the production of ideas and therefore culture and communication do not stand outside the economy, but are part of the economy, although they have emergent qualities that also make them different from the economy. Culture and communication are material production processes resulting in knowledge and meaning. This approach is therefore also called communicative materialism, or cultural materialism.

In Marxist theory, there are a number of authors who represent the approach of cultural and communicative materialism. They include, for example, Raymond Williams, Georg Lukács, Erich Fromm, Horst Holzer, Lucien Goldmann, Henri Lefebvre, Herbert Marcuse, Ferruccio Rossi-Landi, and E. P. Thompson.[33] My own work also uses this approach. All of these authors, in contrast to structural Marxism, stress the importance of human beings and human production processes in society. In the remainder of this chapter, I will briefly focus on two of these approaches, the ones of Raymond Williams and Georg Lukács.

Raymond Williams's Cultural Materialism

Raymond Williams (1921–1988) was a Marxist literary, cultural, social and media theorist, and a novelist. For Williams, culture is not simply a cultural work (a novel, a painting, a movie, a piece of music, a radio broadcast, a theatre piece, etc.), but "a distinctive way of life" that includes cultural works, but also cultural "practice and behaviour" that produce, distribute, or consume cultural works.[34] Williams describes the "separation of 'culture' from material social life", as is the case in structural Marxism, as a form of philosophical idealism.[35] He says that Marx's Feuerbach chapter tells us that "language is material"[36] and an activity.[37] "'[C]onsciousness and its products' are always, though in variable forms, parts of the material social process".[38] Language and communication are, for Williams, means of production: "Signification, the social creation of meanings through the use of formal signs, is then a practical material activity: it is indeed, literally, a means of production".[39] Aspects of the materiality of culture are that sign systems are social relations, operates in groups, organisations and institutions, and is "a cultural technology and a specific form of practical consciousness".[40]

Williams responded, in an interview with *New Left Review*, to a question about the importance of culture in capitalism and the base/superstructure problem in the following way:

> NLR: *Even a bourgeois liberal will admit, on reflection, that if all novelists stopped writing for a year in England, the results would scarcely be of the same order as if all car workers halted their labour. To take a more relevant example for your argument, a complete cessation of the main communications industries – television, radio and press – would seriously affect the life of any modern capitalist society: but its effects would not be comparable to major strikes in the docks, mines or power stations. The workers in these industries have the capacity to disrupt the whole fabric of social life, so decisive is the importance of their productive activity.* [...]
>
> Raymond Williams: I would not be willing to say that at the top of the hierarchy is productive industry, then come political

> institutions or means of mass communication, and then below them the cultural activities of philosophers or novelists. Not that there wouldn't be a certain scale of that kind, but it is increasingly in the nature of modern capitalist economy that there is a slide in the first bracket from indispensable needs to the dispensable conditions of reproduction of this order or of the ability to maintain life within it, for we can imagine certain breakdowns to which human beings could make adaptations of a very difficult kind by living in different ways. The hierarchies, while in general following a line from activities which answer to basic physical needs down through to those of which you at least can state negatively that if they were not performed, human life would not be immediately threatened, are not immutable. After all, stoppages of electrical power or oil would now make life impossible in the very short term, yet it is obvious enough historically that our society didn't possess them until recently, yet life could be sustained by other methods. To take another example: there have been some estimates that over half the employed population of the United States, the most advanced capitalistic country, is now involved in various kinds of information handling and parcelling. If that were so, an information strike would call the maintenance of human life *in that social order* very quickly into question.[41]

Williams stresses that cultural work, such as work in advertising, is not superstructural or unproductive, but has become an important realm of capitalism.

Georg Lukács's Ontology of Social Being

Georg Lukács (1885–1971) was a Hungarian Marxist philosopher who became well known for his early work *History and Class Consciousness*. His final work was titled *Ontology of Social Being* and gave particular attention to the role of work and culture in society. For Lukács, materialism means that work is "the model for social being".[42] He argues that humans are goal-oriented beings, which means that they act in order to achieve defined goals. He therefore characterises work as teleological positing. It posits means in order to achieve defined goals. It involves "positing of the goal and investigation of the means".[43] In the work process, humans achieve certain goals by making use of means of production in order to transform parts of the world so that new qualities that certain satisfy human needs and certain human goals emerge. Human subjects work with objects in order to create new objects that are used by subjects in society. "Through labour, a teleological positing is realized within material being, as the rise of a new objectivity".[44]

Work requires consciousness, which means that culture operates within work: "Every teleological process involves the positing of a goal, and therefore a goal positing consciousness".[45] Human consciousness is "called into being in labour, for labour, and by labour".[46] But work also operates inside and outside the economy in every social practice. Work "becomes the model for any social practice, for in such social practice – no matter how ramified its mediations – teleological positings are always realized, and ultimately realized materially".[47] Society is the totality of all complexes of teleological positing. Teleological positing is not confined to economic production, but extends into all realms of society. This means that all non-economic realms of society are at the same time economic because they involve processes of production, and non-economic because the created phenomena have emergent qualities that go beyond the economy. There is "identity of identity and non-identity" of the economic and the non-economic.[48]

Language, communication, and culture form a particular complex of society, in which teleological positing creates understanding and meanings so that social relations can be organised. Communication and language enable the organisation of society over distance because they mediate social relationships.[49] Human language enables humans to repeat production processes at different times in different spaces.

> "In this way what is depicted by the verbal sign is separated from the objects it describes, and hence also from the subject uttering it, becoming the mental expression for an entire group of

> particular phenomena, so that it can be applied in a similar way in completely different contexts and by completely different subjects".[50]

Language and communication are a form of teleological positing that enables teleological positing,[51] a kind of meta-level of teleological positing.

3.5 CONCLUSION

Materialism asks the question of how being and consciousness and the economy and culture are related. Structuralist Marxism uses the spatial metaphor of an edifice and posits the economic as the base that determines the superstructure, to which ideas, consciousness, culture, and communication belong. The problem of this model is that it is static, mechanistic, and anti-humanist.

Cultural materialists like Williams and Lukács stress that Marx wanted to avoid, and argued against, separating ideas from matter and the economy. But orthodox and structuralist Marxists have arrived at a new separation that forgets about the dialectic, human beings, and production as social process. Cultural materialists solve the base/superstructure problem in a dialectical manner: The economic and the non-economic are identical and non-identical. Communication and culture are processes of production, which is an aspect of work, production, and the economy. At the same time communication and culture have a non-economic quality, namely that they are means for and processes of creating social relations between humans, understanding between humans (social meaning), and individual understanding and interpretation of the world (individual meaning). Cultural and communicative materialism explodes the static base/superstructure model by positing a dialectical model, in which the economy/work and culture/communication are identical and different at the same time.

Cultural and communicative materialism does not imagine society as an edifice as vulgar materialism does. Instead, it uses the metaphor of a river, where the main current is the economy from which non-economic realms such as culture and politics branch out, taking qualities of the river's main current with them but at the same time taking on new dynamics that might flow back into the river's main current (see Figure 3.1).

Figure 3.1 The river as metaphor for society

Recommended Further Readings About Materialism and the Base/Superstructure Problem

Karl Marx. 1845/46. Feuerbach: Opposition of the Materialist and Idealist Outlooks. In Karl Marx and Friedrich Engels: *The German Ideology. Critique of Modern German Philosophy According to Its Representatives Feuerbach, B. Bauer and Stirner, and of German Socialism According to Its Various Prophets. MECW Volume* 5, 27–93. London: Lawrence & Wishart.

This chapter is a key reading in the understanding of Marx's approach of dialectical materialism. It also contains some elaborations of Marx on language and the means of communication.

Christian Fuchs. 2016. Georg Lukács as a Communications Scholar: Cultural and Digital Labour in the Context of Lukács's Ontology of Social Being. *Media, Culture & Society* 38(4): 506–524.

This article shows that Georg Lukács' forgotten final book *The Ontology of Social Being* provides a dialectical approach to cultural and communicative materialism.

Raymond Williams. 1977. *Marxism and Literature*. Chapters I.1: Culture, II.1: Base and Superstructure, II.3: Productive Forces, II.10: The Sociology of Culture. Oxford: Oxford University Press.
In *Marxism and Literature*, Williams does not so much give an introduction to literary studies, but rather to his approach of cultural materialism, which is why the book would be better being called *Marxism and Culture*. These chapters discuss some foundations of cultural materialism.

Raymond Williams. 1983/1989. Marx on Culture. In *What I Came to Say*, ed. Neil Belton, Francis Mulhern and Jenny Taylor, 195–225. London: Hutchinson Radius.
This essay is a thorough discussion of some writings of Marx on culture, including the Feuerbach chapter in *The German Ideology*.

Christian Fuchs. 2017. Raymond Williams's Communicative Materialism. *European Journal of Cultural Studies* 20 (6): 744–762.
In this article, Raymond Williams's approach of cultural materialism is interpreted as a communicative materialism.

Christian Fuchs. 2019. Revisiting the Althusser/E. P. Thompson Controversy: Towards a Marxist Theory of Communication. *Communication and the Public* 4 (1): 3–20.
This article discusses the problems of Louis Althusser's structural Marxism; E. P. Thompson's humanist Marxist critique of Althusser; and the implications of both approaches for cultural materialism.

Cinzia Arruzza, Tithi Bhattacharya, and Nancy Fraser. 2019. *Feminism for the 99 Percent: A Manifesto*. London: Verso.
This book is a manifesto of an anti-capitalist feminism for the 99 percent. It criticises liberal feminism as "equal opportunity domination" and argues that the realm of social reproduction is just like production an inherent aspect of capitalism. As a consequence, struggles for a better world have to unite as an international movement against capitalism.

Notes

1. Karl Marx. 1852. The Eighteenth Brumaire of Louis Bonaparte. In *MECW Volume 1*. London: Lawrence & Wishart. pp. 99–197.
2. Karl Marx and Friedrich Engels. 1848. The Manifesto of the Communist Party. In *MECW Volume 6*. London: Lawrence & Wishart. pp. 477–519.
3. Karl Marx and Friedrich Engels. 1845. The Holy Family, or Critique of Critical Criticism. Against Bruno Bauer and Company. In *MECW Volume 4*. London: Lawrence & Wishart. p. 93.
4. Karl Marx. 1859. A Contribution to the Critique of Political Economy. In *MECW Volume 29*. London: Lawrence & Wishart. pp. 257–417.
5. Karl Marx and Friedrich Engels. 1845/46. The German Ideology. Critique of Modern German Philosophy According to Its Representatives Feuerbach, B. Bauer and Stirner, and of German Socialism According to Its Various Prophets. In *MECW Volume 5*. London: Lawrence & Wishart. pp. 15–539.
6. Friedrich Engels. 1884. The Origin of the Family, Private Property and the State. In the Light of the Researchers by Lewis H. Morgan. In *MECW Volume 26*. London: Lawrence & Wishart. pp. 129–276
7. See: Zillah Eisenstein, ed. 1979. *Capitalist Patriarchy and the Case for Socialist Feminism*. New York: Monthly Review Press. Mariarosa Dalla Costa and Selma James. 1972. *The Power of Women and the Subversion of Community*. Bristol: Falling Wall Press.
8. Cinzia Arruzza, Tithi Bhattacharya and Nancy Fraser. 2019. *Feminism for the 99 Percent: A Manifesto*. London: Verso. p. 21.
9. Ibid., p. 21.
10. Ibid., p. 68.
11. Ibid., 70.
12. Ibid., pp. 24–25.
13. Karl Marx. 1859. Preface to A Contribution to the Critique of Political Economy. In *MECW Volume 29*. London: Lawrence & Wishart. pp. 261–265.
14. Karl Marx.1845/46. Feuerbach: Opposition of the Materialist and Idealist Outlooks. In Karl Marx and Friedrich Engels: *The German Ideology. Critique of Modern German Philosophy According to Its Representatives Feuerbach, B. Bauer and Stirner, and of German Socialism According to Its Various Prophets. MECW Volume 5*. London: Lawrence & Wishart. p. 27–93.

15 Marx, Preface to A Contribution to the Critique of Political Economy, p. 262.
16 Marx, Preface to A Contribution to the Critique of Political Economy, p. 263.
17 Louis Althusser. 1965/2005. *For Marx*. London: Verso. p. 110.
18 Ibid., p. 100.
19 Ibid., p. 106.
20 Ibid., p. 232.
21 Ibid., p. 110.
22 Ibid., p. 111.
23 Louis Althusser. 1971. *Lenin and Philosophy and Other Essays*. New York: Monthly Review Press. pp. 135–136.
24 Ibid., p. 136.
25 Althusser, *For Marx*, p. 100.
26 Engels to Joseph Bloch, 21–22 September 1890. In *MECW Volume 49*. London: Lawrence & Wishart. pp. 33–37.
27 Ibid., p. 34.
28 Marx and Engels, The German Ideology, p. 31.
29 Ibid., pp. 31–32.
30 Karl Marx and Friedrich Engels. 1845/46. Die deutsche Ideologie. Kritik der neuesten deutschen Philosophie in ihren Repräsentanten Feuerbach, B. Bauer und Stirner, und des deutschen Sozialismus in seinen verschiedenen Propheten. In *MEW Band 3*. Berlin: Dietz. pp. 9–530.
31 Ibid., p. 44.
32 Marx and Engels, The German Ideology, p. 36.
33 For more detailed discussions, see:

Christian Fuchs. 2016. Georg Lukács as a Communications Scholar: Cultural and Digital Labour in the Context of Lukács' Ontology of Social Being. *Media, Culture & Society* 38 (4): 506–524.

Christian Fuchs. 2016. *Critical Theory of Communication: New Readings of Lukács, Adorno, Marcuse, Honneth and Habermas in the Age of the Internet*. London: University of Westminster Press.

Christian Fuchs. 2017. Raymond Williams' Communicative Materialism. *European Journal of Cultural Studies* 20 (6): 744–762.

Christian Fuchs. 2017. Preface: Horst Holzer's Marxist Theory of Communication [Preface to Christian Fuchs' translation of Horst Holzer's article "The Forgotten Marxist Theory of Communication & Society"]. *tripleC: Communication, Capitalism & Critique* 15 (2): 686–706.

Christian Fuchs. *2018*. Towards A Critical Theory of Communication with Georg Lukács and Lucien Goldmann. *Javnost – The Public* 25 (3): 265–281.

Christian Fuchs. 2018. Postface: Horst Holzer's "Communication & Society: A Critical Political Economy Perspective". *tripleC: Communication, Capitalism & Critique* 16 (1): 398–401.

Christian Fuchs. 2019. Henri Lefebvre's Theory of the Production of Space and the Critical Theory of Communication. *Communication Theory* 29 (2): 129–150.

Christian Fuchs. 2019. Revisiting the Althusser/E. P. Thompson Controversy: Towards a Marxist Theory of Communication. *Communication and the Public* 4 (1): 3–20.

Christian Fuchs. Erich Fromm and the Critical Theory of Communication (in preparation).

Christian Fuchs. *Communication and Capitalism: A Critical Theory.* London: University of Westminster Press (in press).

34 Raymond Williams. 1983/1989. Marx on Culture. In Raymond Williams: *What I Came to Say*, ed. Neil Belton, Francis Mulhern and Jenny Taylor. London: Hutchinson Radius. pp. 195–225.
35 Raymond Williams. 1977. *Marxism and Literature.* Oxford: Oxford University Press. p. 19.
36 Ibid., p. 29.
37 Ibid., p.31
38 Ibid., p.61.
39 Ibid., p. 38.
40 Ibid., p. 140.
41 Raymond Williams. 1979. *Politics and Letters. Interviews with New Left Review.* London: Verso. pp. 354–355.
42 Georg Lukács. 1980. *The Ontology of Social Being. 3. Labour.* London: The Merlin Press. p. v.
43 Ibid., p. 11.
44 Ibid., p. 3.
45 Ibid., p. 5.
46 Ibid., p. 52.
47 Ibid., p. 3.
48 Ibid., p. 59.
49 Ibid., pp. 99–102.
50 Ibid., p. 100.
51 Georg Lukács. 1986. *Zur Ontologie des gesellschaftlichen Seins. Zweiter Halbband Bände. Georg Lukács Werke, Band 14.* Darmstadt: Luchterhand. p. 119.

4

COMMODITIES, CAPITAL, CAPITALISM

4.1 INTRODUCTION

Marx begins his main work *Capital Volume 1* with the following famous sentence: "The wealth of societies in which the capitalist mode of production prevails appears as an 'immense collection of commodities'; the individual commodity appears as its elementary form".[1] Marx also, in the preface to the first edition of *Capital Volume 1*, argues that "for bourgeois society, the commodity-form of the product of labour, or the value-form of the commodity, is the economic cell-form".[2]

A commodity is a good that a company sells on a market in order to achieve a monetary profit, which is a sum of money that goes beyond the investment costs. In order to understand capitalism, one needs to understand the commodity form and how commodities are produced, distributed, and consumed. This is the task of political economy. What makes political economy a "critical political economy" or "critique of the political economy" is that such an approach sets out to understand and outline how capitalism and class societies in general create crises, inequalities, are based on social antagonisms, and create the objective need for an alternative framework of society, a socialist society, where there is wealth for all and political decisions are made in a participatory manner so that everyone benefits.

The task of this chapter is to look at the logic of commodities and capital as outlined by Marx. Section 4.2 focuses on commodities, Section 4.3 on cultural commodities, Section 4.4 on capitalism, and Section 4.5 on cultural and digital capitalism.

4.2 COMMODITIES

Chapter 1.1 in Marx's *Capital Volume 1* analyses the commodity's dimensions: A commodity has a qualitative aspect (use-value) and a quantitative one (exchange-value). "The commodity is, first of all, an external object, a thing which through its qualities satisfies human needs of whatever kind. The nature of these needs, whether they arise, for example, from the stomach, or the imagination, makes no difference".[3] "The usefulness of a thing makes it a use-value".[4] Use-values "constitute the material content of wealth".[5]

"Exchange-value appears first of all as the quantitative relation, the proportion, in which use-values of one kind exchange for use-values of another kind".[6] If something is a commodity, then one can only get hold of it if one exchanges something else for it. A quantitative exchange relationship mediates how people obtain use-values: x commodity A = y commodity B. In the commodity form, use-value is subordinated to exchange-value. You cannot obtain a commodified use-value without entering a quantitative exchange relationship. Exchange-value is the quantitative side of the commodity.

Commodities have the "same phantom-like objectivity", "human labour is accumulated in them".[7] Here Marx introduces a third term that characterises the "common factor in the exchange relation"[8]: value. "A use-value, or useful article, therefore, has value only because abstract human labour is objectified or materialized in it".[9] Exchange-value is the form of appearance of value.[10] Labour is the substance of value.[11] Value's measure or magnitude is labour-time:

> How, then, is the magnitude of this value to be measured? By means of the quantity of the 'value-forming substance', the labour, contained in the article. This quantity is measured by its duration, and the labour-time is itself measured on the particular scale of hours, days etc.[12]

A commodity has an individual value, a specific number of minutes it takes to produce it. To tap a pint of beer sometimes takes a minute, sometimes just half a minute. Writing a new song takes an artist sometimes an hour, sometimes a month. Marx says that the average production time is a decisive economic phenomenon that shapes how well a company can survive in the economy. Marx speaks in this context of socially necessary labour-time, the average time it takes to produce a specific commodity: "Socially necessary labour-time is the labour-time required to produce any use-value under the conditions of production normal for a given society and with the average degree of skill and intensity of labour prevalent in that society".[13] Value has an individual and a social dimension. What is decisive is the average kind of commodity – "the average sample of its kind"[14] that is produced in a typical, average amount of minutes. Marx's labour theory of value is a theory of time in capitalism. It argues that labour-time is a key resource in capitalism and that the value of a commodity is the higher the more average labour-time is expended in its production.

As different as a song and a beer may be as use-values, if on average it takes 2 minutes to write a song and 2 minutes to produce and tap a pint of beer, then the song and the pint "have therefore the same value" because they "contain equal quantities of labour"[15] (130). In reality we know that on average it takes longer to write a song than to tap a pint of beer.

4.3 CULTURAL COMMODITIES

Use-Value, Exchange-Value, Value

For Marx, a use-value is something that satisfies human needs. He says that these needs can arise from the stomach or from imagination.[16] With this formulation he indicates that use-values are not just physical things that we can touch and feel, such as food that satisfies the need of nourishment, and intangible products of the human mind – information that satisfies the need of humans to understand the world and each other. It is not only physical goods such as food, coffee, carbon, bricks, air, soil, meadows, or forests that are use-values. Cultural goods that have an informational character, are primarily consumed with the help of the human mind, and foster communication, are use-values too. Examples of cultural use-values are: books, computer games, concerts, educational courses, Internet websites, newspapers, magazines, mobile phone applications, movies, online communities, operating systems, phone calls, radio programmes, software, songs, television programmes, and theatre plays, etc. For Marx, use-values constitute the material content of wealth.[17] The logical implication is that information and culture are material and constitutes parts of the material content of human wealth.

Information's Use-Value

Information is a use-value with peculiar characteristics:[18] it is not used up in consumption, it is not scarce, can be easily, cheaply and endlessly shared and copied, and it can be used simultaneously by many people. Drinking a pint of beer uses up the beer, so another person cannot drink it. Listening to a song does not use up the music. Others can still consume it without the artist having to re-record it. Creating the prototype, first edition, or first exemplar of a piece of information is labour intensive and often expensive. The "sunk cost rule" says that the initial production costs and labour-times of information are high: large costs are sunk into information. At the same time, it is uncertain whether there is a big demand for a specific kind of information and whether people will be interested in it. Information commodities are therefore a high-risk good. This is the "nobody knows anything" rule of information. Cultural corporations try to offset this risk by creating large varieties of cultural commodities. A record label or publishing house may, for example, produce 1,000 new albums or publish 1,000 new books a year. Only five of them may become "hits", which may suffice in making the company profitable. This is the "hit rule" of information. Another strategy is that media companies window their products to different channels: There is a different price for seeing a movie in a movie theatre, downloading it on iTunes, buying a DVD, or watching it on TV.

The theory of public goods considers information to be a public good because of its non-rival and non-excludable consumption.[19] The song is not used up in consumption like the beer. Humans are not rivals in the consumption of a song. If there is just one bottle of beer in the world, then the owner of this bottle can easily exclude others from drinking beer. Given that songs can easily be copied and shared, it is much more difficult to exclude others from listening to a song. Even if there are just two copies of one song, the owner of one of these copies may make 100 copies and distribute them to ten friends, who again distribute copies to ten friends, etc. The second person wanting to keep the song limited in reach will therefore not be able to exclude others from consumption. The theory of public goods points out important features of culture. But it is false to use the terminology of a public or common good for culture, knowledge, and information because such a move abstracts from class relations. Almost any good and service can be turned into a commodity. Public and common goods are not commodities created by means of production that are privately owned, but are available to all and created by means of production that are publicly owned by the state or a municipality or commonly owned by self-managed corporations, where workers own the means of production collectively.

The theory of public goods poses the danger of naturalising physical goods as commodities and cultural goods as not subsumable under the commodity form. In what Marx terms a communist society, most goods are available to all. They are common goods. There are no commodities in communism.

Information and culture are more difficult to subsume under the commodity form than physical goods. But there are special strategies for accumulating capital in the culture industry. These include monopolies that control the distribution of information, legal mechanisms such as copyrights and intellectual property rights, advertising that sells audiences to advertisers and provides information without payment to audiences, the re-formatting of information onto new channels or into new media formats that allow re-selling, charging for access to distribution channels, the constant updating of information so that re-consumption is required to stay up-to-date (e.g. news changes constantly; you are not happy to just watch the 1962 James Bond movie *Dr. No*, you also want to see later ones and the latest one; the obsolescence of media products – you do not and probably cannot use MS Word 1.0 because you do not have a computer and operating system that supports it but, rather, you use a newer version).

A Typology of Public Forms of Communication

Table 4.1 shows an overview of major forms of public communication and some of their characteristics.

What all of the forms of communication shown in Table 4.1 have in common is that they are public, i.e. accessible to a relatively large audience. The term culture is sometimes used in a narrow sense for public forms of communication that are live and performed face-to-face, such as theatre performances, concerts, or dances. But all forms of public communication create and distribute meanings and result in an audience's construction of meanings in everyday life. Therefore, all forms of public communication are forms of culture. All forms of public communication make use of the human mind and the human body (such as the sense organs). Mediated forms of communication make use of communication technologies for the production, distribution, and consumption of technologies. For example, a news show is produced in a television studio and live-screened by making use of broadcast technologies. Audiences watch it on their television screens, mobile phones, or computers.

There are broadcast, distribution, and consumption technologies involved in audio-visual media. In traditional media, the technological means of production and distribution are different from the technological means of consumption. In digital

Table 4.1 A typology of forms of public communication/culture

Form of communication	*Means of production*	*Means of consumption*	*Time and space*	*Examples*
Face-to-face culture	Body, brain, mouth, ears	Brain, ears, eyes, body (applause, bodily gestures of agreement or disagreement)	Synchronous, face-to-face, in the same place at the same time	Theatre, concerts, speeches, public debates, artistic live performances
Written communication	Brain, hands, technologies	Eyes, brain, technologies	Asynchronous, producer and consumer are in different places, texts are read later than they are written	Books, newspapers, magazines, letters to the editor
Oral communication	Brain, mouth, technologies	Ears, brain, technologies	Synchronous or asynchronous	Synchronous: live radio/audio broadcast Asynchronous: recorded radio programmes, recorded music
Visual communication	Brain, body, technologies	Eyes, brain, technologies	Asynchronous	Photographs, visual artworks, exhibitions, photo books, visual art books, charts, graphs, illustrations, drawings, paintings, maps,

				silent films, silent animations, posters, advertising posters, etc.
Audio-visual communication	Brain, body, mouth, technologies	Ears, eyes, brain, technologies	Synchronous or asynchronous	Synchronous: live television broadcasts (e.g. news, debates, etc.). Asynchronous: films broadcast on television or shown in the cinema, television news, television ads, entertainment programmes, audio-visual animations
Digital communication	Brain, body, eyes, ears, mouth, converging digital technologies	Brain, body, eyes, ears, mouth, converging digital technologies	Convergence of face-to-face, written, oral, visual and audio-visual communication, synchronous or asynchronous	Synchronous digital communication: live Internet radio or television, text-based chat rooms, voice over IP, video chat. Asynchronous digital communication: podcasts,

(Continued)

Table 4.1 (Cont.)

Form of communication	*Means of production*	*Means of consumption*	*Time and space*	*Examples*
				blogs, video blogs, pictures, postings, comments, and videos uploaded to social media and user-generated content sites, audio, and video streaming services, electronic books, online newspapers

communication, the networked computer is a converging technology that: (a) results in the convergence of the production, distribution and consumption in one digital technology, and (b) results in the convergence of live communication, written communication, oral communication, visual communication, and audio-visual communication through the digitisation of information and the use of digital platforms that support multiple modes of communication. For example, social networking sites such as Facebook allow the upload of images, written text, videos, and written comments. The traditional hierarchy between producers and consumers of information is sublated on networked digital media. Consumers have the potential to act as producers (so-called prosumers, short for producing consumers). When culture takes place in a synchronous manner, then humans produce and consume information live at the same point of time. They can do so in the same place or with the help of communication technologies over a distance. In asynchronous communication, the production of information takes place at a different point of time than its reception.

A Typology of Cultural Commodities in the Culture Industry

Capitalist media, culture and organisations organise the forms of communication shown in Table 4.1 based on the logic of the commodity in order to yield monetary profits. Table 4.2 shows a typology of cultural commodities.

The Culture Industry

In "The Culture Industry: Enlightenment as Mass Deception" in the book *Dialectic of Englightenment*, the philosophers Max Horkheimer and Theodor W. Adorno introduce the notion of the culture industry.[20] In the 20th century, culture became commodified; it became a realm of commodity production, commodity sale, and consumer culture. The culture industry is the sphere of "the total assimilation of culture products into the commodity sphere".[21] The exchange-value of culture that yields profit for cultural corporations became dominant over cultural use-values:

Table 4.2 A typology of cultural commodities in the culture industry

Cultural commodity type	*Exchange-value*	*Use-value*	*Value*	*Examples*
Cultural labour-power	Wage-labour: cultural workers sell their labour-power to cultural corporations in order to earn a living. In exchange for achieving a wage, they help creating cultural products that the companies sell as commodities	Creation and distribution of meanings and ideas	The average value of cultural labour-power is the average number of hours of reproductive labour that it takes to create its means of subsistence	Artists, musicians, journalists, designers, software engineers, actors, dancers, presenters, technicians, printers, etc.
Access to cultural events	Audience members pay a one-time fee for access to a live event, where they are either present in the space where the event is performed or watch via cultural consumption technologies over a distance. Consumption	Entertainment, education, information, distraction, enjoyment	The value of a cultural event is the average amount of labour-time that it takes to organise and perform the event	Theatre performances, exhibitions, talks, lectures, readings, discussions, concerts, live performances, movie screening in the cinema, pay-per-view access to live television events, etc.

	occasion			
Cultural content	Audience members pay for having access to a copy of cultural content that they can consume repeatedly	Entertainment, education, information, distraction, enjoyment	The value of a certain cultural content is the average amount of hours that its production, organisation, and distribution take. The value of a single copy is the total amount of utilised labour divided by the number of created copies	Books, newspapers, magazines, audio recordings (e.g. vinyl records), recorded audio-visual content (e.g. movies distributed on DVDs, Blu-ray discs, computer hard disks, or downloaded on the Internet) purchased artworks, posters, or prints
Advertising space	Advertisers sell advertising space and audiences' attention to ad clients, who in return reach audiences with their product propaganda	Companies advertise their commodities	The more regular audience members there are, the higher the ad price can be set	Outdoor and transit ads, direct mail, newspaper and magazine ads, radio ads, television ads, digital, and online ads
Subscriptions for regular access to cultural content	Regular payment of money for securing the access to content for	Entertainment, education, information,	The value of a subscription service is the average amount of	Newspaper and magazine subscriptions, theatre subscription, museum

(*Continued*)

Table 4.2 (Cont.)

Cultural commodity type	*Exchange-value*	*Use-value*	*Value*	*Examples*
	a particular subscription period	distraction, enjoyment	hours it takes to organise and maintain this service	subscription, cinema subscription, pay television
Technologies for the production, distribution, and consumption of information	Audiences purchase technologies that enable the production, distribution, or consumption of information	Humans are enabled to produce, distribute, or consume information	The value of a communication technology is the average amount of hours that it takes to plan, produce, market, and sell the technology	Record player, stereo, television set, computer, mobile phone, laptop, camera, audio recorder
Mixed models of cultural commodities	Cultural corporations make use of capital-accumulation strategies, where they combine the sale of several types of cultural commodities	Entertainment, education, information, distraction, enjoyment	Mixed models combine different cultural commodities and therefore involve multiple forms of value	Newspaper and magazine models that combine the sale of advertising, printed copies and subscriptions, one-time digital access and digital subscriptions; cultural corporations that sell technologies and access to content

> What might be called use value in the reception of cultural assets is being replaced by exchange-value; enjoyment is giving way to being there and being in the know, connoisseurship by enhanced prestige. The consumer becomes the ideology of the amusement industry, whose institutions he or she cannot escape.[22]

All commodity types shown in Table 4.2 are cultural in character. Cultural labour-power is a special commodity type. Cultural workers are human beings who produce culture. In capitalism, many of them do so as wage workers or freelance workers. They sell their labour-power as commodity. But what is the value of labour-power? Marx writes that "the value of labour-power is the value of the means of subsistence necessary for the maintenance of its owner". The value of labour-power is therefore the average labour-time necessary for making the worker fit for exploitation, which includes the time for child-rearing, pregnancy, shopping, cleaning, self-care, housework, preparing meals, spending time with friends and family, sleeping, education, sexuality, enjoyment, entertainment, washing clothes and dishes, and consuming media, etc. All of these activities are, in capitalism, labour that produces a commodity, namely human subjectivity, i.e. the labour-power that is sold on the market as a commodity to capitalists in order for the working class to earn a living and survive. In Marxist feminism, the notion of reproductive labour was coined for labour that reproduces labour-power. Mariarosa Dalla Costa and Selma James argue that reproductive labour "produces not merely use values, but is essential to the production of surplus value".[23] Reproductive labour produces a commodity "unique to capitalism: the living human being – 'the labourer himself'"[24] (6). The German Marxist-feminist sociologist Maria Mies (1986) argues that capitalist production is based on the:

> *superexploitation* of non-wage labourers (women, colonies, peasants) upon which wage labour exploitation then is possible. I define their exploitation as superexploitation because it is not based on the appropriation (by the capitalist) of the time and labour over and above the 'necessary' labour time, the *surplus* labour, but of the time and labour *necessary* for people's own survival or subsistence production. It is not compensated for by a wage.[25]

Mixed models of capital accumulation in the culture industry combine the sale of several cultural commodities. Many newspapers sell subscriptions, copies, and ads. In 2018, Apple was the world's eighth largest transnational corporation.[26] In the same year, the company had total annual sales of US$265.6 billion and its annual profits amounted to US$59.6 billion[27]. In 2018, Apple achieved 56 percent of its revenues from the sale of communication technologies, namely iPhones (18 percent), iPads (2 percent), Macs (1 percent) and other products (35 percent, including Apple Watch, AirPods, HomePod, iPod Touch, and Beats products, etc.). Twenty-four percent was achieved from digital content and services such as iTunes, AppleCare, Apple Pay, iTunes store (music, films, TV programmes, e-books, podcasts, audiobooks). Apple combines two major capital-accumulation strategies that are interlinked: the sale of communication technologies, and digital services and content. Apple aims at accumulating capital by selling technologies on which users purchase and consume content sold by Apple. One can of course also consume and purchase from other content providers (such as Amazon Prime, Netflix, Spotify, Hulu, Disney+, and Virgin TV, etc.) but a significant degree of users will use Apple's digital services and content because they prefer the Apple brand name and the convenience of access to such content on Apple technologies. In respect to digital content, Apple uses both a subscription model (e.g. Apple Music, Apple TV+, iCloud) and a content model where one pays for the download of single pieces of cultural content (single songs, albums, movies, e-books, and audiobooks, etc.).

Digital Communication

Networked digital communication technologies such as computer networks, mobile phones, or the Internet differ in a number of respects from the forms of communication shown in Table 4.1:

- *Interactivity*: Users can respond to software dialogues, which enables that behaviour of software depends on user inputs.

- *Technological convergence*: Convergence of production, distribution, and consumption of information in one digital technology.
- *Convergence of information activities*: Convergence of processes of cognition, communication, and co-operation on digital technologies and platforms.
- *Convergence of communication*: Convergence of different forms of communication in one digital technology (interpersonal communication, group communication, organisational communication, mass communication, international communication, global communication, one-to-one-communication, one-to-many communication, many-to-many communication, many-to-one communication).
- *Convergence of modes of time*: Convergence of synchronous and asynchronous communication in one technology.
- *Hypertext*: Hypertextual information spaces that contain links between information; decontextualised pieces of information can be remixed and put together in new forms so that new meanings and contexts emerge.
- *Multimedia*: Written, oral, visual, and audio-visual communication converge in digital communication.
- Prosumption (productive consumption): Consumers of information can produce user-generated content.
- *Digital machines*: Digital technologies are not just information and communication technologies, but also digital machines that enable digital work, digital co-operation, and computer-supporter co-operative work.
- *Data, databases, data analysis*: Computers operate based on data (information stored in the form of bits of zeros and ones). Networked computing allows the collection, storage, processing, analysis, combination, and comparison of data from different sources. In the 21st century, databases have developed into big data[28] that is characterised by three Vs: <u>v</u>ast amounts and <u>v</u>arieties of data that can no longer be overseen by humans are processed and analysed at high <u>v</u>elocity.

Table 4.3 A typology of digital commodities and capital accumulation models in the digital culture economy

Model	*Commodity*	*Exchange-value*	*Use-value*	*Value*	*Example*
Digital labour model	Labour-power	Digital labour is either sold on a labour market so that digital workers achieve money in order to create digital goods, or there is the unremunerated creation of digital goods (as in the case of targeted advertising and unremunerated crowdsourcing)	Digital labour creates and organises digital technologies (hardware, software) or digital content or digital services	The average value of cultural labour-power is the average number of hours of reproductive labour that it takes to create its means of subsistence	Miners who extract minerals from which components are created, Foxconn assemblage workers, software engineers, crowd workers/platform workers, online freelancers, e-waste workers
The digital content as commodity model	Digital content, digital code, software	Users pay money in order to obtain access to and to be able to use digital	Software and content that enables human information, communication, co-	The value of a particular piece of digital content is the average amount of	Microsoft, Adobe, Oracle, SAP, Electronic Arts (computer games)

		content or software. Use can be unrestricted or restricted to a specific time period.	operation, education, entertainment	labour-time it takes to produce and maintain it. The value of a single copy of digital content is the total annual amount of labour-time that a company utilises for the creation and update of this commodity divided by the number of created copies	
Digital finance model	Financial services sold online	Users pay money online for financial services that are organised electronically. The digital finance company	Payments can be made electronically	Financial services yield profit by consuming value created in other parts of the economy that is	eBanking, PayPal, Google Checkout, Amazon Payments, cryptocurrency and digital currency exchanges (e.g.

(*Continued*)

Table 4.3 (Cont.)

Model	*Commodity*	*Exchange-value*	*Use-value*	*Value*	*Example*
		charges a fee for the service.		channelled into the finance system.	Bitstamp, Coinbase, Coinmama, Kraken)
Hardware model	Computing hardware	Sale of computing hardware	Computing devices can be used for work, information, communication, and co-operation	The value of a piece of hardware is the average amount of time it takes to produce it	Apple, HP, Dell, Fujitsu, Lenovo
Network model	Access to digital networks	Sale of the access to digital networks	Access to digital networks such as mobile telephony and the Interne	The value of a digital network is the average amount of labour-time that is used to set up and maintain the network per year	Telecommunications and Internet service providers: AT&T, Verizon, China Mobile, Deutsche Telecom, Orange, BT
The online advertising model	Targeted ads	Companies, organisations or individuals pay money in order to be able to	Buyers of ads are enabled to target users with messages in order to convince	Users create the value of targeted online ads. The more time a particular	Google, Facebook, Twitter

		present online ads to a targeted audience. The ads are often personalised, targeted with the help of digital surveillance and sold with algorithmic auctions	them to buy certain commodities or follow certain ideas	group spends online, the more valuable it is as an audience targeted by online ads	
The online retail model	Various commodities ordered online	Users purchase tangible and intangible commodities (goods and services) in online shops or on online auction sites. The goods are delivered to them physically or electronically	Goods can be purchased from everywhere without having to physically go to a shop; consumption of goods	The value of the purchased commodities is created by the workers who create them. The value of a single online retail process is the average amount of labour-time involved in the packaging, transportf delivery of the	Amazon, Alibaba, Apple iTunes, eBay,

(*Continued*)

Table 4.3 (Cont.)

Model	*Commodity*	*Exchange-value*	*Use-value*	*Value*	*Example*
				purchased commodity	
The sharing economy – pay-per-service model	Services organised via an online platform	Users purchase a service via a digital platform. The platform mediates the economic relationship between the producer and the buyer of the service, for which it charges a fee	Ordering of services from a distance via Internet platforms and apps	The average time it takes the platform workers to create the digital service is the service's value. The platform companies derive profit by charging fees for the mediation of the sales process of the service. These fees are charged on the generated revenue and are paid for by the worker and/or the buyer	Uber, Upwork, Deliveroo

The sharing economy – rent-on-rent model	Renting of goods via an online platform	Users rent the use of a good (e.g. a property, a flat, or a car) for a limited period of time via a digital platform. The platform mediates the rent relationship between the lessor and the renter, for which it charges a fee (a rent-on-rent)	Renting of goods over Internet platforms or apps; use of property over a limited amount of time	Rent-seeking digital platforms generate their win from the transfer of wages or profits from other parts of the economy	Airbnb, Hiyacar, Drivy
Digital subscription model	Access to a collection of digital resources	Users pay a subscription fee in order to obtain access to a library of digital content. The subscription is in most cases time-limited so that after	Information, education, entertainment	The value of a single subscription is the average amount of labour-time that those who work for the platform expend per year. The value of a single	Netflix, Spotify, Amazon Prime, Apple Music

(*Continued*)

Table 4.3 (Cont.)

Model	*Commodity*	*Exchange-value*	*Use-value*	*Value*	*Example*
		expiration a renewed purchase is necessary for maintaining access		subscription is the total amount of labour-time that workers conducted for the platform per year divided by the number of created subscriptions	
Mixed models	Combination of various digital commodities	In such models, companies sell different kinds of digital commodities in order to accumulate capital	Information, education, entertainment	Mixed models combine different forms of digital value generation.	Spotify, online newspapers, Apple

A Typology of Commodities in the Digital Culture Industry

The rise of the Internet and the World Wide Web (WWW) in the 1990s, the mobile phone and social media in the first decades of the second millennium, and big data in the 2010s has created a digital culture industry that features capital accumulation models and commodification strategies that are slightly different from traditional culture industry models (as listed in Table 4.2). Table 4.3 provides an overview of such models.

4.4 CAPITALISM

What Is Capital?

Capital is money that is invested into the production of commodities so that a monetary profit is generated, a sum of money that is larger than the investment made. Marx characterises capital as: "valorization of value", "an end in itself", "limitless",[29] "ceaseless augmentation of value [...] achieved by the [...] capitalist by [...] throwing his money again and again into circulation",[30] "self-valorization", value that as "subject [...] lays golden eggs" and adds "value to itself",[31] "making still more money out of money", "value [...] as a self-moving substance", "value in process, money in process" that "preserves and multiplies itself within circulation, emerges from it with an increased size, and starts the same cycle again and again", "money which begets money", "buying in order to sell dearer",[32] "money which is worth more money, value which is greater than itself".[33] The point is that the capitalist's aim is to constantly increase capital by investing and re-investing money and buying and selling commodities at prices that are higher than the investment costs.

A capitalist is "the conscious bearer of this movement" of capital accumulation. "His person, or rather his pocket, is the point from which the money starts, and to which it returns".[34] The "appropriation of ever more wealth in the abstract is the sole driving force behind his operations that he functions as a capitalist, i.e. as capital personified and endowed with consciousness and a will. [...] the capitalist is a rational miser".[35] Capital is a social structure that compels capitalists and workers to act within class relations and on markets.

Capital Accumulation

In *Capital Volume 2*'s Chapter 1, "The Circuit of Money Capital", Marx introduces the formula of capital accumulation:[36] M – C (Mp, L) .. P .. C' – M'. Figure 4.1 visualises the capital-accumulation process. Capitalists invest money capital M (that they often obtain from banks, to which they pay interest for loans) for buying labour-power L and means of production Mp. The monetary value of labour-power is called variable capital, the monetary value of the means of production is called constant capital. Marx distinguishes between two forms of constant capital: circulating constant capital and fixed constant capital. Circulating constant capital is comprised of resources that lose their

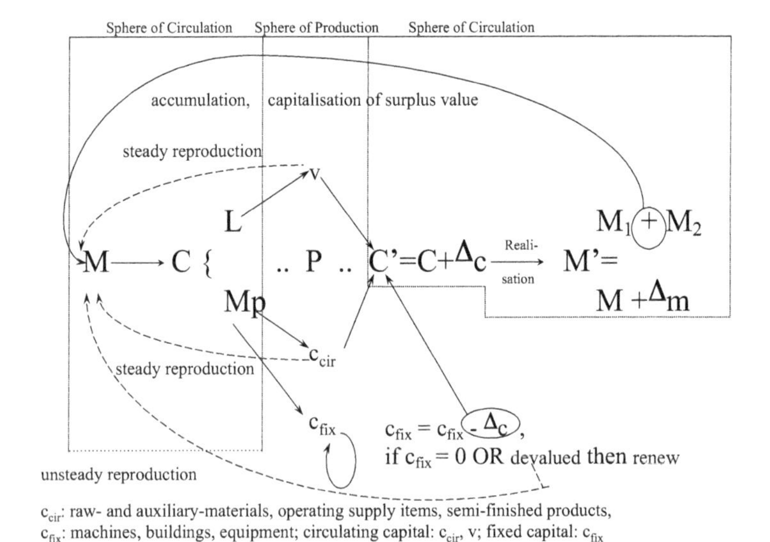

Figure 4.1 The process of the accumulation of capital

value through full productive consumption in the production process. It includes raw and auxiliary materials, operating supply items, and semi-finished products. Fixed constant capital, in contrast, stays in the production process for a longer time and only gradually loses and transfers value to the commodity. One can count machines, buildings, and equipment as this form of capital.

In the production process P, workers conduct labour in order to transfer the value of parts of the means of production to a new commodity, creating the value of their labour-power as well as new surplus-value. The new commodity's value C' is $c + v + s$; it is larger than the value of the initial commodities. The commodity value has been increased by a surplus-value (measured in hours of labour) and surplus product Δc. The new commodity C' is sold at a price M' that is larger than the initial capital M so that a monetary profit p emerges and $M' = M + p = M + \Delta m$. Part of the profit is re-invested for expanding economic operations, while other parts are used for other purposes, such as paying interest to banks and dividends to shareholders. The main goal and purpose of capitalism is that capital increases, i.e. is accumulated. Profit is generated by exploiting human labour.

Marx argues in *Capital Volume 3* that the general definition of the capitalist economy, i.e. its basic quality, is the combination of generalised commodity production and the exploitation of surplus-value generating labour, so that capital is accumulated.[37] For Marx, the capitalist economy is the system of expanded capital reproduction in the form M – C .. P .. C' – M', in which capitalists buy with money M the commodities C (labour-power, means of production) so that labour creates in the production process a new commodity C' that contains a surplus-value that upon sale on the market realises a profit p that increases the invested capital M by a surplus and allows capital to be accumulated and new investments to be made. For Marx, capitalism turns labour-power and means of production into instruments for the production of the chief end of accumulating capital, i.e. "money breeding money, value breeding value"[38] (Marx 1885, 160).

The capitalist economy is a form of generalised commodity production: The commodity is the main form of the organisation of property. Labour is compelled to produce commodities that are sold in order that capitalists can accumulate ever more capital, i.e. money that is intended to increase itself. The capitalist economy is a unity of many elements – money, the commodity, the exploitation of labour-power, the means of production, commodity production, and capital. This functional unity has emergent qualities so that the sum of these elements is more than any of the separate elements. Capital accumulation is enabled by all of these elements, but is itself a new quality of capitalist society in comparison to other economic formations. Commodities are one of the cells of capitalism. The accumulation of capital is the whole body. Capital is a body that tries to increase its size by letting labour produce commodities that are sold on markets so that capital grows.

There is a difference between the capitalist economy and capitalist society. Capitalism can signify both a mode of the organisation of the economy and of society. One can argue that the capitalist mode of economic production shapes modern society at large: Modern society is a form of society dominated by the accumulation of money capital in the economy, power in politics, and reputation/distinction in culture. These forms of accumulation are all interlinked. The economy shapes modern society and its subsystems in the form of the logic of accumulation that takes on specific forms with relative autonomy in each of these subsystems that mutually shape each other. Society's subsystems are therefore identical and different at the same time.

4.5 CULTURAL AND DIGITAL CAPITALISM

In the culture industry, the commodity C' has a cultural character. In the digital culture industry, the commodity C' is digital hardware, software, digital content, or a digital service. The capital accumulation process, as visualised in Figure 4.1, can be applied in a straightforward manner to cultural and digital commodities. Advertising (and digital advertising) is a special case that is more complex, which we will therefore discuss in more detail.

Advertising

Dallas W. Smythe (1907–1992) was a Canadian political economist of communication. He stressed that, in advertising, the commodity sold is not content, but the attention of the users. He therefore coined the notion of the audience commodity. "Because audience power is produced, sold, purchased, and consumed, it commands a price and is a commodity. [...] You audience members contribute your unpaid work time and in exchange you receive the program material and the explicit advertisements".[39] Audiences "work to market [...] things to themselves"[40] (Smythe 1981, 4). The "main function of the mass media [...] is to produce audiences prepared to be dutiful consumers".[41]

Smythe asked the question: Who produces the commodity of the commercial, advertising-financed media?

> I submit that the materialist answer to the question – What is the commodity form of mass-produced, advertiser-supported communications under monopoly capitalism? – is audiences and readerships (hereafter referred to for simplicity as audiences). The material reality under monopoly capitalism is that all non-sleeping time of most of the population is work time. This work time is devoted to the production of commodities-in-general (both where people get paid for their work and as members of audiences) and in the production and reproduction of labor power (the pay for which is subsumed in their income). Of the off-the-job work time, the largest single block is time of the audiences which is sold to advertisers.[42]
>
> The work which audience members perform for the advertiser to whom they have been sold is to learn to buy particular 'brands' of consumer goods, and to spend their income accordingly. In short, they work to create the demand for advertised goods which is the purpose of the monopoly capitalist advertisers. While doing this, audience members are simultaneously reproducing their own labour power.[43]

Smythe stressed the importance of reproductive labour for capitalism and that the engagement with commercial media and culture in consumer capitalism is an important form of reproductive labour:

> The material reality under monopoly capitalism is that all non-sleeping time of most of the population is work time. [...] Of the off-the-job work time, the largest single block is time of the audiences, which is sold to advertisers. [...] In 'their' time which is sold to advertisers workers (a) perform essential marketing functions for the producers of consumers' goods, and (b) work at the production and reproduction of labour power.[44]

The modern advertising industry came into existence around 1890 as part of the emergence of the "new 'monopoly' (corporate) capitalism"[45] and took full effect in the 20th century with the rise of the culture industry, the mass media, mass production, and mass consumption. Digital advertising on the Internet and on mobile phones has, since the first decade of the second millennium, undergone massive growth and has to a certain degree substituted print advertising. Table 4.4 shows the development of global advertising revenues since 1980.

In the early 1980s, print advertising accounted for almost two-thirds of global ad revenue. By the mid-1990s, its share had decreased to about 50 percent and television ad revenue's share had increased from a quarter in the early and mid-1980s to

Table 4.4 Share of the revenue of certain forms of advertising in total global ad sales (data source: WARC)

Year	*Print (newspapers & magazines)*	*TV*	*Radio*	*Cinema*	*Outdoor*	*Digital (Internet & mobile)*	*Mobile*
1980	64.4%	23.9%	8.1%	0.2%	3.3%		
1985	60.0%	26.4%	9.1%	0.2%	4.3%		
1990	57.6%	28.4%	8.1%	0.2%	5.7%		
1996	51.4%	34.1%	8.3%	0.3%	5.8%	0.1%	
2000	47.8%	34.2%	9.3%	0.3%	5.2%	3.1%	
2005	42.4%	37.0%	8.6%	0.4%	5.9%	5.7%	0.1%
2010	29.4%	41.4%	7.1%	0.5%	6.4%	15.2%	0.3%
2015	16.8%	39.2%	6.3%	0.6%	6.5%	30.6%	9.3%
2019	9.5%	31.7%	5.3%	0.8%	6.1%	46.7%	26.9%

about a third. The 1990s also saw the rise of the Internet and the WWW as platforms of advertising. Digital advertising started growing massively after 2005, the time when Google and Facebook started conquering advertising. In 2019, digital advertising accounted for 46.7 percent of global ad revenue. Print advertising's share had dropped to less than 10 percent and television advertising amounted to 31.7 percent. Since 2010, mobile phone advertising has, with the rising popularity of apps and smartphones, become a new trend in digital advertising. In 2019, mobile advertising accounted for 26.9 percent of global ad revenue and 57.7 percent of digital advertising.

Digital Advertising

In 2018, Alphabet/Google achieved profits of US$30.7 billion and Facebook made profits of US$22.1 billion.[46] In the same year, Alphabet/Google was the world's 23rd biggest transnational corporation (TNC) and Facebook was the world's 77th largest TNC.[47] In 2018, there were more than one billion users of Google Search and YouTube[48] per month. And there were 2.4 billion Facebook users[49] per month. Google and Facebook are the world's two largest advertising agencies. In 2018 their combined revenues were US$192.6 billion (Google: US$136.8 billion; Facebook: US$55.8 billion).[50] Facebook derived 98.5 percent of its revenues (US$55.0 billion) from ads, Google 85.4 percent (US$ 116.3 billion).[51] The two digital giants' combined ad revenues amounted to US$171.3 billion. In 2018, global digital ad revenue was US$256.4 billion, and global ad revenue amounted to US$590.4 billion.[52] In 2018, Google and Facebook's ad sales together made up 66.8 percent of the world's digital ad revenue and 29 percent of the global advertising revenues. Google and Facebook hold a duopoly in digital advertising. They are also known for having avoided paying taxes.

On Facebook and other commercial social media, the law of value means that the more time a certain group spends on the platform, the more valuable the corresponding data commodity becomes, on average. A group that spends on average many minutes per day on Facebook (e.g. the group of those aged

15–25) compared to another group (e.g. the group of those aged 75–85) constitutes a more valuable data commodity because (a) it has a higher average labour/online time per day, which generates more data that can be sold, and (b) it spends more time online, during which targeted ads are presented to this group. Figure 4.2 visualises the capital accumulation model of targeted-ad-based platforms such as Facebook and Google.

The targeted-ad model is shown at the bottom of the figure. The platforms themselves are not commodities because users do not pay for access. They are gifts and a "free lunch". The software engineers working for Google and Facebook do not create a commodity. Their labour (v1) creates the platform technologies. These companies sell ad space and the attention of their users. Based on Smythe, we can say that the use of Facebook and Google is labour, a particular form of digital labour that is unremunerated and creates attention and big data. Users' digital labour (v2) creates

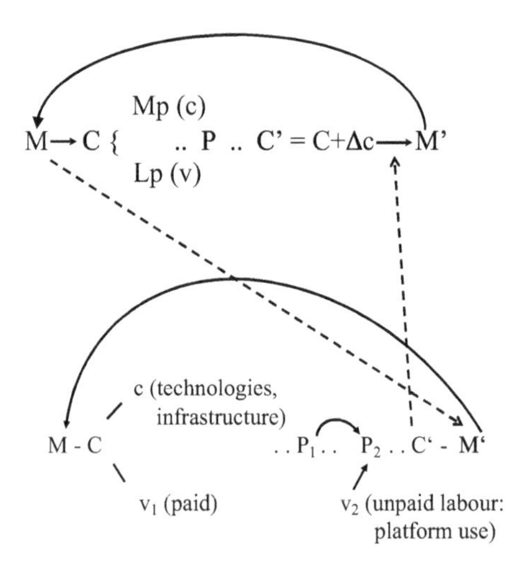

Figure 4.2 The capital accumulation process of targeted-ad-based digital platforms such as Google and Facebook

personal data, content and usage data that Facebook and Google use to make the ads they sell to specific targeted user groups. For advertisers, the advantage of advertising on such platforms is that they can select audiences with certain characteristics to whom the ads are presented. Facebook and Google's commodity C' is targeted-ad space and the attention that users give to ads. The targeted-ad capital-accumulation circuit interacts with regular capital-accumulation cycles in other parts of the economy. Such companies are visualised by the cycle in the top of Figure 4.2. A particular company invests a certain amount of its capital into purchasing targeted ads. Therefore, there is a flow of money from this company to the social media company. In return, the social media company enables the ad-purchasing company or organisation to present targeted ads, which feeds back into the sales process of the latter organisation so that the realisation of profit and commodity sales are supported.

How Does Targeted Advertising Differ from Traditional Advertising?

Social media users are partly audiences who read texts, comments, or e-mails; watch videos or images; listen to music, etc. They tend, however, also to be prosumers in that they create texts, comments, e-mails, videos, images, or music. Prosumers' labour on social media platforms that use targeted ads differs in a number of respects from audience labour in broadcasting:

- *Creativity and social relations*: Broadcasting audiences produce meanings of programmes, whereas social media prosumers don't just produce meanings, but also content, communications with other users, and social relations. Users of social media do not always create content, but to a specific degree behave like audiences watching content.
- *Surveillance*: Broadcasting requires audience measurements, which are approximations, in order to sell audiences as commodities. Social media corporations monitor, store, and assess all online activities of users

on their platforms and also on other platforms. They have very detailed profiles of users' activities, interests, communications, and social relations. Constant real-time surveillance of users is an inherent feature of prosumers' labour on capitalist social media. Personal data is sold as a commodity. Measuring audiences has, in broadcasting and print, traditionally been based on studies with small samples of audience members. Measuring and monitoring user behaviour on social media is constant, total, and algorithmic.

- *Targeted and personalised advertising*: Advertising on capitalist social media can therefore more easily target user interests and personalise ads, whereas this is more difficult in commercial broadcasting.
- *Algorithmic auctions*: Algorithms organise the pricing of the user-data commodity in the form of auctions for online advertising spaces on the screens of a specific number of users. The ad prices on social media vary depending on the number of auctioneers, whereas the ad prices in newspapers and on radio and TV are set in a relatively fixed manner and are publicly advertised. User measurement uses predictive algorithms (if you like A, you may also like B because 1,000,000 people who like A also like B).

Capitalism and the Information Society

Claims that we live in an information society, post-industrial society, knowledge society, network society, or Internet society have proliferated since the 1960s. They have to do with the rising importance of computing and knowledge-labour. Such theories often have a bourgeois character: They claim that society has been *radically* transformed by technology and that we therefore live today in a new society. For example, Daniel Bell argued that the "post-industrial society", a term by which he means an information society, has brought about "the emergence of a new kind of society [that] brings into question the distributions of wealth, power, and status that are central to any society".[53] The problem of such claims is that they imply that capitalism is over, which poses the danger of the ideological denial of the existence of class conflict and inequalities. Terms such as "information society" and "network society" are positivist: They sound positive and thereby hide the problems of capitalist society.

But it is also wrong to assume that capitalism has not changed since the 19th century, when Marx lived. Capitalism develops as a unity of contradictions so that crises result in the emergence of a new regime of accumulation, a new mode of regulation, and a new ideological mode. Capitalist society remains the same at the most basic level by changing at upper levels of organisation. There is a dialectic of continuity and change in capitalist development: Capitalism remains the same system of exploitation and domination by changing dynamically. And capitalism changes through its basic invariant antagonisms, such as class antagonism and the antagonism between productive forces and relations of production.

Cultural/Digital Capitalism

Cultural capitalism is that part of capitalist society and the capitalist economy that is organised around the production of cultural commodities and cultural products. Digital capitalism is that part of capitalist society and the capitalist economy that is organised around the production of digital commodities and digital products. Capitalism exists as the dialectical unity of many capitalisms. Cultural and digital capitalism are just two dimensions of capitalism. Table 4.5 provides an analysis of some aspects of global capitalism via an analysis of the sales, profits and assets of the world's 2,000 largest transnational corporations.

The data underlying Table 4.5 was grouped according to economic sectors. The culture/digital industry was conceived of consisting of the following sub-industries: advertising, broadcasting and cable, business supplies, casinos and gaming, communications equipment, computer and electronics retail, computer hardware, computer services, computer storage devices,

Table 4.5 Share of specific industries in the profits, revenues and assets of the world's largest 2,000 transnational corporations (data source: Forbes 2000 List of the World's Largest Public Companies, 2018)

Industry	*No. of companies*	*Share of sales*	*Share of profits*	*Share of assets*
Conglomerates	36	2.0%	1.1%	0.9%
Culture & Digital	260	14.6%	17.7%	5.1%
Energy & Utilities	199	14.3%	9.8%	5.7%
Fashion	26	1.0%	0.9%	0.0%
FIRE (Finance, Insurance & Real Estate)	634	22.5%	33.7%	74.8%
Food	86	3.6%	5.8%	1.2%
Manufacturing & Construction	352	15.2%	13.1%	5.4%
Mobility & Transport	169	11.6%	9.4%	3.6%
Pharmaceutical & Medical	105	7.2%	4.9%	1.9%
Retail	86	6.9%	2.5%	0.9%
Security	1	0.0%	0.0%	0.0%
Various Services	46	1.1%	1.1%	0.4%

consumer electronics, diversified media, electronics, Internet retail, publishing and printing, recreational products, semiconductors, software and programming, and telecommunications services.

Finance, insurance and real estate (FIRE) dominates the structure of the sales, profits and capital assets of the world's largest 2,000 corporations. The culture/digital industry is the third largest sector in respect to sales, the second largest in respect to profits, and the fourth largest in respect to capital assets. Other sectors that are fairly large are energy and utilities (which includes the oil industry), classical manufacturing and construction, and the mobility and transport sector (that includes aerospace, air couriers, airlines, car manufacturing, hotels and motels, railroads, and trucking). It is evident from this data that capitalism is several capitalisms at the same time: finance capitalism, culture/digital capitalism (that can also be termed informational capitalism or communicative capitalism), hyper-industrial capitalism, and mobility capitalism. There is a dialectic of these types of capitalism. They are distinct, but interlinked: For example, digital capitalism is linked to finance capitalism via venture capital investments into digital start-ups and the listing of digital corporations on stock markets. Digital and cultural capitalism requires energy inputs, which links to classical resources and hyper-industrial capitalism. Global communication also advances increased transportation of people and goods, which is why the digital/culture industry and the mobility/transport industries are interacting.

4.6 CONCLUSION

The commodity is capitalism's cell-form. The capitalist economy is a system of capital accumulation. Capitalist society is a form of society that is shaped by the logic of accumulation.

The culture industry is that part of the capitalist economy in which culture is organised as commodity. There are different forms of cultural commodities. The digital culture industry differs in a number of respects from the traditional culture industry, such as in the capacity that consumers become producers/consumers (prosumers) of information, which has resulted in new capital-accumulation models.

Capitalism is a dialectical unity of many different capitalisms. Cultural and digital capitalism forms a significant moment of contemporary capitalism. It interacts with other forms of capitalism such as finance capitalism, hyper-industrial capitalism, or mobility capitalism.

Recommended Further Readings about Commodities, Capital, and Capitalism

Karl Marx. 1867. *Capital Volume 1*. Chapter 1: The Commodity:

1.1. The Two Factors of the Commodity: Use-Value and Value (Substance of Value, Magnitude of Value), pp. 125–131.

1.2. The Dual Character of the Labour Embodied in

Commodities, pp. 131–137. 1.3. The Value-Form, or Exchange-Value. London: Penguin. pp. 138–163.

Marx opens *Capital Volume 1* with a discussion of the commodity, use-value, value, and exchange-value.

Dallas W. Smythe. 1977. Communications: Blindspot of Western Marxism. *Canadian Journal of Political and Social Theory* 1 (3): 1–27.

This text is a classical reading in the critical political economy of communication. Smythe argues that advertising has not been taken serious in previous Marxist theory. He introduces the notions of the audience commodity and audience labour for the analysis of the political economy of advertising.

Notes

1 Karl Marx. 1867. *Capital Volume 1*. London: Penguin. p. 125.
2 Ibid., p. 90.
3 Ibid., p. 125.
4 Ibid., p. 126.
5 Ibid., p. 126.
6 Ibid., p.126.
7 Ibid., p. 128.
8 Ibid., p. 128.
9 Ibid., p. 129.
10 Ibid., p. 128.
11 Ibid., p. 129.
12 Ibid., p. 129.
13 Ibid., p. 129.
14 Ibid., p. 130.
15 Ibid., p. 130.
16 Marx, *Capital Volume 1*, p. 125.
17 Ibid., p. 126.
18 See: Richard E. Caves. 2000. *Creative Industries: Contracts Between Art and Commerce*. Cambridge, MA: Harvard University Press. John Micklethwait. 1989. The Entertainment Industry. *The Economist*, 23 December 1989: 3–4.

19 See: Charlotte Hess and Elinor Ostrom. 2007. *Understanding Knowledge as Commons: From Theory to Practice*. Cambridge, MA: MIT Press.
20 Max Horkheimer and Theodor W. Adorno. 1947/2002. *Dialectic of Enlightenment: Philosophical Fragments*. Stanford, CA: Stanford University Press. pp. 94–136.
21 Ibid., p. 129.
22 Ibid., p. 128.
23 Mariarosa Dalla Costa and Selma James. 1973. *The Power of Women and the Subversion of Community*. Bristol: Falling Wall Press. Second edition. p. 31.
24 Ibid., p. 6.
25 Maria Mies 1986. *Patriarchy & Accumulation on a World Scale: Women in the International Division of Labour*. London: Zed Books. p. 48.
26 Data source: Forbes 2000 List of the World's Largest Public Companies, year 2018, available onwww.forbes.com/global2000/list/#tab:overall, accessed on 12 May 2019.
27 Data source: Apple Investor Relations, SEC Filings for the financial year 2018: form 10-K, available on https://investor.apple.com/investor-relations/sec-filings, accessed on 12 May 2019.
28 Rob Kitchin. 2014. *The Data Revolution: Big Data, Open Data, Data Infrastructures & Their Consequences*. London: Sage. p. 68.
29 Marx, *Capital Volume 1*, p. 253.
30 Ibid., pp. 254–255.
31 Ibid., p. 255.
32 Ibid., p. 256.
33 Ibid., p. 257.
34 Ibid., p. 254.
35 Ibid., p. 254.
36 Karl Marx. 1885. *Capital Volume 22*. London: Penguin. p. 109.
37 Karl Marx. 1894. *Capital Volume 33*. London: Penguin. pp 1019–1021.
38 Marx, *Capital Volume 2*, p. 160.
39 Dallas W. Smythe. 1981. The Audience Commodity and Its Work. In *Dependency Road: Communications, Capitalism, Consciousness, and Canada*. Norwood, NJ: Ablex. pp. 22–51, 233.
40 Ibid., p. 4.
41 Ibid., p. 250.
42 Dallas W. Smythe. 1977. Communications: Blindspot of Western Marxism. *Canadian Journal of Political and Social Theory* 1 (3): 1–27. p. 3.
43 Ibid., p. 6.

44 Ibid., p. 3.
45 Raymond Williams, 1960/1969. Advertising: The Magic System. In *Culture and Materialism*. London: Verso. pp. 170–195.
46 Data source: Alphabet and Google SEC-filings, forms 10-K for the financial year 2018, accessed on 2 October 2019.
47 Data source: Forbes Global 2000 list for the year 2018, available on www.forbes.com/global2000/list, accessed on 13 May 2019.
48 https://abc.xyz/investor/static/pdf/20180204_alphabet_10K.pdf?cache=11336e3, accessed on 13 May 2019.
49 https://newsroom.fb.com/company-info/, accessed on 13 May 2019.
50 Data source: Alphabet and Google SEC-filings, forms 10-K for the financial year 2018, accessed on 2 October 2019.
51 Ibid.
52 Data source: WARC ad spend data (www.warc.com/data), accessed on 13 May 2019.
53 Daniel Bell. 1974. *The Coming of Post-Industrial Society. A Venture in Social Forecasting*. London: Heinemann. p. 43.

5

LABOUR AND SURPLUS-VALUE

5.1 INTRODUCTION

Marx's critical theory analyses capitalism as a class society. This means that wherever there is capital there is also the exploitation of labour in a class relationship. Labour produces capital and commodities. Without labour, there is no capital. There is a dialectic of capital and labour. Just like the commodity and capital, labour is a key category of Marx's critique of the political economy.

This chapter introduces Marx's concept of labour and how it matters in the context of communication and culture. Section 5.2 introduces the notions of work and labour, Section 5.3 discusses the concepts of surplus-value and surplus-labour, and Section 5.4 focuses on cultural labour.

5.2 WORK AND LABOUR

Work

Marx defines work as:

> a process between man and nature, a process by which man, through his own actions, mediates, regulates and controls the metabolism between himself and nature. [...] He sets in motion the natural forces which belong to his own body, his arms, legs, head and hands, in order to appropriate the materials of nature in a form adapted to his own needs. Through this movement he acts upon external nature and changes it, and in this way he simultaneously changes his own nature.[1]

Marx systematically develops and analyses moments of the work process: "The simple elements of the work ['labour' in the original English translation] process are (1) purposeful activity, that is work itself, (2) the object on which that work is performed, and (3) the instruments of that work."[2] In any work process, we find one or more human subjects who change an object by using other objects on them so that a new subject-object, a product of work that is a use-value that satisfies specific human needs, emerges. Figure 5.1 visualises the work process's dialectic of subject and object.

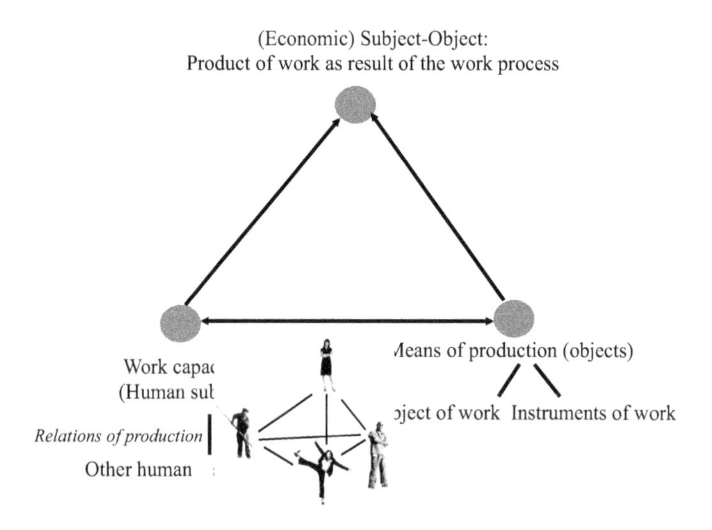

Figure 5.1 The work process's dialectic of subject and object

The Productive Forces

What Marx terms the work process, in which humans use technologies in order to create new use-values from nature or culture, is also called the productive forces. The productive forces are not mere objects, things, and technologies, but the process of how humans use objects in order to create use-values. In work processes, humans stand in specific social relations to others because they, under normal circumstances, are not as alone as Robinson Crusoe was on his island. Marx terms the social relations or the economy the relations of production. Class relations are specific relations of production organised within class-based societies: one class owns the means of production and the created products, whereas another one is without property and is forced to work for the propertied class in order to survive.

Marx defines an instrument of work as "a thing, or a complex of things, which the worker interposes between himself and the object of his work ['labour' in the original translation] and which serves as a conductor, directing his activity onto that object."[3] Marx supports Benjamin Franklin's assumption that man is a "tool-making animal."[4] He argues that different economic epochs distinguish each other not by what is made, but how and with the help of which instruments it is made. [5] We can therefore, for example, distinguish between the Stone Age (approximately 3.4 million years BC–2,000 BC),[6] the Bronze Age (approximately 4,000 years BC–1000 BC),[7] and the Iron Age (approximately 1,000 BC–400 AD).[8] Different materials were used for making tools in these eras.

Humans apply the instruments of work to objects – specific resources that act as raw materials – in order to produce new objects: the products of work. To be able to conduct a particular type of work, humans have and need certain capacities. Marx speaks in this context of *Arbeitsvermögen*, the capacity to work. Work capacity is "the aggregate of those mental and physical capabilities existing in the physical form, the living personality, of a human being, capabilities which he sets in motion whenever he produces a use-value of any kind."[9] Work capacity includes physical and mental abilities, skills, and experience, etc. For example, a good translator needs excellent language skills, linguistic sensitivity, specialist knowledge, and experience in reading and translating.

Concrete Work

Marx argues that the commodity's use-value and value translate into two types of human activity: concrete work and abstract labour. The first creates the commodity's use-value, the second its value. Concrete work is "productive activity of a definite kind, carried on with a definite aim."[10] As a concrete worker, the human being is "the creator of use-values"[11] that satisfy certain human needs. "Use-values like coats, linen, etc., in short, the physical bodies of commodities, are combinations of two elements, the material provided by nature, and [work] ['labour' in the original translation]."[12]

Abstract Labour

Whereas concrete work is "a matter of the 'how' and the 'what'" (qualities of work), abstract labour is a matter:

> of the 'how much', of the temporal duration of labour. Since the magnitude of the value of a commodity represents nothing but the quantity of labour embodied in it, it follows that all commodities, when taken in certain proportions, must be equal in value.[13]

The values of specific quantities of specific, qualitatively different, kinds of labour equal each other. If it takes on average six hours to produce a table and three hours to write a poem, then the abstract labour for the production of one table equals the one for the production of two poems, and the abstract labour of a carpenter required for producing one table equals the abstract labour of two poets who each write one poem, or the labour of one poet writing two poems.

The German words *Werk* and *werken* and the English word *work* have their etymological roots in the Indo-European word *uerg*, which means doing, acting, or creating something.[14] In contrast, the German word *Arbeit* goes back to the Germanic term *arba*, which meant slave.[15] The English word labour comes from the French word *labor* and the Latin term *laborem* and first appeared in the English language around 1300 AD.[16] It was associated with hard work, pain, and trouble. Whereas work is a general process of production characteristic of all societies, labour means types of work that are organised in class relations, where one class produces goods that another one owns. Labour as wage-labour that one has to conduct in order to earn a living and survive is so deeply entrenched in the logic of class society that it is hard for us to imagine a society without labour, class, and commodities. But nonetheless, labour is a historical phenomenon, which means that it is a necessary constituent of class society and is sublated in a communist society, where everyone gets what they need for free and works according to their abilities. In this context Marx speaks of the communist principle, "From each according to his abilities, to each according to his needs"[17] as the way the economy is organised in a communist society.

5.3 SURPLUS-VALUE AND SURPLUS-LABOUR

The Valorisation Process

For Marx, capitalist production is a dialectical unity of the work process and the valorisation process: "a unity, composed of the labour process and the process of creating value."[18] The capitalist's aim is "to produce a use-value which has exchange-value" and "a commodity greater in value than the sum of the values of the commodities used to produce it."[19]

Marx asks where profit comes from and what its source is. He argues that workers' production of surplus-value is the riddle of capital accumulation. Capital and profit do not come from the activities of capitalists, managers, or technology, but from the unpaid part of workers' labour conducted in class relations. The valorisation process is inherently linked to Marx's notions of surplus-value and surplus-labour, which are key theoretical innovations of his critical theory.

Marx uses the notion of profit as a monetary increment/surplus ΔM over the invested sum of money M in the capital accumulation process: M' = M + ΔM. Profit is measured in monetary units of a specific currency. Sometimes Marx refers to profit as surplus-value, but surplus-value also refers to the amount of unpaid labour-time that workers perform. A commodity has certain investment costs and yields a monetary profit. It is produced during a certain average production time. This production time can be divided into one part that represents the investment costs and another part that represents profit. The labour-time that represents profit is unpaid labour-time or surplus-labour time. Marx also uses the notion of surplus-value for this part of the working day.

Surplus-Value as Surplus-Labour-Time

The Argentinian–Mexican Marxist philosopher Enrique Dussel argues that in his work on the *Grundrisse*, Marx had "for the first time in his work [...] discovered the category of surplus value"[20] in December 1857:

> The matter can also be expressed in this way: if the worker needs only half a working day in order to live a whole day, then, in order to keep alive as a worker, he needs to work only half a day. The second half of the day is forced labour; surplus-labour. What appears as surplus value on capital's side appears identically on the worker's side as surplus-labour in excess of his requirements as worker, hence in excess of his immediate requirements for keeping himself alive.[21]

In *Capital Volume 1*, Marx describes the production of surplus-value in the following manner:

> We have seen that the worker, during one part of the labour process, produces only the value of his labour-power, i.e. the value of his means of subsistence. [...] I call the portion of the working day during which this reproduction takes place necessary labour-time, and the labour expended during that time necessary labour; necessary for the worker, because independent of the particular social form of his

> labour; necessary for capital and the capitalist world, because the continued existence of the worker is the basis of that world. During the second period of the labour process, that in which his labour is no longer necessary labour, the worker does indeed expend labour-power, he does work, but his labour is no longer necessary labour, and he creates no value for himself. He creates surplus-value which, for the capitalist, has all the charms of something created out of nothing. This part of the working day I call surplus-labour-time, and to the labour expended during that time I give the name of surplus-labour.[22]

Marx writes that "economic formations of society" distinguish themselves from each other "in the form in which this surplus-labour is in each case extorted from the immediate producer, the worker."[23] A mode of production is the dialectical unity of the productive forces and the social relations of production (see Figure 5.1). Marx distinguishes a number of modes of production based on the question who produces and who controls and owns the means of production and the surplus-product that a society creates. Table 5.1 provides an overview of the modes of production that Marx distinguishes in his works.

Communism is a classless society, which implies that the workers collectively own the means of production and products are made available to everyone who needs them as gifts without exchange. In capitalism, the dominant class does not, like in slavery, own the body and mind of workers. Workers own themselves, but they do not own the means of production. This separation necessitates that they sell their labour-power in order to be able to purchase the commodities they need in order to survive. The capitalist class relation is shaped by the commodity form, a labour market that coerces humans into wage-labour and the state's legal protection of capitalists' private ownership of the means of production.

Class societies are based on divisions of labour. In a division of labour, there is an institutionalised separation of tasks:

> For as soon as the division of labour comes into being, each man has a particular, exclusive sphere of activity, which is forced upon

Table 5.1 The main forms of ownership in various modes of production

Mode of production	*Class relation*	*Owner of labour-power*	*Owner of the means of production*	*Owner of the products of work*
Patriarchy	Patriarch/ family	Patriarch	Patriarch	Family
Slavery	Slave master/ slaves	Slave master	Slave master	Slave master
Feudalism	Feudal lords and serfs, aristocracy/ peasants	Partly self-controlled, partly lord	Partly self-controlled, partly lord	Partly self-controlled, partly lord
Capitalism	Capitalists/ working class (proletariat)	Worker	Capitalist	Capitalist
Communism	Classless society	Self	All	Partly all, partly individual

> him and from which he cannot escape. He is a hunter, a fisherman, a shepherd, or a critical critic, and must remain so if he does not want to lose his means of livelihood.[24]

Education systems that are based on the idea of specialisation sustain the division of labour by providing specialised branches of education that train individuals for particular jobs.

Marx and Engels in *The German Ideology* characterise the first division of labour as one that occurred in tribes and families: the gender division of labour, in which patriarchal family chieftains dominate over their family and slaves. In the family, "the wife and children are the slaves of the husband."[25] The class relationship between capital and labour implies a division between executing and planning work: capitalists and management strategically and operationally plan production and workers carry out these plans by producing commodities. One implication of any class division of labour is that the production process is not democratic, but a form of political economic dictatorship. In commodity-producing societies, the division of labour between town and country is foundational. In modern society, there is also a division of labour between the various sectors and branches of the economy (such as agriculture, manufacturing, services, the information economy). In an international division of labour, different parts of a commodity are produced in different countries in order to save labour costs and weaken unions and class struggles by separating workers geographically from each other. In a communist society, there are no divisons of labour. Such divisions are sublated into the emergence of what Marx calls well-rounded individuals, who have time for engaging in a multitude of different activities. In a communist society:

> nobody has one exclusive sphere of activity but each can become accomplished in any branch he wishes, society regulates the general production and thus makes it possible for me to do one thing today and another tomorrow, to hunt in the morning, fish in the afternoon, rear cattle in the evening, criticise after dinner, just as I have a mind, without ever becoming hunter, fisherman, shepherd or critic.[26]

5.4 CULTURAL LABOUR

The Dialectic of Mental and Bodily Activities in the Work Process

For Marx, work is a productive relationship between humans that transforms resources into new products. The resources that are transformed can originate in nature or in society, i.e. in the physical world external to humans or in the social relations internal to humanity. Marx argues that all work is necessarily a dialectical combination of the brain and the rest of the human body, especially the muscles and hands: "Tailoring and weaving, although they are qualitatively different productive activities, are both a productive expenditure of human brains, muscles, nerves, and hands etc., and in this sense both human [work] ['labour' in the original translation}."[27] A tailor doesn't just use their hands for creating a dress, but also has to imagine what the product will look like; a writer doesn't just use their brain but also their fingers for writing and typing, and the mouth for discussing the ideas in their books with others, etc. In the work process, the human being "sets in motion the natural forces which belong to his own body, his arms, legs, head and hands."[28] In all human work, humans use their brains and the rest of their bodies, including their limbs and sense organs.

Distinguishing physical and information-based work has mainly to do with the quality of the final product. Physical work produces tangible products, information work produces intangible, information-based products. Both forms of work require, as Marx points out, the human brain and the rest of the body.

Human Creativity: How Humans Differ from Animals

Marx points out a difference between humans and animals:

> A spider conducts operations which resemble those of the weaver, and a bee would put many a human architect to shame by the construction of its honeycomb cells. But what distinguishes the worst architect from the best of bees is that the architect builds the cell in his mind before he constructs it in wax. At the end of every labour process, a result emerges which had already been conceived by the worker at the beginning, hence already existed ideally. Man not only effects a change of form in the materials of nature; he also realizes [*verwirklicht*] his own purpose in those materials. And this is a purpose he is conscious of, it determines the mode of his activity with the rigidity of a law, and he must subordinate his will to it.[29]

Humans have the capacity to mentally anticipate what the future could look like. They are not just anticipatory beings, but also moral beings who are capable of drawing a distinction between what they find desirable and undesirable; between good and evil. The architect has a specific taste and there are particular requirements for the building they design, which are considerations that let them make specific choices and construct models before the actual construction begins. A writer anticipates what they want to write about before starting. So it needs to be decided if the focus is on a novel, an art book, or a social science book; where the novel is set; what kind of art the book covers; or what part of society the social science study shall cover. A bee, in contrast, acts much more driven by instincts and immediate needs. Creativity, self-consciousness, empathy, and morality are crucial forms of the human constitution that also shape the work process.

Three Modes of Organisation of the Productive Forces

The human brain, the human body, mechanical tools, and complex machine systems can act as instruments of work. They also include specific organisations of space–time, i.e. locations of production that are operated at specific time periods. The most important aspect of time is the necessary work time that depends on the level of productivity. At the level of society, it is the work time that is needed per year for guaranteeing the survival of a society. The objects and products of work can be natural, industrial, or informational resources, or a combination thereof.

The productive forces are a system of production that creates use-values. There are different modes of organisation of the productive forces, such as agricultural productive forces, industrial productive forces, and cultural/informational productive forces. Table 5.2 provides an overview.

In Chapter 4, models of commodities in the culture and digital industry were introduced (see Tables 4.2 and 4.3). We have seen in this chapter that Marx shows there is no commodity without the exploitation of labour. The implication is that wherever there is a cultural commodity or a digital commodity there is a class relationship organising the exploitation of cultural or digital workers. Tables 5.3 and 5.4 provide examples of workers in the culture industry and the digital industry.

Table 5.2 Three modes of organisation of the productive forces

Mode of the organisation of the productive forces	*Instruments of work*	*Objects of work*	*Products of work*
Agricultural productive forces	Body, brain, tools, machines	Nature	Basic products
Industrial productive forces	Body, brain, tools, machines	Basic products, industrial products	Industrial products
Informational/cultural productive forces	Body, brain, tools, machines	Experiences, ideas	Informational products

Table 5.3 Examples of cultural labour in the culture industry

Cultural commodity type	*Example commodities*	*Example workers*
Access to cultural events	Theatre performances, exhibitions, talks, lectures, readings, discussions, concerts, live performances, movie screenings in the cinema, pay-per-view access to live television events, etc.	Actors, dancers, musicians, museum workers, performance artists, theatre and cinema employees, event technicians, sound engineers, advertising, and public relations workers, etc.
Cultural content	Books, newspapers, magazines, audio recordings (e.g. vinyl records), recorded audio-visual content (e.g. movies distributed on DVDs, Blu-ray discs, computer hard	Writers, novelists, journalists, musicians, recording engineers, advertising and public relations workers, visual artists, filmmakers, etc.

(*Continued*)

Table 5.3 (Cont.)

Cultural commodity type	*Example commodities*	*Example workers*
	disks, or downloaded on the Internet) purchased artworks, posters, or prints	
Advertising space	Outdoor and transit ads, direct mail, newspaper and magazine ads, radio ads, television ads, digital, and online ads	Audiences producing attention for advertisements, advertising workers, advertising technology engineers, etc.
Subscriptions for regular access to cultural content	Newspaper and magazine subscriptions, theatre subscriptions, museum subscriptions, cinema subscriptions, pay-television	Subscription sales and management personnel, PR and advertising workers responsible for marketing subscriptions
Technologies for the production, distribution, and consumption of information	Record player, stereo, television set, computer, mobile phone, laptop, camera, audio recorder	Miners extracting minerals used for the production of components, scientists and engineers, sales, advertising and public relations workers who brand and market technologies, etc.
Mixed models of cultural commodities	Newspaper and magazine models that combine the sale of advertising, printed copies and subscriptions, one-time digital access and digital subscriptions; cultural corporations that sell technologies and access to content	Combination of various workers creating different cultural commodities

Table 5.4 A typology of digital commodities and capital accumulation models in the digital culture industry

Model	*Example commodities*	*Example workers*
The digital content as commodity model	Microsoft, Adobe, Oracle, SAP, Electronic Arts (computer games)	Software engineers, designers, digital content marketers, etc.
Digital finance model	eBanking, PayPal, Google Checkout, Amazon Payments, cryptocurrency and digital currency exchanges (e.g. Bitstamp, Coinbase, Coinmama, Kraken)	Software engineers, designers, digital service marketers, etc.
Hardware model	Apple, HP, Dell, Fujitsu, Lenovo	Miners in developing countries extracting minerals (known as "conflict minerals") out of which digital technologies are produced, hardware assemblage workers working for companies such as Foxconn, hardware engineers, scientists, advertising and public relations workers who brand and market hardware, sales workers, e-waste workers, etc.
Network model	Telecommunications and Internet service providers: AT&T, Verizon, China Mobile, Deutsche Telecom, Orange, BT	Telecommunications technicians, network engineers, sales workers, telecommunications marketing workers,
	Google, Facebook, Twitter	

(*Continued*)

Table 5.4 (Cont.)

Model	*Example commodities*	*Example workers*
The online advertising model		Users as workers, software engineers, advertising workers, etc.
The online retail model	Amazon, Alibaba, Apple iTunes, eBay	warehouse workers, transport workers, advertising workers, etc.
The sharing economy pay-per-service model	Uber, Upwork, Deliveroo	Uber and Deliveroo drivers, Upwork freelancers
The sharing economy-rent on rent model	Airbnb, Hiyacar, Drivy	Waged workers employed by the platforms mediating the rental process, no productive labour is conducted by the owners of the leased property and the leasers
Digital subscription model	Netflix, Spotify, Amazon Prime, Apple Music	Engineers, salespersons, subscription managers and other waged employees
Mixed models	Spotify, online newspapers, Apple	Various workers producing different commodities

Typologies of Labour in the Culture Industry and the Digital Culture Industry

In the culture and digital industries, we find a variety of workers and working conditions. In culture and digital industries, there is a relatively high share of freelance workers. The reason is that such work can be individualised, does not require very expensive means of production, and uses knowledge as the object of work.

Freelancers in the Culture/Digital Industry

Marx points out that the population size and the maximum possible length of the working day present limits to the mass of surplus-value that can be produced.[30] He furthermore argues that if a capitalist participates "directly in the process of production, [...] he is only a hybrid, a man between capitalist and worker, a 'small master'."[31] In the 21st century, freelancers are such hybrid workers. Freelancers are single-person companies. In many countries, freelancing is particularly prevalent in the media, cultural, and digital industries. A freelancer is at the same time the only capitalist and the only worker in the company. Freelancers own all capital and exploit themselves. A freelancer is a hybrid worker-capitalist. Many companies outsource parts of their labour in such a way that they tell all people working for them that they have to become freelancers.

Marx argues that capitalists participating in labour tend to strive to increase their capital to such a degree that they are:

> able to devote the whole of the time during which he functions as a capitalist, i.e. as capital personified, to the appropriation and therefore the control of the labour of others, and to the sale of the products of that labour.[32]

A certain amount of capital is required to be able to employ and exploit others. Marx says that there is a certain sum of capital that poses a point at which "merely quantitative differences pass over by a dialectical inversion into qualitative distinctions"[33] so that the capitalist can become a pure capitalist, not a worker-capitalist, and can devote himself/herself to management and control purposes. "The capitalist, who is capital personified, now takes care that the worker does his work regularly and with the proper degree of intensity."[34] The capitalist is an "extractor of surplus labour and an exploiter of surplus-labour"[35]. Freelancers are part of the working class. Freelancers, who start having enough capital that they utilise to employ others as wage-workers, are capitalists and therefore not part of the working class.

Ten Typical Features of Labour in the Digital/Culture Industry

Based on empirical studies she conducted in the culture and digital industry, the sociologist Rosalind Gill describes ten typical features of labour in the digital and culture industry:[36]

1. *Love of the work*: Digital and cultural workers love their activities and are emotionally attached to and engaged in them.
2. *Entrepreneurialism*: Digital and cultural workers have the aspiration to innovate, create something and be pioneers.
3. *Short-term, precarious, insecure work*: Work is often conducted on a project-basis that does not guarantee a stable, continuous flow of income.
4. *Low pay*: There is heavy competition and in some segments there are low levels of income, whereas in others (such as software engineering) the total income is relatively high.
5. *Long-hours culture*: Freelancers in the culture/digital industry regularly work 60, 80, or more hours per week.
6. *Keeping up*: Knowledge, standards and technology constantly change and one needs to constantly keep up with these changes and educate oneself about them, which is time-consuming.
7. *DIY learning*: Learning is not a paid part of the job, but a self-organised activity conducted when no new projects are available, or on top of projects as unremunerated activities.
8. *Informality*: Digital/cultural work has a playful ethos; finding work and getting clients is based on friends and personal networks, networking as an obligation, a compulsory sociality.
9. *Exclusions and inequality*: In the culture/digital industry, there are high inequalities relating to gender, age, class, race, ethnicity, and disability, etc. It is "extremely difficult for a woman to combine child-rearing with the bulimic patterns of the portfolio new media career"[37].

10 *No future*: Cultural/digital workers cannot think about how life will look like in five years because they are so engaged with their work in the present.

The International Division of Labour

In the old or first international division of labour, colonies were markets for commodities and sources of slaves and raw materials that were plundered. In the new international division of labour that emerged in the second half of the 20th century, the periphery often provides the raw materials and manufacturing steps while the knowledge, research, and technological innovations are situated in the capitalist centres. Transnational corporations have become important in the capitalist world economy and outsource labour in a flexible manner to countries and regions where they can minimise wages and other investment costs in order to maximise profits.

The production of computers, laptops, mobile phones, and peripheral computing devices is based on an international division of digital labour (IDDL).[38] Figure 5.2 visualises the IDDL. In the IDDL, different forms of alienation and exploitation can be encountered. Examples are slave workers in mineral extraction (e.g. so-called conflict mineral extraction in the Congo), Taylorist hardware assemblers (e.g. the highly exploited assemblage workers in Foxconn factories), software engineers, professional online content creators (e.g. online journalists), call centre agents, social media prosumers, and platform workers. The IDDL shows that various forms of labour that are characteristic of various stages of capitalism, capitalist, and pre-capitalist modes of production interact so that different forms of separated and highly exploited forms of double free-wage labour, unpaid "free" labour, casualised labour, and slave labour form a global network of exploited labour that creates value and profits for companies involved in the capitalist information and communication technology (ICT) industry.

The IDDL shows that stages of capitalist development and historical modes of production (such as patriarchal housework, classical slavery, feudalism, capitalism in general) and modes of

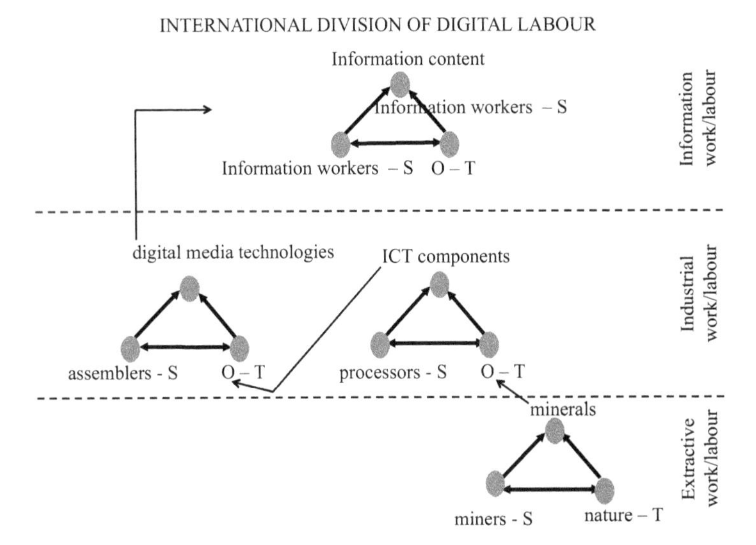

Figure 5.2 The international division of digital labour

organisation of the productive forces (such as agriculture, industrialism, informationalism) are not simply successive stages of economic development, where one form substitutes for an older one, but that they are all dialectically mediated. Capitalism has not destroyed the possibility of slavery, but slavery on the one hand exists in a new form as wage slavery, and on the other hand possibilities for the existence of classical and feudal forms of slavery remain and, as the example of slavery in mining shows, exist today in a way that benefits Western ICT companies.

"Digital labour" doesn't only describe the production of digital content. Rather, it signifies the entire interconnected international division of labour in the production of digital media technologies and content that involves various modes of production and different forms of the organisation of the productive forces (extractive/agricultural work, industrial work, and information work). The IDDL contains a network of agricultural/extractive, industrial, and informational forms of work that enables the existence and usage of digital media. The subjects involved in the digital mode of production (S) – miners, processors, assemblers, information workers, and related workers – stand in specific relations to production that are either class related or non-class related. So what is designated as S in Figure 5.2 is actually a relationship S_1 –S_2 between different subjects or subject groups. The IDDL combines agricultural, classical industrial, and informational productive forces, which means extractive labour that extracts natural resources from nature and thereby creates basic materials, industrial labour that processes and transforms natural resources into components and assembles components into digital technologies, and information labour that uses digital technologies for producing digital goods and services.

In contemporary capitalist society, most of these digital relations of production tend to be shaped by wage-labour, slave labour, unpaid labour, precarious labour, and freelance labour. The political task is that people working under such class relations emancipate themselves so that a communist mode of production can emerge that contains a communist mode of digital production as well as non-digital communist modes of production.

Slave Labour in the International Division of Digital Labour

In order to produce computer hardware, minerals need to be extracted. This is partly done under slave-like conditions in war-ridden regions of Africa, which is why such minerals are also called "conflict minerals". They include beryllium, cobalt, coltan, gallium, indium, palladium, platinum, rare earths, tantalum, and tin, etc. Studies have documented slavery in the extraction of conflict minerals, including, for example, in conflict-ridden parts of the Democratic Republic of Congo.[39]

The capitalist economy is not purely based on wage-labour, but also contains other class relations, such as slavery. According to the Global Slavery Index, there were 40.3 million people toiling in modern slavery in 2018,[40] including 8 million in India, 3.8 million in China, 3.2 million in Pakistan, 2.6 million in North Korea, 1.4 million in Nigeria, 1.3 million in Iran, 1.2 million in Indonesia, and 1 million in the Democratic Republic of Congo.[41]

In 2018, there were more than 200,000 slaves in Malaysia.[42] A study conducted in 2014 interviewed 501 workers in more than 100 electronics factories in Malaysia and documented modern slavery in this industry. It documented the existence of debt peonage, a particular form of modern slavery where slavery is enforced by debt:

> Twenty-eight percent of all workers in the study sample were found to be in situations of forced labor. [...] Ninety-two percent of all foreign workers surveyed paid recruitment fees in order to get their jobs. [...] Of respondents that had not yet paid off their debt, 92% reported feeling compelled to work over me hours to pay off their debt, and 85% felt it was impossible to leave their job before paying off their debt. [...] Ninety-four percent of foreign workers in the sample reported that their passports were held by the facility or their broker/agent, and 71% reported it was impossible or difficult to get their passports back when they wanted or needed them.[43] (10-11)

Quanta Computer is a hardware manufacturer based in Taiwan. It assembles laptops and other hardware for companies such as Apple, Dell, Fujitsu, Lenovo, and LG. In 2017, the company's net income after tax was NT$14.5 billion (around US$465 million).[44] In 2018, Apple made profits of US$59.5 billion, an increase of 23 percent in comparison to the financial year 2017.[45] In the same year, Apple was the world's largest digital and media company and the eighth largest transnational corporation.[46] In 2018, the Apple Watch cost between US$399 and US$799. The watches are manufactured in Quanta Computer factories. In 2017, a study conducted by Students and Scholars Against Corporate Misbehaviour (SACOM) documented modern slavery in the form of forced internships in Quanta factories:

> Many of the students reported that there is a high ratio of students in the production lines where they are working. When asked to state the portion of students in their line, many reported "more than half", "almost half" or "I can't tell the exact number

> but anyway there are a lot". [...] During the interviews, student workers were asked if they had voluntarily applied for internships at Quanta. All replied negatively, saying that their schools assigned the positions and required the students to take them. They had no right to choose where or when to carry out the internships. The schools had simply notified them that they had been assigned to internships in the factory.[47]

The Condition of the Industrial Working Class in the 19th Century and the 21st Century

In his book *The Condition of the Working Class in England*, Engels analyses the bad working conditions in British manufacturing industry in the 1840s. He for example describes dress-making manufacturers in London:

> "They employ a mass of young girls – there are said to be 15,000 of them in all – who sleep and eat on the premises, come usually from the country, and are therefore absolutely the slaves of their employers. During the fashionable season, which lasts some four months, working hours, even in the best establishments, are fifteen, and, in very pressing cases, eighteen a day; but in most shops work goes on at these times without any set regulation, so that the girls never have more than six, often not more than three or four, sometimes, indeed, not more than two hours in the twenty-four, for rest and sleep, working nineteen to twenty-two hours, if not the whole night through, as frequently happens! The only limit set to their work is the absolute physical inability to hold the needle another minute."[48]

Reports about assemblage and other manufacturing labour in contemporary China remind us of Engels's analysis. China has developed from a society dominated by agricultural labour into one where manufacturing and services have been rapidly growing. Here is an example. In 2017, China Labor Watch published a report about the working conditions in the Chinese factories of the Apple suppliers Foxconn, Pegatron, Compel, and Green Point:

> In all of the four factories, weekly working hours surpassed 60 hours and monthly overtime hours surpassed 90 hours, with most overtime amounting to of 136 hours over a month. [...] Workers were required to sign an agreement to voluntarily do overtime, opt out of paying for social insurance and opt out of housing funds. These acts are blatant attempts to evade responsibilities and are clear violations against China's Labor Law. [...] Workers at Pegatron and Green Point were continuously working overtime without compensation. [...] Both excessive working hours and tremendous pressure are severe problems at Foxconn. Since 2010, there have been more than 10 suicides, indicative of the terrible working conditions and rigid management. In September 2016, [a] CLW [China Labour Watch] investigator launched another undercover investigation at Foxconn. [...] Most workers there had accumulated 122 hours of overtime each month [...], far exceeding the legal limit of 36 hours per month as per China's labor laws.[49]

Platform Labour

The European Foundation for the Improvement of Living and Working Conditions (Eurofound) defines crowd labour or platform labour as "an employment form that uses an online platform to enable organisations or individuals to access an indefinite and unknown group of other organisations or individuals to solve specific problems or to provide specific services or products in exchange for payment."[50] In 2018, Eurofound published a study of platform labour in ten European countries. A total of 41 interviews were conducted in eight European countries. Typical conditions that platform workers face are labour insecurity, insecure income, digital surveillance, and low levels of unionisation:

> Platform work was not the main source of income for the large majority of the interviewees; it is a side activity. [...] New technologies allow platforms to continuously monitor these workers while they work, the results of which are in some cases communicated to the workers, indicating their relative performance. [...] Most of the platforms automatically suspend the worker after a number of 'strikes' (negative marks of their performance) or when their rating falls

> below a certain threshold. [...] Earnings are highly uncertain for most types of platform work. [...] In most cases, platform workers do not have collective representation, and when they do, it is generally through their own initiatives or trade unions. [...] When platform workers are self-employed, however, it becomes more complicated since many trade unions and business organisations do not consider self-employed workers eligible for membership.[51]

There are different forms of working conditions in the IDDL, including slave labour in mineral extraction and hardware assemblage, highly exploited manufacturing labour, highly paid, and highly stressed software engineers whose poverty is a lack of free time, relatively low-paid software engineers in developing countries, precarious platform and service workers, etc.[52] What these digital workers have in common is that transnational digital corporations that yield high profits from the international division of digital labour exploit them.

5.5 CONCLUSION

Commodities stand in a dialectical relationship to labour. Wherever there is a commodity, it has been produced by labour. Abstract and concrete labour are the two labour dimensions of the commodity. Surplus-value and surplus-labour are two of the key categories of Marx's theory. They are at the heart of the analysis of class relations between an exploiting class and an exploited class.

The combination of love of the work and precarious labour is a feature of cultural and digital labour that is frequently found. Transnational cultural and digital corporations exploit workers in an international division of labour that features a range of different forms of exploitation. Workers in the international division of cultural/digital labour have in common that they coproduce the value, commodities and profits of transnational capital in the culture/digital industries. The exploitation of global digital/cultural labour can only be overcome if they unite to organise class struggles against digital/cultural capital.

A better world can only be won through class struggles. The slogan under which the digital workers of the world should unite needs to reflect *The Manifesto of the Communist Party*'s dictum: "Let the [digital] ruling classes tremble at a Communistic revolution! [...] [Digital workers] of all countries, unite!"[53]

Recommended Further Readings About Labour and Surplus-Value

Karl Marx. 1867. *Capital Volume 1*. Chapter 4: The General Formula for Capital, pp. 247–256. Chapter 7: The Labour Process and the Valorization Process. London: Penguin. pp. 283–306.

In *Capital Volume One*, Chapter 4, Marx introduces the notion of surplus-value. In Chapter 7, Marx explains the production of the commodity as the dialectic of the labour process and the valorization process.

Rosalind Gill. 2011. "Life is a Pitch": Managing the Self in New Media Work. In *Managing Media Work*, ed. Mark Deuze. London: Sage. pp. 249–262.

Rosalind Gill. 2002. Cool, Creative and Egalitarian? Exploring Gender in Project-Based New Media Work in Europe. *Information, Communication & Society* 5 (1): 70–89.

In these two works, Rosalind Gill documents results of empirical research she conducted about the working conditions in the digital media industry.

Christian Fuchs. 2014. *Digital Labour and Karl Marx*. New York: Routledge.

Christian Fuchs. 2015. *Culture and Economy in the Age of Social Media*. New York: Routledge.

These two books provide an introduction to how Marxist theory helps us to understand digital capitalism and digital labour. There are case study chapters that focus on specific themes. I recommend you read a number of the following chapters:

- *Digital Labour and Karl Marx*, Chapter 6: Digital Slavery: Slave Work in ICT-Related Mineral Extraction.
- *Digital Labour and Karl Marx*, Chapter 7: Exploitation at Foxconn: Primitive Accumulation and the Formal Subsumption of Labour.

- *Digital Labour and Karl Marx*, Chapter 8: The New Imperialism's Division of Labour: Work in the Indian Software Industry.
- *Digital Labour and Karl Marx*, Chapter 9: The Silicon Valley of Dreams and Nightmares of Exploitation: The Google Labour Aristocracy and Its Context.
- *Digital Labour and Karl Marx*, Chapter 10: Tayloristic, Housewifized Service Labour: The Example of Call Centre Work.
- *Digital Labour and Karl Marx*, Chapter 11: Theorizing Digital Labour on Social Media.
- *Culture and Economy in the Age of Social Media*, Chapter 6: Social Media's International Division of Digital Labour.
- *Culture and Economy in the Age of Social Media*, Chapter 7: Baidu, Weibo and Renren: The Global Political Economy of Social Media in China.

Notes

1 Karl Marx. 1867. *Capital Volume 1*. London: Penguin. p. 283.
2 Ibid., p. 284.
3 Ibid., p. 285.
4 Ibid., p. 286.
5 Ibid., p. 286.
6 See: http://en.wikipedia.org/wiki/Stone_Age.
7 See: http://en.wikipedia.org/wiki/Bronze_Age.
8 See: http://en.wikipedia.org/wiki/Iron_Age.
9 Marx, *Capital Volume 1*, p. 270.
10 Ibid., p. 133.
11 Ibid., p. 133.
12 Ibid., p. 133.
13 Ibid., p. 136.
14 Hannah Arendt. 1958. *The Human Condition*. Chicago, IL: University of Chicago Press. 2nd edition. pp. 80–81. Brigitte Weingart. 1997. *Arbeit – ein Wort mit langer Geschichte*. www.ethikprojekte.ch/texte/arbeit.htm, accessed on 31 December 2015. Raymond Williams. 1983. *Keywords*. New York: Oxford University Press. pp. 176–179.
15 Ibid.

16 Ibid.
17 Karl Marx. 1875. Critique of the Gotha Programme. In *MECW Volume* 24. London: Lawrence & Wishart. pp. 75–99.
18 Marx, *Capital Volume 1*, p. 293.
19 Ibid.
20 Enrique Dussel. 2008. The Discovery of the Category of Surplus Value. In *Karl Marx's Grundrisse: Foundations of the Critique of the Political Economy 150 Years Later*, ed. Marcello Musto. New York: Routledge. pp. 67–78.
21 Karl Marx. 1857/1858. *Grundrisse: Foundations of the Critique of Political Economy*. London: Penguin. pp. 324–325.
22 Marx, *Capital Volume 1*, pp. 324–325.
23 Ibid., p. 325.
24 Karl Marx and Friedrich Engels. 1845/46. The German Ideology. Critique of Modern German Philosophy According to Its Representatives Feuerbach, B. Bauer and Stirner, and of German Socialism According to Its Various Prophets. In *MECW Volume* 5. London: Lawrence & Wishart. pp. 15–539.
25 Ibid., p. 52.
26 Ibid., p. 47.
27 Marx, *Capital Volume 1*, p. 134.
28 Ibid., p. 283.
29 Ibid., p. 284.
30 *Volume 1*Ibid., p. 422.
31 Ibid., p. 423.
32 Ibid., p. 423.
33 Ibid., p. 423.
34 Ibid., p. 424.
35 Ibid., p. 425.
36 Rosalind Gill. 2011. "Life is a Pitch": Managing the Self in New Media Work. In *Managing Media Work*, ed. Mark Deuze. London: Sage. pp. 249–262. Rosalind Gill. 2002. Cool, Creative and Egalitarian? Exploring Gender in Project-Based New Media Work in Europe. *Information, Communication & Society* 5 (1): 70–89.
37 Gill, Cool, Creative and Egalitarian?, p. 84.
38 Christian Fuchs. 2014. *Digital Labour and Karl Marx*. New York: Routledge. Christian Fuchs. 2015. *Culture and Economy in the Age of Social Media*. New York: Routledge.
39 For an overview and a Marxist interpretation of empirical reports, see: Fuchs, *Digital Labour and Karl Marx*, Chapter 6: Digital Slavery: Slave Work in ICT-Related Mineral Extraction, pp. 155–181.

40 Walk Free Foundation. 2018. *The Global Slavery Index 2018*. Nedlands: Walk Free Foundation.
41 Ibid., pp. 69–70, 87–88, 178.
42 Ibid., p. 88.
43 Verité. 2014. *Forced Labor in the Production of Electronic Goods in Malaysia. A Comprehensive Study of Scope*. Amherst, MA: Verité. pp. 10–11.
44 Data source: Quanta Computer Inc. Annual Report 2017, available on www.quantatw.com, accessed on 15 May 2019.
45 Data source: Apple Investor Relations, SEC-filings form 10-K for financial year 2018, available on https://investor.apple.com/, accessed on 15 May 2019.
46 Data source: Forbes 2000 List of the World's Largest Public Companies, year 2018, available on www.forbes.com/global2000/, accessed on 15 May 2019.
47 Students and Scholars Against Corporate Misbehaviour (SACOM). 2014. *Apple Watch 3 – Exploit Students Workers Further. An Investigative Report on Apple Watch's Exclusive Manufacturer*. Hong Kong: SACOM. pp. 12, 16.
48 Friedrich Engels. 1845. The Condition of the Working Class in England. From Personal Observation and Authentic Sources. In *MECW Volume 4*. London: Lawrence & Wishart. pp. 295–596.
49 China Labor Watch. 2017. *A Year of Regression in Apple's Supply Chain. Pursuing Profits at the Cost of Working Conditions*. New York: China Labor Watch. pp. 1, 3.
50 Eurofound. 2015. *New Forms of Employment*. Luxembourg: Publications Office of the European Union. p. 107.
51 Eurofound. 2018. *Employment and Working Conditions of Selected Types of Platform Work*. Luxembourg: Publications Office of the European Union. pp. 60–62.
52 Compare: Fuchs, *Digital Labour and Karl Marx* and Fuchs, *Culture and Economy in the Age of Social Media*.
53 Karl Marx and Friedrich Engels. 1848. The Manifesto of the Communist Party. In *MECW Volume 6*. London: Lawrence & Wishart. pp. 477–519.

6

THE WORKING CLASS

6.1 INTRODUCTION

This chapter asks: What is class? What is the working class? How has the working class changed since Marx's time? How has the working class changed in the age of digital capitalism?

Section 6.2 discusses Marx and Engels's understanding of the working class. In Section 6.3, attention focuses on the soci[et]al worker.

6.2 THE WORKING CLASS

In *The Manifesto of the Communist Party*, Marx and Engels not only point out the foundations of the classless society, but also argue that there is a long history of class societies that ranges from ancient slavery, to feudalism, to capitalism:

> In the earlier epochs of history, we find almost everywhere a complicated arrangement of society into various orders, a manifold gradation of social rank. In ancient Rome we have patricians, knights, plebeians, slaves; in the Middle Ages, feudal

> lords, vassals, guild-masters, journeymen, apprentices, serfs; in almost all of these classes, again, subordinate gradations.[1]

Marx and Engels write that the capitalist class antagonism is one between the bourgeoisie and the working class:

> Our epoch, the epoch of the bourgeoisie, possesses, however, this distinct feature: it has simplified class antagonisms. Society as a whole is more and more splitting up into two great hostile camps, into two great classes directly facing each other – Bourgeoisie and Proletariat. [...] In proportion as the bourgeoisie, i.e., capital, is developed, in the same proportion is the proletariat, the modern working class, developed – a class of labourers, who live only so long as they find work, and who find work only so long as their labour increases capital.[2]

Marx and Engels argue that capitalism is based on a social antagonism between the capitalist class and the working class. The first exploits the labour of the second in order to accumulate capital and wealth. Marx argues in *Capital* that in capitalism, workers are "merely a machine for the production of surplus-value" and capitalists are "a machine for the transformation of this surplus-value into surplus capital".[3] Capitalism is based on an instrumental logic that reduces humans to their labour-power and treats them like dead things, machines, and resources. The proletariat is the class that signifies "the *complete loss* of" the human being and whose emancipation is "the *complete rewinning*" of the human.[4] The working class is the manifestation of economic alienation in capitalism.

The working class does not own means of production and is therefore forced to live from its labour and from entering into class relations that force it to produce commodities that are owned by the capitalist class:

> But the worker, whose sole source of livelihood is the sale of his labour, cannot leave the *whole class of purchasers, that is, the capitalist class,* without renouncing his existence. *He belongs not to this or that bourgeois, but to the bourgeoisie, the bourgeois class,* and it is his business to dispose of himself, that is to find a purchaser within this bourgeois class.[5]

> The proletariat is that class of society which procures its means of livelihood entirely and solely from the sale of its labour and not from the profit derived from any capital; whose weal and woe, whose life and death, whose whole existence depend on the demand for labour, hence, on the alternation of times of good and bad business, on the fluctuations resulting from unbridled competition. The proletariat, or class of proletarians, is, in a word, the working class of the nineteenth century.[6]

Marx argues that the working class faces a "double freedom". It is free from the ownership of the means of production. As a consequence, it is forced to work and produce surplus-value for capitalists in order to survive. It is also different from slaves who are owned by slave masters. The members of the working class own their own bodies and minds but are forced to sell their labour-power. Marx calls this situation the "double freedom" of the working class:

> The wageworker is "the free proprietor of his own labour-capacity, hence of his person. [...] For the transformation of money into capital, therefore, the owner of money must find the free worker available on the commodity-market; and this worker must be free in the double sense that as a free individual he can dispose of his labour-power as his own commodity, and that, on the other hand, he has no other commodity for sale, i.e. he is rid of them, he is free of all the objects needed for the realization of his labour-power".[7]

> Free workers, in the double sense that they neither form part of the means of production themselves, as would be the case with slaves, serfs, etc., nor do they own the means of production, as would be the case with self-employed peasant proprietors. The free workers are therefore free from, unencumbered by, any means of production of their own.[8]

Marx argues that the working class's freedom of the person has turned into another form of unfreedom in capitalism. Given that not everyone owns means of production, most humans in modern society are compelled to work for others in order to earn a living. The legal structure of private property and commodity production compels humans to enter class relationships in which their labour is exploited and which creates goods owned by others.

The working class produces advantages for the capitalist class that mean disadvantages for itself. Therefore, the working class is the class "which has to bear all the burdens of society without enjoying its advantages, which, ousted from society, is forced into the most decided antagonism to all other classes; a class which forms the majority of all members of society".[9] The working class's existence constitutes a capitalist dialectic of poverty and wealth. The working class is poor because it produces wealth that it does not own:

> Labour as *absolute poverty*: poverty not as shortage, but as total exclusion of objective wealth. [...] labour is *absolute poverty as object*, on one side, and is, on the other side, the *general possibility* of wealth as subject and as activity.[10]

These quotes show that Marx and Engels outlined several features of the working class:

- *Class position*: Class position is determined by a group's role in the production process and its relation to the means of production.
- *Class antagonism*: The working class stands in an antagonistic class relation to the capitalist class (the bourgeoisie).
- *Structural coercion*: The working class does not own means of production and capital and is therefore structurally forced into class relations in order to live and survive from its labour and from producing commodities and capital for the capitalist class that owns these goods.
- *Production of surplus-value*: The working class produces surplus-value in class relations. The working class produces advantages for the capitalist class that mean disadvantages for itself.
- *Double freedom*: Unlike slaves, the members of the working class have freedom of the person, but the structures of capitalism force them into surviving by selling their labour-power.

- *Dialectic of poverty and wealth*: The working class's existence constitutes a capitalist dialectic of poverty and wealth. It is poor because it produces wealth that the capitalist class owns and without which the capitalist class cannot exist, which also constitutes the power of the working class.
- *Economic alienation*: The working class is the manifestation of economic alienation in capitalism. Capitalism is based on instrumental reason that reduces workers to the status of machines, instruments, and things. The working class's emancipation is the emancipation of humanity from class society.

Workers are "the majority of society".[11] In 2019, 5.7 billion people, or 74 percent of the world's population of 7.7 billion humans, were part of the working class.[12] There were 105.1 million employers, which is just 1.4 percent of the world's population. The working class is the largest group of humans. The capitalist class is, in contrast, the most financially powerful group of humans, but is relatively small in absolute numbers. Because they are exploited by capital, face the threat of insecurity when they lose their jobs, and surrender their autonomy to bosses, workers have an objective interest in the abolishment of class society. The working class is the only social group "positioned to bring capital to heel".[13]

6.3 THE SOCIAL WORKING CLASS

In order to think about the working class today, the Marxist media and communication scholar Peter Goodwin provides a number of helpful questions that any Marxist needs to answer in order to make sense of class today:

> "First, and most fundamental: Is it possible to be a Marxist without accepting the self-emancipation of the working class as an integral part of Marxism?" For those who want to reply 'Yes' two further questions follow:

(a) How does this make Marxism different from any other critique? In other words whatever happened to 'the point is to change it'?
(b) Or is there perhaps some other agency of change – perhaps a reconstituted "people" for the 21st century? If so we need to know the details.

For those whose reply to our fundamental question is a firm 'No' three further questions follow:

(a) Is the proletariat still centred around blue-collar workers and/or manufacturing but has the weight of these now decisively relocated from its previous bases in Europe and North America?
(b) Is the proletariat, on the other hand, equally centred among the new white-collar occupations, particularly those associated with information technology? And if so are the tools developed by Marxists in the seventies to analyse these groups still adequate? If not what are the new ones?
(c) And finally – whether we choose positive answers to (a) and/or (b) – what leads us to believe that this 21st-century proletariat will act as a class seeking its self-emancipation?

These are not easy questions and they don't have easy answers. But any of us who wants to be called a Marxist two hundred years after Marx's birth needs to ask them, and make a serious start on giving answers".[14]

The Complexity of Capitalism's Class Structure

Capitalism's class structure is complicated by a number of social phenomena:

1. *Houseworkers:* In capitalism, houseworkers are unremunerated reproductive workers who produce and reproduce labour-power as a commodity so that it is fit and ready for being sold on the labour market. Houseworkers are part of the working class and exploited by capital.

2. *Managers:* The 20th century has seen the rise of managers and chief executive officers (CEOs) who are paid high salaries for planning, organising, and controlling the production process. Many, but not all of them, also have ownership shares. Given that managers' role in the production process is the control of the working class, they are part of the capitalist class and not of the working class.
3. *The unemployed:* Automation causes structural unemployment. The unemployed do not have a regular wage-income, but are what Marx terms the industrial reserve army,[15] workers in waiting who are "human material always ready for exploitation by capital" and "a condition for the existence of the capitalist mode of production".[16] Often the state forces them to conduct low-paid or unremunerated labour or they take a very active role in reproductive labour. The existence of the unemployed helps capital to keep down wage demands because labour-power is not a scarce commodity if there is a significant level of unemployment. The unemployed are part of the working class.
4. *Workers in poor ("developing") countries:* The economies of poor countries tend to have low technological productivity and a relatively high average amount of labour-time utilised per commodity. These economies therefore not competitive on the world market, which creates uneven global geographical economic development, a dependence on investment from capital in rich countries, and loans that create a debt spiral. Internationally mobile capital invests in developing countries in order to find cheap labour. Uneven development, dependence, and the international division of labour create poverty and high rates of exploitation in poor countries. There is not a class contradiction between rich and poor countries, but between global capital and poor countries' poor and workers.
5. *Global capitalism:* Global capital outsources labour globally in order to reduce its labour costs and increase its profits. Transnational corporations often exploit workers

in many countries. Global capital has created a global working class. The problem is that capital has resources for organising the exploitation of labour, whereas the workers in a global corporation's international division of labour are often separate, which requires international trade unions to unite them in class struggles.

6. *Farm workers:* Farmers who rent the land from land owners produce rent and form a class of vassals. Farmer-workers who do not own the land and work for land-owning farmers are part of the working class. Members of family-owned farms that are run and owned by families and that depend on selling their products to profit-making corporations are part of the working class. Examples are family farmers who produce crops, meat, or milk for global capitalist agrobusinesses and food and drink corporations such as Monsanto or Nestlé. The owners of large farms that employ wage workers and yield profit are not part of the working class, but the agricultural workers employed on these farms are.
7. *Knowledge workers and professionals:* The 20th century has seen a massive growth of the number of people who do not work with their hands in factories, but are knowledge workers employed in offices. Although the content and activities of the labour of such white-collar workers are different from blue-collar labour, they are also part of the working class insofar as they produce cultural commodities for capitalist corporations. Professionals such as lawyers, medical doctors, architects, engineers, lawyers, or medical doctors are university-educated. A share of them works for capitalist businesses and are therefore part of the working class. Others are entrepreneurs who run their own companies that employ workers. Such professionals are part of the capitalist class. A third type of professionals are freelancers. They belong to a separate group of freelance workers.
8. *Freelancers and the self-employed:* Freelancers are self-employed workers who own their means of production, do not employ other workers, and depend on selling the

results of their labour on the market. Insofar as they do not employ others, they are self-exploiting workers and are therefore part of the working class. Many of them face precarious working conditions and have a relatively low income. Freelancing is very common in the culture/digital industry. Freelancers own the means of production such as a car, a computer, and their brains. The total amount of capital assets tends to be small, which is why they cannot employ others. Freelancers who accumulate lots of capital in order to stop exploiting themselves and start exploiting others whom they employ are part of the capitalist class and cease to be freelancers.

9. *Public service workers:* Public service workers are workers in publicly owned companies such as hospitals, schools, universities, public service media organisations, local, regional, or federal administration, etc. They often do not produce commodities that are sold on the market for yielding profit. Rather they are paid reproductive workers who are remunerated by taxes. Their labour helps to reproduce the health and skills of labour-power, which is why they reproduce commodities and are part of the working class.
10. *Children, youth, and students:* Children, youth, pupils and students who are not yet part of the working population depend on their parents and/or the state. Pupils, students, preschoolers, and children in nurseries are part of educational organisations where skills for the capitalist economy are created. They can therefore be seen as reproductive workers whose future status is not fixed. Some of them become capitalists or managers, many of them become workers. Babies, infants and children who do not attend educational institutions are part of the working class insofar as their parents are members of the working class. Young people who conduct apprenticeships are highly exploited members of the working class.
11. *Consumer labour, prosumption:* Since the 20th century, there has been a steady growth of companies' outsourcing of parts of the labour process to unremunerated

consumers in order to save labour costs and increase profits. Examples are self-service restaurants, self-service checkouts in supermarkets, self-service gas stations, the self-assemblage of furniture, the crowdsourcing of design and strategic labour over the Internet, etc. Consumers thereby become producers of commodities. The labour of productive consumption, so-called prosumption, is that of the working class. Prosumers working for profit-yielding companies are unremunerated members of the working class. Also, the audience labour of the consumers of advertising-funded media is a form of prosumption (see the discussion in Chapter 4).

12. *Digital labour:* The rise of digital technologies such as the computer, the Internet, laptops, and mobile phones has changed the world of work. The office has diffused into society so that the boundaries between labour-time and leisure-time and between the office, the private sphere, and the public sphere have become fluid. The effect is that there is hidden labour outside of the office and that unremunerated labour-time is increased via the use of digital technologies as tools for organising work and producing commodities. The users of targeted-advertising-funded corporations such as Facebook or Google produce attention, data, metadata, content, and social relations that are used as resources for selling targeted ads. They constitute an unremunerated form of digital labour. Companies today often crowdsource labour to fans and consumers over the Internet. An example is the running of competitions, where the best idea or design wins and is realised by a business. Crowdsourcing is a form of unremunerated or low-paid digital labour. Platform workers conduct labour whose organisation is mediated via digital platforms that are owned by profit-yielding companies such as Uber, Deliveroo, Upwork, or Amazon. The freelancers performing services via such platforms are digital workers who are exploited by platform capitalists. They are part of the working class.

13. *Prisoners:* Prisons are today often outsourced from the state to private, profit-oriented businesses. Inmates in private prisons and state prisons are often forced or encouraged to work for nothing or extremely low wages. Such prisoners are highly exploited, enslaved members of the working class.
14. *Modern slavery:* Slavery has not ceased to exist, but continues to exist in various forms such as forced labour, debt bondage, sex trafficking and sex slavery, domestic servitude, forced marriage, child labour, prison labour, or government-forced labour within the global capitalist economy. Slaves are highly exploited workers who are coerced by physical violence, which includes the unfreedom of their person and which puts their lives at risks if they refuse to work. According to the Global Slavery Index for the year 2018, there were 40.3 million individuals living and working in modern slavery.[17]
15. *Migrant workers and racialised workers:* There are members of the capitalist class who move to other countries in order to take up positions as managers or CEOs. Capital is highly flexible. Well-paid professional workers, to a certain degree, move voluntarily to other countries in order to obtain better jobs and higher wages. Whereas migrating managers are not part of the working class, well-paid migrant workers are because they are exploited by capital. Involuntary migration is caused by structures of domination that result in wars, environmental degradation, the explosion of inequalities, precarious labour, genocide, gender oppression, and racism, etc. Workers who leave the countries they live in because of economic, political, or ideological domination often lose a lot or everything. They end up in other countries as refugees, asylum seekers, illegal immigrants, or legal migrant workers. A certain number of them enter the labour market in the countries they migrate to. Once there they very frequently become highly exploited labour because they are vulnerable and face class relations that are ideologically shaped by

racism. Often, it is not just migrant workers but also citizens of a country who look different to the majority and face racist exploitation.

The working class is a dialectically differentiated unity. It is differentiated by divisions in respect to wages, income, education, language, skills, geography, citizenship, gender, origin, racism, ability, occupation, industry, sector, status of (un) employment, remuneration, class mobility, beliefs, worldviews, lifestyles, and tastes, etc. The point is that these divisions are united by the fact that all workers stand in, and together constitute, a class relation to capital. The divisions within the working class help capital in its attempt to try to politically separate the working class and repress class struggles.

The class antagonism and capital "circulation and accumulation" constitute "the economic engine of capitalism".[18] Class relations and the economic logic of production for accumulation shape all realms of capitalist society and these realms' antagonisms, including environmental degradation, patriarchy, racism, fascism, nationalism, and ethnic hatred, etc. Non-economic antagonisms, beyond production and accumulation, have their internal dynamics and emergent qualities that influence each other and the economy. There are dialectical "intersections and interactions"[19] of the class antagonism and non-economic antagonisms. For example, racism has: (a) political-ideological dynamics, and (b) economic dynamics that are intersecting and interacting: (a) There are ideologues who foster racism in the political realm in order to accumulate power, which distracts attention from the class conflict, and (b) racism operates in the form of a racist class relation with high levels of exploitation in the economy.

The Collective Worker

Marx's notion of the collective worker helps us to theorise the complex structure of the working class. In *Capital Volume One*, Chapter 16 "Absolute and Relative Surplus-Value", Marx introduces the concept of the collective worker:

> With the progressive accentuation of the co-operative character of the labour process, there necessarily occurs a progressive extension of the concept of productive labour, and of the concept of the bearer of that labour, the productive worker. In order to work productively, it is no longer necessary for the individual himself to put his hand to the object; it is sufficient for him to be an organ of the collective labourer, and to perform any one of its subordinate functions.[20]

Elsewhere, Marx speaks of the collective worker as the "aggregate worker" performing a "combined activity" of labour:

> An ever increasing number of types of labour are included in the immediate concept of *productive labour*, and those who perform it are classed as *productive workers*, workers directly exploited by capital and *subordinated* to its process of production and expansion. If we consider the aggregate worker, i.e. if we take all the members comprising the workshop together, then we see that their *combined activity* results materially in an *aggregate* product which is at the same time a *quantity of goods*. And here it is quite immaterial whether the job of a particular worker, who is merely a limb of this aggregate worker, is at a greater or smaller distance from the actual manual labour. But then: the activity of this aggregate labour-power is its *immediate productive consumption by capital*, i.e. it is the self-valorization process of capital, and hence, as we shall demonstrate, the immediate production of surplus-value, the *immediate conversion of this latter into capital*.[21]

The concept of the collective worker is an extended version of the concepts of productive labour, the labour theory of value, and the working class. It is not limited to wage-labour. It can explain the complexity of the working class and includes a multitude of workers such as blue-collar wage workers, white-collar wage workers, the unemployed, workers and the poor in developing countries, freelancers, farm workers, public service workers, pupils, students, preschoolers, kindergarten children, apprentices, consumer and prosumer labour, digital labour, prison labour, slave labour, migrant workers, or racialised workers. It is not just wage-labour's unpaid part (surplus-labour) that is exploited and productive, but it is also unwaged labour, which contributes to the production of commodities and capital accumulation, that is exploited and productive.

Antonio Negri: The Social Worker

Antonio Negri introduced the notion of the social worker for the collective working class that extends beyond the walls of the factory and the office, goes beyond wage-labour and includes precarious, atypical, and unremunerated labour.

The social worker is "a new working class" that is "now extended throughout the entire span of production and reproduction".[22] The socialisation of labour has resulted in the "emergence of a massified and socialised working class".[23] The social worker signifies "a growing awareness of the interconnection between productive labour and the labour of reproduction",[24] the emergence of "diffuse labour",[25] and mobile labour[26] (= labour flexibility). The term "societal worker" is more suitable than "social worker" because what Negri designates is that the working class has diffused from the offices and factories into capitalist society that is a social factory of value production. To a certain degree, homes, cafés, public spaces, co-working spaces, and the Internet, etc., are factories that operate as temporally fixed constant capital that workers use as work environments that enable them to produce commodities. In later works written together with Michael Hardt, Toni Negri uses the term "the multitude" for the societal working class. The multitude stands in a class contradiction to global capital ("empire") and is constituted by "all those who labour and produce under the rule of capital"[27] and "all those whose labour is directly or indirectly exploited by and subjected to capitalist norms of production and reproduction".[28]

Marx and Engels's dictum that "the history of all hitherto existing society is the history of class struggles"[29] not only means that class struggles are decisive at the passage point from one class society to the next and from capitalism to communism, but also that in phases of struggle, multiple class struggles, i.e. the struggles of various factions and sub-groups of the working class, intersect and unite. Marx and Engels anticipated Hardt and Negri's concept of the working class as the multitude.

The Subsumption of Nature, the City, Culture, Cultivated Nature, and Human Subjectivity under Capital

The natural environment is the human being's external nature. Natural systems are self-producing systems; they create, maintain, and reproduce themselves. It is not human labour but nature itself that creates and reproduces nature, although human labour transforms and uses nature as constant capital. Class relations are social relations, in which human labour is exploited. The relation between capital and nature, in which the natural environment is polluted and destroyed, is not a class relationship but an antagonistic relationship of appropriation and extraction through which nature is turned into commodities and constant capital. Capitalism uses nature as a free resource that is treated in a ruthless manner in order to yield profit. The human–nature relation is in capitalism subsumed under capital, which does not imply that the abolition of capital results in an automatic end of environmental degradation. Non-capitalist forms of production can also appropriate nature in a destructive manner, which implies that socialism needs to be combined with environmental consciousness in order to guarantee the sustainability of nature and society. Struggles against capital's environmental degradation are anti-capitalist struggles, but not automatically class struggles. In the ideal case, they are linked to and therefore also part of class struggles.

The city is a social, physical, and natural space, where humans live and work. In capitalism, it is the infrastructural space, where social systems of commodity production are organised. The city is not produced and reproduced by a single company but by all humans living and working in it. It is an urban common that is available to all. In capitalism this means that both citizens and capital use urban infrastructures for their purposes. The city therefore always acts simultaneously as fixed capital for many corporations. But it also consists of social spaces that are accessible to all without a profit imperative and relatively autonomous from capital. Parks that are used for recreation are an example. When such parks are privatised so that either you have to pay an entry fee that yields profit for a private owner, or the park's land is turned into property that is rented out to businesses, then parts of the city are subsumed under the logic of capital. The urban common that is created by all humans living in it is expropriated and people are excluded from access. Monetary access that yields rent becomes the governing principle that benefits a class of rentiers. David Harvey argues that an urban space is "a product of collective human labor".[30] Hardt and Negri write that the "metropolis is a factory for the production of the common. [...] In fact, production of the common is becoming nothing but the life of the city itself".[31] Understood in this way, the subsumption of the city under capital is a class relation between citizens living in the city and real estate capital that yields a rent-profit that emerges from citizens' collective labour.

For most of us, the properties we live in are the most expensive resources we pay for. This becomes evident if you think of the amount of money you pay each month for renting a house or flat or for paying back a mortgage and its interest to a bank. In many cases, rent, mortgage instalments, and interest make up the largest share of a household's annual expenses. In capitalist society, real estate in the city is therefore a realm that promises the highest rates of return for rentiers and finance capital. As a consequence, falling profits rates in the 1970s resulted in the financialisation of the real estate market, which created high-risk speculative financial derivatives based on mortgages. Pension funds, insurance, consumer credit, student loans, the Internet economy, and the stock market are other examples of highly financialised spheres. In 2008, the real estate financial bubble burst in the USA, which triggered a new world-economic crisis and a long depression that led to austerity, bailouts of banks and large corporations, a fiscal crisis of nation-states, the strengthening of nationalists, and the far-right, etc. Expropriation via the financialisation of social systems such as the city promises high profits, but entails high risks such as new inequalities arising from debt and crises, economic and political crisis, and the rise of fascism, etc.

The history of human knowledge constitutes a cultural heritage. Current and future cultures build on older cultures and their knowledge. Language is the most evident example of a cultural heritage. Culture is the outcome of the collective cultural work of all members of a society. In the context of science, discovery, and invention, Marx argues that culture is created by the "universal labour" of humans; it "is brought about partly by the cooperation of men now living, but partly also by building on earlier work".[32] Cultivated nature is based on and develops through the collective labour of agricultural workers. Certain crops reflect the whole history of the labour that cultivated the same land over generations. The human subject's bodily and mental features and capacities are the historical result of life in society, human procreation, and women's work of child-bearing. The human being is a biological and social being, a product of nature and society. If property rights are used to commodify, create private ownership of, and start extracting value from cultural resources such as traditional songs passed on over generations, cultivated nature such as crops, or human subjectivity such as genetic information, then the collective labour of human groups is expropriated and a class relation between the property rights of owners and humanity is created.

Struggles for the right to the city as common, culture as common, cultivated nature as common, and the human subject's control of the body are particular forms of class struggle.

Marxist Feminism

Certain versions of Marxist feminism have, just like autonomist Marxism (Negri and others), advanced the insight that exploitation goes beyond wage-labour. They have argued that reproductive work in capitalism is productive labour. Mariarosa Dalla Costa and Selma James point out that "domestic work produces not merely use values, but is essential to the production of surplus value" and that the "productivity of wage slavery" is "based on unwaged slavery" in the form of productive "social services which capitalist organization transforms into privatized activity, putting them on the backs of housewives".[33] Zillah

Eisenstein writes that the gender division of labour guarantees "a free labor pool" and "a cheap labor pool" for capital.[34] Maria Mies argues that capitalism is based on the:

> *superexploitation* of non-wage labourers (women, colonies, peasants) upon which wage labour exploitation then is possible. I define their exploitation as superexploitation because it is not based on the appropriation (by the capitalist) of the time and labour over and above the 'necessary' labour time, the *surplus* labour, but of the time and labour *necessary* for people's own survival or subsistence production. It is not compensated for by a wage.[35]

These Marxist-feminist approaches have in common that they stress that capitalism requires for its existence unremunerated and low-paid spheres that are highly exploited. The Marxist theorist Rosa Luxemburg (1871–1919), who together with Karl Liebknecht founded the Spartakusbund (Spartacus League), which in 1919 became the Kommunistische Partei Deutschlands (KPD, Communist Party of Germany), argued in this context that capitalism requires the exploitation of non-capitalist milieus: "Capital feeds on the ruins of such organisations, and, although this non-capitalist milieu is indispensable for accumulation, the latter proceeds, at the cost of this medium nevertheless, by eating it up".[36] Capital searches for social milieus of unremunerated and low-paid labour and free resources that it subjects and subsumes under capital in order to maximise profits.

Clara Zetkin (1857–1933) was a German Marxist, socialist, women's rights and labour activist. She worked together with Rosa Luxemburg and Karl Liebknecht and like them was involved in founding the Spartacus League in 1916 and the Communist Party of Germany (KPD) in 1919. Zetkin argues that it is "capitalism's need to exploit and search incessantly for a cheap labor force that has created the women's question".[37] We can add that the drive for accumulation has also shaped questions related to imperialism, globalisation, uneven global development, environmental problems, and racism, etc.

Global Precarity, Global Austerity

The soci(et)al working class stands in a class antagonism to global capital. The global class antagonism is an antagonism between precarity and austerity. There are precariously living and working individuals who face insecure living conditions and create the wealth that is owned and controlled by the global class of capitalists and managers that are supported by the power of the capitalist state which keeps capital taxation and wages low, subsidises capital, deregulates labour laws, advances the privatisation, financialisation and commodification of public services, public resources and nature, bails out crisis-ridden capital, enforces debt regimes on countries, citizens, consumers, workers, tenants, and students, etc. The managers and functionaries of the austerity state are part of the global capitalist class. Austerity, debt, financialisation, commodification, imperialist wars, dispossession, etc. are mechanisms of the global capitalist class's struggle against the societal working class. As a result, the world's 2,000 largest corporations in 2018 made combined revenues of US$41.2 trillion.[38] In 2018, the global gross domestic product was US$84.74 trillion.[39] This means that just 2,000 companies controlled economic power that amounts to 48.5 percent of the world total of monetised economic activities. The global class antagonism means an extreme polarisation of wealth between the capitalist class on the one hand and the rest of the world on the other.

6.4 CONCLUSION

Capitalism is based on the class antagonism between capital and labour. Capital exploits the working class in order to yield profits and accumulate capital. The working class does not own means of production and capital and is therefore structurally forced into class relations. The working class's existence constitutes a capitalist dialectic of poverty and wealth. It is poor because it produces wealth that the capitalist class owns and without which the capitalist class cannot exist, which also constitutes the power of the working class.

Marx's notion of the collective worker helps us to theorise the complex structure of the working class as a class doesn't just work in factories and offices, but in social spaces all over society. The social working class includes a multitude of workers, such as blue-collar wage workers, white-collar wage workers, the unemployed, workers and the poor in developing countries, freelancers, farm workers, public service workers, pupils, students, preschoolers, kindergarten children, apprentices, consumer, and prosumer labour, digital labour, prison labour, slave labour, migrant workers, and racialised workers.

Recommended Further Readings about the Working Class

Peter Goodwin. 2018. Where's the Working Class? *tripleC: Communication, Capitalism & Critique* 16 (2): 535–545. https://doi.org/10.31269/triplec.v16i2.1005.

This article traces the perceived role of the working class in Marxist theory, from Marx and Engels, through the Second and Third Internationals, Stalinism and Maoism, to the present day. It situates this in political developments and changes in the nature of the working class over the last 200 years. It concludes by suggesting a number of questions about Marxism and the contemporary working class that anyone claiming to be a Marxist today needs to answer.

Antonio Negri. 1982/1988. Archaeology and Project. The Mass Worker and the Social Worker. In *Revolution Retrieved. Selected Writings on Marx, Keynes, Capitalist Crisis & New Social Subjects 1967–1983*. London: Red Notes. pp. 199–228.

In this text, Antonio Negri discusses the concept of the social worker and aspects of class struggles.

Christian Fuchs. 2010. Labor in Informational Capitalism and on the Internet. *The Information Society* 26 (3): 179–196.

This paper first points out the foundations of Marxist class theory and the soci(et)al worker. It applies these foundations in order to understand the unremunerated digital labour performed by users on Facebook, Google, YouTube, and Twitter, etc.

Notes

1 Karl Marx and Friedrich Engels. 1848. The Manifesto of the Communist Party. In *MECW Volume 6*. London: Lawrence & Wishart. pp. 477–519.
2 Ibid., pp. 485, 490.
3 Karl Marx. 1867. *Capital Volume One*. London: Penguin. p. 742.
4 Karl Marx. 1843. Contribution to the Critique of Hegel's Philosophy of Law. In *MECW Volume 3*. London: Lawrence & Wishart. pp. 3–129, 186.
5 Karl Marx. 1847. Wage Labour and Capital. In *MECW Volume 9*. London: Lawrence & Wishart. pp. 197–228.
6 Friedrich Engels. 1847. Principles of Communism. In *MECW Volume 6*. London: Lawrence & Wishart. pp. 341–357.
7 Marx, *Capital Volume One*, pp. 271–273.
8 Ibid., p. 874.
9 Karl Marx and Friedrich Engels. 1845/46. The German Ideology. Critique of Modern German Philosophy According to Its Representatives Feuerbach, B. Bauer and Stirner, and of German Socialism According to Its Various Prophets. In *MECW Volume 5*. London: Lawrence & Wishart. pp. 15–539.
10 Karl Marx. 1857/1858. *Grundrisse: Foundations of the Critique of Political* Economy. London: Penguin. p. 296.
11 Vivek Chibber. 2018. *Capitalism and Class Struggle. Catalyst: The ABCs of Capitalism*. Brooklyn, NY: Jacobin Foundation. p. 4.
12 See: Christian Fuchs. 2020. *Communication and Capitalism. A Critical Theory*. Chapter 7: Communication Society. London: University of Westminster Press.
13 Chibber, *Capitalism and Class Struggle*, p. 11.
14 Peter Goodwin. Where's the Working Class? *tripleC: Communication, Capitalism & Critique* 16 (2): 535–545.
15 Marx, *Capital Volume One*, pp. 781–794.
16 Ibid., p. 784.
17 Walk Free Foundation. 2018. *The Global Slavery Index 2018*. Nedlands: Walk Free Foundation.
18 David Harvey. 2014. *Seventeen Contradictions and the End of Capitalism*. Oxford: Oxford University Press. pp. 7–8.
19 Ibid., p. 8.
20 Marx, *Capital Volume One*, pp. 643–644.
21 Karl Marx. 1867. *Capital Volume One*, p. 1039.

22 Antonio Negri. 1982/1988. Archaeology and Project. The Mass Worker and the Social Worker. In Antonio Negri: *Revolution Retrieved. Selected Writings on Marx, Keynes, Capitalist Crisis & New Social Subjects 1967–1983*. London: Red Notes. pp. 199–228.
23 Antonio Negri. 1971/1988. Crisis of the Planner-State. Communism and Revolutionary Organisation. In Antonio Negri: *Revolution Retrieved. Selected Writings on Marx, Keynes, Capitalist Crisis & New Social Subjects 1967–1983*. London: Red Notes. pp. 91–148.
24 Negri, Archaeology and Project, p. 209.
25 Ibid., p. 214.
26 Ibid., p. 218.
27 Michael Hardt and Antonio Negri. 2005. *Multitude*. New York: Penguin. Reprint edition. p. 106.
28 Michael Hardt and Antonio Negri. 2000. *Empire*. Cambridge, MA: Harvard University Press. p. 52.
29 Marx and Engels, The Manifesto of the Communist Party, p. 482.
30 David Harvey. 2012. *Rebel Cities: From the Right to the City to the Urban Revolution*. London: Verso. p. 80.
31 Michael Hardt and Antonio Negri. 2009. *Commonwealth*. Cambridge, MA: Belknap Press. pp. 250–251.
32 Karl Marx. 1894. *Capital Volume Three*. London: Penguin. p. 199.
33 Mariarosa Dalla Costa and Selma James. 1972. *The Power of Women and the Subversion of Community*. Bristol: Falling Wall Press. p. 31.
34 Zillah Eisenstein, ed. 1979. *Capitalist Patriarchy and the Case for Socialist Feminism*. New York: Monthly Review Press. p. 31.
35 Maria Mies. 1986. *Patriarchy & Accumulation on a World Scale: Women in the International Division of Labour*. London: Zed Books. p. 48.
36 Rosa Luxemburg. 1913/2003. *The Accumulation of Capital*. New York: Routledge. p. 363.
37 Clara Zetkin. 2015. Only in Conjunction with the Proletarian Women Will Socialism be Victorious. In *Selected Writings*, ed. Philip S. Foner. Chicago, IL: Haymarket Books. p. 76.
38 Data source: Forbes 2000 List of the World's Largest Public Companies for year 2019, www.forbes.com/global2000/list, accessed on 26 May 2019.
39 Data source: International Monetary Fund (IMF): World Economic Outlook (April 2019), available on www.imf.org, accessed on 29 May 2019.

7

ALIENATION

7.1 INTRODUCTION

Alienation is a concept that Marx used throughout his life, from the early philosophical works like the *Economic and Philosophic Manuscripts* to *Capital*. The concept on the one hand is Marx's version of the general notion of domination. On the other hand, it has a more specific meaning, namely the objective conditions and the process of the exploitation of labour in class societies.

This chapter introduces Marx's concept of alienation and its relevance for studying communication and culture. Section 7.2 focuses on economic alienation. Section 7.3 deals with political and cultural alienation. Section 7.4 discusses the relevance of alienation in the critical analysis of communication and culture.

7.2 ECONOMIC ALIENATION

In class societies, the physical and symbolic externalisation of human activities turns into economic alienation and turns work into labour: we are not in control and do not own the means of production or the products of our labour. In capitalism, these externalised products become private property, sold and acquired as commodities. This is true for both physical (e.g., tables) and informational (e.g., software) goods that are sold as commodities.

The Alienation of Labour

In *Capital*, Marx argues that labour in capitalism has two characteristics:

1. Labour belongs to the capitalist who controls and monitors the workers[1];
2. The product belongs to the capitalist and not the worker.[2]

> The labour process is a process between things the capitalist has purchased, things which belong to him. Thus the product of this process belongs to him just as much as the wine which is the product of the process of fermentation going on in his cellar.[3]

For Marx, the workers' non-ownership of the means of production (the instruments and objects of labour) and the labour product is an important characteristic of capitalism. Marx also says that the workers are alienated from the means of production and their products of labour. Workers also face the compulsion to let capitalists exploit them in order to survive, which means that they cannot fully control their lives and are facing alien forces that compel them to do something – to work for a capitalist – that they may otherwise not freely do. In *Capital* Marx describes the violence of the market and capitalism as the "silent compulsion of economic relations" that "sets the seal on the domination of the capitalist over the worker".[4] "Direct extra-economic force is still of course used, but only in exceptional cases".[5]

Figure 7.1 visualises the multidimensional alienation of the worker in capitalism.

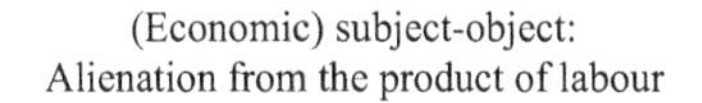

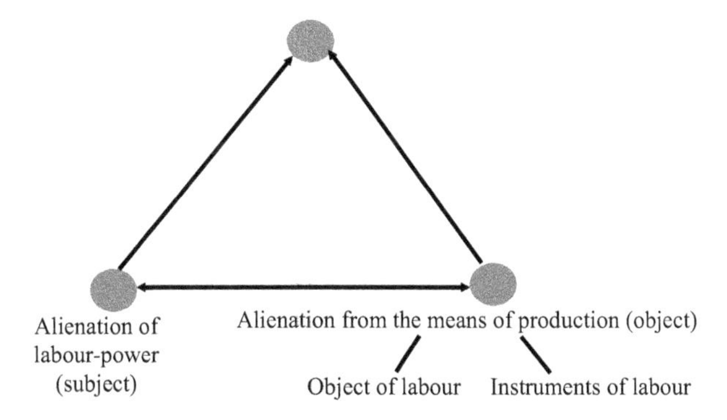

Figure 7.1 The economic alienation of labour

There are several dimensions of economic alienation:

1. Humans are not in full control of their labour-power. They are forced to enter class relations in order to survive (by means such as physical violence, the structural dominance of commodity markets, ideology, etc.).
2. Workers do not collectively own the means of production they use in the production process.
3. Workers do not collectively own the created products.

Alienation is the condition and process of workers' lack of control, property, and ownership in the economy. Alienation is an antagonistic relationship between workers and the ruling class. There is a dialectic of control and non-control in alienation: The ruling class controls the conditions and results of production, whereby the workers are excluded from control and forced into exploitation.

Marx used the concept of economic alienation the first time in the essay *On the Jewish Question* from 1844: "Money is the estranged essence of man's work and man's existence, and this alien essence dominates him, and he worships it".[6]

Alienation in the 1844 Economic and Philosophic Manuscripts'

Marx developed the notion of economic alienation in a detailed, systematic manner in the *Economic and Philosophic Manuscripts'* section, "Estranged Labour".[7] There he identifies four forms of alienation:

1. the alienation of humans from the product.
2. the alienation of humans from the labour process in the form of forced labour.
3. the alienation of humans from themselves:

   > Estranged labour turns thus: (3) *Man's species being*, both nature and his spiritual species property, into a being *alien* to him, into a *means* for his *individual existence*. It estranges from man his own body, as well as external nature and his spiritual aspect, his *human* aspect.[8]

4. the alienation from other humans and society.

Marx formulated the foundations of the concept of economic alienation in the *Economic and Philosophic Manuscripts* and later, systematically and in more detail, analysed the economic foundations of alienation.

Alienation in the Grundrisse: *Alienation as Class Relation*

In the *Grundrisse*, Marx analyses economic alienation in respect to class. He argues that the antagonism between capital and labour constitutes alienation:

> The emphasis comes to be placed not on the state of being objected, but on the state of being alienated, dispossessed, sold [Der Ton wird gelegt nicht auf das *Vergegenständlichtsein*, sondern das *Entfremdet-*, Entäußert-, Veräußertsein]; on the condition that the monstrous objective power which social labour itself erected opposite itself as one of its moments belongs not to the worker, but to the personified conditions of production, i.e. to capital.[9]

Slavery as Alienation: Django Unchained

Alienation is not just a feature of capitalism, but of all class societies. The defining feature of class societies is that the dominated class does not own the means of production and the products of labour and is forced to enter class relations in which the dominant class exploits it. In slave economies, the slave does not own the objects and products of his/her work. One difference from capitalism is that the slave is, like a machine, the physical property of the slave master. The coercion the slave is confronted with is not a dull compulsion of the market but the physical violence of the whip and the gun, as movies such as Steve McQueen's *12 Years a Slave* or Quentin Tarantino's *Django Unchained* show.

In *Django Unchained*, the former slave Django and the bounty hunter King Schultz fight against the plantation owner Calvin Candie. Django's wife Broomhilda works on Candie's Candyland plantation as house servant. In one scene, Calvin Candie says: "You see, under the laws of Chickasaw County, Broomhilda here is my property. And I can choose to do with my property whatever I so desire". He threatens to kill Broomhilda by smashing a hammer on her head and shouts: "What I'm gonna desire to do is … take this goddamn hammer here and beat her ass to death with it! Right in front of both y'all! Then we can examine the three dimples inside Broomhilda's skull".

This scene in its brutal faithfulness to slaves' reality makes clear that slaves are unfree because they are the property of slave masters who can choose to kill them if they please without having to fear any legal consequences. Marx writes in Chapter 7 of *Capital Volume One* that, in slavery, "the worker is distinguishable only as *instrumentum vocale* [vocal instrument] from an animal, which is *instrumentum semi-vocale* [semi-vocal instrument], and from a lifeless implement, which is *instrumentum mutum* [silent instrument]".[10] The slave is for the slave owner a thing, an instrument that can be treated and mistreated as the owner pleases.

Louis Althusser's Rejection of Marx's Notion of Alienation

Louis Althusser (1918–1990) was a French structuralist philosopher. He argued that Marx's notion of alienation is an "ideological concept" used in "his Early Works".[11] "In his later works, however, the term appears very rarely".[12] Althusser speaks of an "epistemological break" that "divides Marx's thought into two long essential periods: the 'ideological' period before, and the scientific period after, the break in 1845".[13] This means that Althusser considers the notion of alienation and works such as the *Economic and Philosophic Manuscripts* as esoteric. But Marx did not give up the notion of alienation, but it is, rather, a concept that he first created in his early works and that is present also in his major later writings. The final passages in *Capital Volume 1*'s Section 7.1 are a good example, showing that Marx saw the concept of alienation as crucial throughout his life.

In Chapter 23 of *Capital Volume 1* ("Simple Reproduction"), there is another passage that shows the importance of the notion of alienation understood as non-ownership and dispossession in *Capital*:

> On the one hand, the production process incessantly converts material wealth into capital, into the capitalist's means of enjoyment and his means of valorization. On the other hand, the worker always leaves the process in the same state as he entered it – a personal source of wealth, but deprived of any means of making that wealth a reality for himself. Since, before he enters the process, his own labour has already been alienated [*entfremdet*] from him, appropriated by the capitalist, and incorporated with capital, it now, in the course of the process, constantly objectifies itself so that it becomes a product alien to him [*fremdes Produkt*]. Since the process of production is also the process of the consumption of labour-power by the capitalist, the worker's product is not only constantly converted into commodities, but also into capital, i.e. into value that sucks up the worker's value-creating power, means of subsistence that actually purchase human beings, and means of production that employ the people who are doing the producing. Therefore the worker himself constantly produces objective wealth, in the form of

> capital, an alien power that dominates and exploits him; and the capitalist just as constantly produces labour-power, in the form of a subjective source of wealth which is abstract, exists merely in the physical body of the worker, and is separated from its own means of objectification and realization; in short, the capitalist produces the worker as a wage-labourer. This incessant reproduction, this perpetuation of the worker, is the absolutely necessary condition for capitalist production.[14]

Marx argues here that labour-power is, in capitalism, alienated labour-power because workers must sell this capacity as a commodity in order to survive and as a result of capitalism do not own the products their labour creates and are facing capital in a class relation, in which workers are dominated and exploited by an alien power.

Why Althusser Misinterpreted Marx

When one reads such passages in *Capital*, one wonders how Althusser could claim that alienation was an esoteric concept that Marx stopped using in his later "scientific" works. Althusser wrote in his autobiography that he only knew "a few passages of Marx"[15] and that his method of getting to know philosophy was "all done by 'hearsay'":

> I learnt from Jacques Martin, who was cleverer than me, by gleaning certain phrases in passing from my friends, and lastly seminar papers and essays of my own students. In the end, I naturally made it a point of honour and boasted that 'I learnt by hearsay'. This distinguished me quite markedly from all my university friends who were much better informed than me.[16]

He described himself as "a trickster and deceiver and nothing more, a philosopher who knew almost nothing about the history of philosophy or about Marx".[17] One wonders how a person who hardly read Marx became one of the most highly regarded French "Marxist" theorists. Althusser's claims about Marx's usage of the term alienation show that he indeed did not understand and had not read Marx.

7.3 POLITICAL AND CULTURAL ALIENATION

Marx on Political and Ideological Alienation

In *On the Jewish Question*, Marx advances an understanding of alienation as not just economic but also political and cultural-ideological process:

> It is indeed *estrangement* which matters in the so-called Christian state, but not *man*. The only man who counts, the *king*, is a being specifically different from other men, and is moreover a religious being, directly linked with heaven, with God. The relationships which prevail here are still relationships dependent on *faith*. Political emancipation is at the same time the *dissolution* of the old society on which the state alienated from the people, the sovereign power, is based.[18]

Here, Marx on the one hand analyses a state that is controlled by a king as a form of political alienation. When humans do not exert democratic control of society, we can speak of political alienation. At the same time, he indicates that faith in God is a form of ideological alienation. Ideology is a feature of class societies. Ideology – distorted and manipulated presentations that do not correspond to reality – distracts attention from domination and exploitation. It is an attempt to alienate humans from their true interests and to construct false consciousness and false interests. Oppressed humans who share ideological views are estranged from their true interests.

Marx argued that the ideological mechanisms of religion can also be found in class society's political economy: ideology presents political-economic entities such as capital, the state, or the nation as unchangeable, natural authorities that have no historical character and cannot be altered. In the Introduction, he writes:

> The immediate *task of philosophy*, which is at the service of history, once the *holy form* of human self-estrangement has been unmasked, is to unmask self-estrangement in its *unholy forms*. Thus the criticism of heaven turns into the criticism of the earth, the *criticism of religion* into the *criticism of law* and the *criticism of theology* into the *criticism of politics*.[19]

Religion is for Marx an ideological form of alienation and the self-alienation of humans. By "self-alienation", Marx means that humans are alienated from their true interests. But he argues that it is not enough for critique to focus on the criticism of religion. Marx also says that the critique of politics and political economy, the critique of the state and capitalism, is needed. In politics, the authoritarian state alienates humans from democratic decision-making. And ideology wants to create false consciousness in order to alienate humans from their true interests. For Marx, alienation has to do with exploitation (economic domination), political domination, and ideological domination. In capitalist society, all three forms of alienation work together in the reproduction of domination and exploitation. Class relations alienate humans from collective ownership and economic democracy, the state alienates humans from collective democratic decision-making (participatory democracy), and ideology alienates them from a collective consciousness oriented on the advantage of all humans.

Three Forms of Alienation and Their Dimensions

Table 7.1 presents an overview of the three forms of alienation.

In economic, political, and cultural processes, we find subjects, objects and products that emerge from the social processes in these systems. Table 7.1 shows how alienated affects subjects, objects, and products across the three forms of alienation. In economic alienation, humans are exploited. In political alienation, humans are excluded from collective decision-making and face an unequal distribution of power. Power is the capacity of humans to influence structures, organisations, and decisions that influence their lives. In alienated culture, their interests are disrespected and ideologues try to manipulate and reify their consciousness so that they speak the language of their oppressors, believe their oppressors' interests are their interests, and act according to these false interests. Alienation is a social relation, in which certain groups dominate others. Class relations are the economic form of alienation; dictatorships and authoritarian states are the political form of alienation; ideology is the cultural form of alienation. In alienation, there are not only

Table 7.1 The three forms of alienation

Type	*Social relations*	*Subjects*	*Object*	*Products*
Economic alienation	Class relations	Exploited workers	Privately owned means of production	Goods and services as private property
Political alienation	Dictatorship	Excluded/ oppressed individuals	Authoritarian state, unequal power structures	Authoritarian laws
Cultural alienation	Ideological relations, disrespect	Disrespected individuals	Ideology	Reified consciousness

dominated subjects, but also dominating subjects. Therefore, alienation is an antagonistic relationship.

Table 7.2 shows the antagonisms that constitute alienation and the subjects acting in these antagonistic relations. Economic alienation is a class antagonism between the exploiters and the exploited; political alienation is an unequal, antagonistic power relation between dictators and the oppressed; cultural alienation is an antagonistic power relation between ideologues and disrespected humans.

Table 7.2 Antagonisms in the three forms of alienation

Form of alienation	*Dominating subjects*	*Dominated subjects*
Economic alienation	Ruling class, exploiters	Exploited class
Political alienation	Dictator, dictatorial group	Excluded individuals and groups
Cultural alienation	Ideologues	Disrespected individuals and groups

David Harvey on Universal Alienation

In his essay "Universal Alienation",[20] the Marxist theorist David Harvey defines alienation as universal in three respects[21]:

1. Alienation in the economy not only entails capital's exploitation of labour, but also the realms of realisation, distribution, and consumption, which means it extends to phenomena such as unemployment, consumerism, land seizure, deindustrialisation, debt peonage, financial scams, unaffordable housing, and high food prices, etc.
2. Alienation entails processes beyond the economy, such as frustration with politics, unaffordable public services, nationalist ideology, racism, police violence, militarism, warfare, alcoholism, suicide, depression, bureaucracy, pollution, gentrification, or climate change.
3. Alienation entails the geographic and social expansion of capital accumulation so that capital relations "dominate pretty much everywhere".[22] "Alienation is everywhere. It exists at work in production, at home in consumption, and it dominates much of politics and daily life".[23]

The universalisation of alienation means it extends beyond production, the economy, and bounded spaces. Capital and capitalist society overcome and break down their own barriers in order to expand. In *Marx, Capital and the Madness of Economic Reason*, Harvey argues that "a great deal of appropriation of value through predation occurs at the point of realization",[24] which results in "[a]lienation upon realization".[25]

In all forms of alienation, humans face asymmetric power relations and conditions that hinder their control over certain objects, structures or products (external nature, the means of production, the means of communication, the political system, and the cultural system, etc.) so that aspects of their subjectivity are damaged (concerning human activities, well-being, consciousness, mind/psyche, body, worldviews, social relations). Alienation is neither purely objective nor purely subjective, but a negative relationship between social structures and humans in heteronomous societies.

In *Seventeen Contradictions and the End of Capitalism*, David Harvey devotes Chapter 17 to the topic of "The Revolt of Human Nature: Universal Alienation". He argues that Marxists have often excluded alienation from consideration and have often dismissed it as a "non-scientific concept".[26] The "scientistic stance failed to capture the political imagination of viable alternatives" and "could not even confront the madness of the prevailing economic and political reason".[27] Universal alienation is therefore a concept that, in light of the danger that we may face "a less-than-human humanity",[28] can provide the prospect of alternatives. Alienation has always been a prominent concept in socialist/Marxist humanism.[29] Radical socialist humanism is the best way of opposing authoritarian capitalism's and neoliberalism's anti-humanism.[30]

Consequently, Harvey argues for both the use of the concept of universal alienation and for revolutionary humanism.[31] Humanism argues that "[w]e can through conscious thought and action change both the world we live in and ourselves for the better".[32] Humanism "measures its achievements in terms of the liberation of human potentialities, capacities and powers".[33] Harvey notes that humanism has been perverted and turned into a particularism that disguises itself as universalism but advances "imperialist and colonial cultural domination".[34] He therefore argues for a "secular *revolutionary* humanism" that counters "alienation in its many forms and to radically change the world from its capitalist ways".[35] The autonomist Marxists Michael Hardt and Toni Negri argue that there are parallels between autonomist and humanist Marxism:[36] Both take subjectivity, social struggles and social change seriously, and oppose dogmatic Marxism and Stalinism.

Exploitation and Domination: Class, Patriarchy, Racism

All social systems have economic, political, and cultural dimensions. Humans in social relations and social systems produce (economic dimension), decide (political dimension) and interpret/signify/create meanings (cultural dimension). Production is the basic model that can be found in all of these dimensions, but each dimension of the social has specific, non-reducible qualities. There are social systems in which one dimension dominates. Let us consider three examples of domination: an economic one, a political one, and a cultural one.

In class relations and class societies, the economic dimension of exploitation is dominant. But class societies also have specific forms of politics and culture.

In the political system of class societies, antagonistic interest groups struggle for the control and accumulation of power. In the cultural system, there is a battle over ideas. These ideas range from fascism at the very right-wing end of the worldview spectrum to communism at the left-wing end.

Patriarchy and gendered power relations form a type of society and a form of social relations, in which there is a gendered political distribution of power so that groups belonging to one gender dominate those belonging to other genders. The classical form is that men dominate the economy, politics, and the household. Power relations, i.e. politics, are the dominant dimension of patriarchal and gendered social relations/societies. But in such societies one often also finds a gender division of labour, in which sexist ideologies advance gender stereotypes.

Racism is a social relation, where the ideological assumptions that different human races exist or that different cultures are radically incompatible and that some of these cultures or illusionary races or are superior to others dominates. Racism demands and wants to enforce either separation or the extermination of the groups perceived as being inferior. Often, racism is not limited to the realms of culture, but extends into the spheres of the economy and politics. In the economy, racism takes on the form of the super-exploitation of racialised groups and the exclusion and discrimination of workers and consumers of colour. In the political system, racism takes on various forms of political exclusion and discrimination, including racist police violence, disadvantaged access to public services, exclusion from political roles (voters, politicians, MPs, and members of government, etc.).

Racism is an ideological mode of the production of racist stereotypes that permeate and shape the economy, politics, and culture. Patriarchy is a political mode of the production of gender inequality that permeates and shapes the economy, politics, and culture. Particular class relations (such as the capital/labour relation) are an economic mode of the production of particularistic property that permeates and shapes the economy, politics, and culture. The point is that production plays a role in all social relations and all forms of alienation. It is the model of the social in society in general and therefore also in dominative, heteronomous societies. Economic production (or what Lukács terms teleological positing[37]) shapes all realms of society in a dialectical manner. At the same time, these realms have emergent qualities that are non-reducible to the economy.

7.4 ALIENATION AND COMMUNICATION

The Ruling Ideas

Communication is the production process of sociality, social relations, social groups, social structures, social systems, organisations, institutions, and society. It mediates the social relations that constitute society and society's moments and spheres. The communication of ideas and experiences is part of the constitutive, material foundations of society.

Marx and Engels say: "The ruling ideas of each age have ever been the ideas of its ruling class".[38] This formulation has sometimes been misinterpreted as meaning that if one knows what the economy of a society looks like, one can decide the structure of worldviews from it.

Forms of production, such as Taylorism, are compatible with a range of political systems and ideologies, such as the Keynesian welfare state, fascism, liberal democracy, etc. A small detail of history is that Taylorism is not compatible with socialism, although Lenin and Gramsci incorrectly assumed it was. The "ruling class" refers to those groups that dominate in a class society. This not only includes the economically dominant class, but also the political rulers, and those groups exerting hegemony in the realm of worldviews. There can be a certain divergence of these realms. For example, socialist parties can rule within a capitalist society, which inevitably leads to contradictions that can only be overcome by the abolition of capitalism. The production of ideas takes place in the cultural domain of society, but shapes, and is part of, all social systems. In a class society, those groups that exert economic, political and cultural power influence the "ruling ideas". Given that there can be contradictions between these groups, ideas are, in class-based societies, often social struggles over meanings, interpretations, and symbols.

Social transformations bring about changes of ideas, but the forms, contents, and antagonisms of new ideas are not predictable. Communism "is the most radical rupture with traditional property relations; no wonder that its development involves the most radical rupture with traditional ideas".[39] In order to be a new society, communist transformation not just has to affect the economy, but also the political system and everyday life.

Alienated Communication(s)

Table 7.3 shows an overview of how alienation affects communication and knowledge in the realms of the economy, politics, and culture.

Communication is the process of the production of social relations. Communications are communication systems. In alienated social relations, we find alienated communication through

Table 7.3 Forms of alienated communication(s)

Type of alienated communication(s)	*Description*
Alienated economic communication(s)	Knowledge and communication as commodities, the exploitation of knowledge labour, means of communication as private property
Alienated political communication(s)	Dictatorial control of knowledge and communication processes
Alienated cultural communication(s)	Ideological knowledge, the production and communication of ideology

which humans shape and construct social relations of domination. We also find communication systems in society. In alienated societies, dominative and exploitative organisations that produce, maintain, and organise communication systems will create alienated communication systems.

Google and Alienation

Let us consider the example of Google/Alphabet. The company produces public, web-based information and communication services such as Google Search, Gmail, Google Scholar, Google Maps, YouTube, and Google Play, etc. It is an information and communication corporation. Google's economic structures are alienated: Its employees and users do not own the company. Rather, all executive directors together control 95.2 percent of the corporation's class B common stock: Larry Page 42.9%, Sergey Brin 41.3%, Eric Schmidt 8.6%, L. John Doerr 2.4%.[40] Along with shareholding power comes decision power: Google's directors control 58 percent of the company's decision power: Larry Page 26.1%, Sergey Brin 25.2%, Eric Schmidt 5.3%, L. John Doerr 1.5%.[41]

Economically, Google is a class-structured information and communication system. Politically, Google is a dictatorship, where a handful of people take fundamental decisions. When capitalists and dictators rule an organisation, there is the possibility that workers, members of the public and consumers develop doubts about it. It is therefore very likely that ideologies are utilised in order to try to manipulate the public perception of the organisation. For example, Google's philosophy stresses "a focus on the user before anything else" (first rule), "democracy on the web works" (fourth rule),[42] "you can make money without doing evil" (sixth rule). Google's privacy violations, secret algorithms, its monopoly in online search, strategies of tax avoidance, its top-down designed privacy policies and terms of use, the exploitation of users and Google employees, etc. show that the company focuses on profit before anything else, is anti-democratic, and is, because of its capitalist character, evil by design. Its philosophy is therefore a mere ideology that tries to distract from Google's negative reality.

7.5 CONCLUSION

Alienation is the process and a social relation of domination. In alienation, humans lack control over products, objects, and themselves as subjects. There are economic, political, and cultural forms of alienation: exploitation, dictatorship, and ideology. These forms of alienation interact with each other in a complex manner.

Marx used the notion of alienation throughout his works, from the early to the late ones. The claim of Louis Althusser that alienation is an esoteric concept that can only be found in Marx's early works is incorrect.

Alienated communication systems feature alienated economic communication(s), alienated political communication(s), and alienated cultural communication(s). In class societies, ideas are often contested, i.e. there are social struggles over meanings, interpretations, and symbols.

Recommended Further Readings about Alienation

Karl Marx. 1844. Economic and Philosophic Manuscripts of 1844. In *MECW Volume 3*, 229–346. London: Lawrence & Wishart. Read especially the section on "Estranged Labour" (pp. 270–282), where Marx discusses the notion of economic alienation.

István Mészáros. 1970/2005. *Marx's Theory of Alienation*. Chapter 2: Genesis of Marx's Theory of Alienation. Chapter 3: Conceptual Structure of Marx's Theory of Alienation. London: Merlin.

In these two chapters, Mészáros provides an overview of the genesis and structure of Marx's concept of alienation.

- Michael Hardt and Antonio Negri. 2018. The Powers of the Exploited and the Social Ontology of Praxis. *tripleC: Communication, Capitalism & Critique* 16 (2): 415–423. www.triple-c.at/index.php/tripleC/article/view/1024
- David Harvey. 2018. Universal Alienation. *tripleC: Communication, Capitalism & Critique* 16 (2):424–439. www.triple-c.at/index.php/tripleC/article/view/1026
- Michael Hardt and Antonio Negri. 2018. The Multiplicities within Capitalist Rule and the Articulation of Struggles.

tripleC: Communication, Capitalism & Critique 16 (2): 440–448. www.triple-c.at/index.php/tripleC/article/view/1025

- David Harvey. 2018. Universal Alienation and the Real Subsumption of Daily Life under Capital: A Response to Hardt and Negri. *tripleC: Communication, Capitalism & Critique* 16 (2): 449–453. www.triple-c.at/index.php/tripleC/article/view/1027
- Christian Fuchs. 2018. Universal Alienation, Formal and Real Subsumption of Society Under Capital, Ongoing Primitive Accumulation by Dispossession: Reflections on the Marx@200-Contributions by David Harvey and Michael Hardt/Toni Negri. *tripleC: Communication, Capitalism & Critique* 16 (2): 454–467. www.triple-c.at/index.php/tripleC/article/view/1028.

This series of articles is a debate between the influential Marxist theorists David Harvey and Michael Hardt/Toni Negri on the occasion of Marx's 200th birthday in 2018. They discuss the relevance of Marx today for changing and understanding capitalism. Harvey stresses the relevance of Marx's notion of alienation; Hardt and Negri stress the concept of the real subsumption of society under capital. The debate engages with questions of class struggle and the relation of exploitation to patriarchy and racism. Christian Fuchs's article is a contextualisation of the debate and a reflection on the commonalities and differences between the approaches of Harvey and Hardt/Negri.

Mark Andrejevic. 2014. Alienation's Returns. In *Critique, Social Media and the Information Society*, ed. Christian Fuchs and Marisol Sandoval, 179–190. London: Routledge.

In this book chapter, Mark Andrejevic applies Marx's notion of alienation to the world of digital capitalism.

Notes

1 Karl Marx. 1867. *Capital Volume One*. London: Penguin. p. 291.
2 Ibid., p. 292.
3 Ibid.
4 Ibid., p. 899.

5 Ibid.
6 Karl Marx. 1844. On the Jewish Question. In *Marx & Engels Collected Works (MECW) Volume 3*. London: Lawrence & Wishart. pp. 146–174.
7 Karl Marx. 1844. Economic and Philosophic Manuscripts of 1844. In *MECW Volume 3*. London: Lawrence & Wishart. pp. 229–346.
8 Ibid., p. 277.
9 Karl Marx. 1857/1858. *Grundrisse: Foundations of the Critique of Political* Economy. London: Penguin. p. 831.
10 Marx, *Capital Volume One*, p. 303, footnote 18.
11 Louis Althusser. 1969. *For Marx*. London: Verso. p. 249.
12 Ibid.
13 Ibid., p. 34.
14 Marx, *Capital Volume One*, p. 716.
15 Louis Althusser. 1993. *The Future Lasts Forever: A Memoir*. New York: The New Press. p. 165.
16 Ibid., p. 166.
17 Ibid., p. 148.
18 Marx, On the Jewish Question, pp. 158, 165.
19 Karl Marx. 1844. Contribution to the Critique of Hegel's Philosophy of Law: Introduction. In *MECW Volume 3*. London: Lawrence & Wishart. pp. 175–187.
20 The passage on Harvey was first published in: Christian Fuchs. 2018. Universal Alienation, Formal and Real Subsumption of Society Under Capital, Ongoing Primitive Accumulation by Dispossession: Reflections on the Marx@200.Contributions by David Harvey and Michael Hardt/Toni Negri. *tripleC: Communication, Capitalism & Critique* 16 (2): 454–467. www.triple-c.at/index.php/tripleC/article/view/1028. Reproduced with permission from *tripleC*.
21 David Harvey. 2018. Universal Alienation. *tripleC: Communication, Capitalism & Criti*que 16 (2): 424–439. www.triple-c.at/index.php/tripleC/article/view/1026
22 Ibid., p. 427.
23 Ibid., p. 429.
24 David Harvey. 2017. *Marx, Capital and the Madness of Economic Reason*. London: Profile. p. 47.
25 Ibid., p. 196.
26 David Harvey. 2014. *Seventeen Contradictions and the End of Capitalism*. London: Profile. p. 269.
27 Ibid.
28 Ibid., p. 264.

29 Erich Fromm, ed. 1966. *Socialist Humanism. An International Symposium*. Garden City, NY: Doubleday. David Alderson and Robert Spencer, eds. 2017. *For Humanism: Explorations in Theory and Politics*. London: Pluto Press.
30 Christian Fuchs. 2018. *Digital Demagogue: Authoritarian Capitalism in the Age of Trump and Twitter*. London: Pluto Press.
31 Harvey, *Seventeen Contradictions and the End of Capitalism*, pp. 282–293.
32 Ibid., p. 282.
33 Ibid., p. 283.
34 Ibid., p. 285.
35 Ibid., p. 287.
36 Michael Hardt and Antonio Negri. 2017. *Assembly*. Oxford: Oxford University Press. pp. 72–76.
37 See: Georg Lukács. 1980. *The Ontology of Social Being. 3. Labour*. London: The Merlin Press.
38 Karl Marx and Friedrich Engels. 1848. The Manifesto of the Communist Party. In *MECW Volume 6*. London: Lawrence & Wishart. pp. 477–519.
39 Ibid., p. 504.
40 Alphabet Inc., 2019 Proxy Statement, available on https://abc.xyz/investor, accessed on 16 May 2019.
41 Ibid.
42 Google's Philosopy, available on www.mattpolsky.com/articles/googles-ten-things-seo-connection/, accessed on 16 May 2019.

8

MEANS OF COMMUNICATION AND THE GENERAL INTELLECT

8.1 INTRODUCTION

Bourgeois thinkers are thinkers who are not critical of the capitalist order and as a consequence not only oppose socialism, but also oppose socialists and their thought, such as Karl Marx's theory.

Jean Baudrillard (1929–2007) was a French philosopher who had a major influence on the development of postmodern theory. Marshall McLuhan (1911–1980) was a Canadian media theorist. Both thinkers argued that Marx's theory ignored communication. Baudrillard argues that the Marxist theory of production is "irredeemable partial, and cannot be generalized" to communication, the media, and culture.[1] McLuhan writes that Marx did not "understand the dynamics of the new media of communication. Marx based his analysis most untimely on the machine, just as the telegraph and other implosive forms began to reverse the mechanical dynamic".[2]

This chapter shows that communication and the means of communication played an important role in Marx's works. It shows that claims such as the ones made by Baudrillard and McLuhan are false. Often such claims are attempts to delegitimise socialism by claiming that Marx's theory is outdated. Baudrillard and McLuhan are bourgeois thinkers who have not read Marx's works thoroughly.

Section 8.2 discusses Marx's analysis of communication and language. Section 8.3 focuses on his concept of the means of communication. Section 8.4 points out the relevance of Marx's notion of the general intellect.

8.2 COMMUNICATION AND LANGUAGE

The Emergence of Language

Friedrich Engels stresses that the emergence of language was part of the development of human work as conscious activity that transforms the world in order to produce use-values that satisfy human needs:

> [The] development of labour necessarily helped to bring the members of society closer together by increasing cases of mutual support and joint activity, and by making clear the advantage of this joint activity to each individual. In short, men in the making arrived at the point where *they had something to say* to each other. Necessity created the organ; the undeveloped larynx of the ape was slowly but surely transformed by modulation to produce constantly more developed modulation, and the organs of the mouth gradually learned to pronounce one articulate sound after another.[3]

Humans started communicating because the complexity of their lives created the need for language and communication in order to co-ordinate social processes. There is a dialectic of the development of human production and the human being's body and mind.

Humans as Material, Social, Communicating, Sensuous Beings

In *The German Ideology*, Marx writes that the "production of ideas, of conceptions, of consciousness, is at first directly interwoven with the material activity and the material intercourse of men – the language of real life".[4] The mind "is from the outset afflicted with the curse of the being 'burdened' with matter".[5] Humans are beings who produce socially. The mind and communication are aspects of material social life. They are part of "the language of real life", which means they are not unreal, but embedded into the everyday social relations of human beings:

> Language is as old as consciousness, language *is* practical, real consciousness that exists for other men as well, and only therefore does it also exist for me; language, like consciousness, only arises from the need, the necessity, of intercourse with other men. Where there exists a relationship, it exists for me: the animal does not '*relate*' itself to anything, it does not '*relate*' itself at all. For the animal its relation to others does not exist as a relation. Consciousness is, therefore, from the very beginning a social product, and remains so as long as men exist at all.[6]

Marx here argues that language is the practical aspect of consciousness, which means that humans enact their consciousness through communication in social relations. Humans communicate because there is a need for it, a need that emerged from the increasing complexity of life.

Marx writes that production, language, and communication have a social character. They emerge from a community and take place as social processes:

> Production by an isolated individual outside society – a rare exception which may well occur when a civilized person in whom the social forces are already dynamically present is cast by accident into the wilderness – is as much of an absurdity as is the development of language without individuals living together and talking to each other.[7]

> As regards the individual, it is clear e.g. that he relates even to language itself as his own only as the natural member of a human community. Language as the product of an individual is an impossibility. But the same holds for property. Language itself is the product of a community, just as it is in another respect itself the presence [*Dasein*] of the community, a presence which goes without saying.[8]

For Marx, language and communication also have a sensuous character, which means that they organise human experience with the help of the sense organs. We communicate with the help of the mouth, the ears, the tongue, the eyes, the body. "The element of thought itself – the element of thought's living expression – *language* – is of a sensuous nature".[9]

Is Communication Comparable to Commodity Exchange?

Marx asks if human relations, communication, and language are comparable to commodity exchange. On the one hand, commodities exist through social relations between humans, and communication and language are processes and means for the organisation of social relations. So both humans and the commodity have a social character. Humans recognise themselves in other humans through communication:

> In a certain sense, a man is in the same situation as a commodity. As he neither enters into the world in possession of a mirror, nor as a Fichtean philosopher who can say 'I am I', a man first sees and recognizes himself in another man. Peter only relates to himself as a man through his relation to another man, Paul, in whom he recognizes his likeness. With this, however, Paul also becomes from head to toe, in his physical form as Paul, the form of appearance of the species man or Peter.[10]

But does this mean that language and communication can be compared to money?

> To compare money with language is not less erroneous. Language does not transform ideas, so that the peculiarity of ideas is dissolved and their social character runs alongside them as a separate entity, like prices alongside commodities. Ideas do not exist separately from language. Ideas which have first to be translated out of their mother tongue into a foreign language in order to circulate, in order to become exchangeable, offer a somewhat better analogy; but the analogy then lies not in language, but in the foreignness of language.[11]

Ideas and language are not two separate entities and goods, like money and the commodity. Money and commodities are exchanged in a relationship of x commodity A = y money (e.g. 1 computer = US$999), which means that the control of the two goods changes hands. Ideas that are communicated are not exchanged for another good. In communication, there is not one quantity of a first good that is exchanged for the control of a quantity of another good whose value is considered of being equal to the first good. Communication is not an exchange because it does not follow the logic of x commodity A = y commodity B.

Communication as Translation

Marx argues that in revolution, revolutionary movements often refer to symbols and events from the past as inspirations for their struggles:

> Men make their own history, but they do not make it just as they please; they do not make it under circumstances chosen by themselves, but under circumstances directly encountered, given and transmitted from the past. The tradition of all the dead generations weighs like a nightmare on the brain of the living. And just when they seem engaged in revolutionising themselves and things, in creating something that has never yet existed, precisely in such periods of revolutionary crisis they anxiously conjure up the spirits of the past to their service and borrow from them names, battle-cries and costumes in order to present the new scene of world history in this time-honoured disguise and this borrowed language. Thus Luther donned the mask of the Apostle Paul, the revolution of 1789 to 1814 draped itself alternately as the Roman Republic and the Roman Empire, and the revolution of 1848 knew nothing better to do than to parody, now 1789, now the revolutionary tradition of 1793 to 1795. In like manner a beginner who has learnt a new language always translates it back into his mother tongue, but he has assimilated the spirit of the new language and can freely express himself in it only when he finds his way in it without recalling the old and forgets his native tongue in the use of the new.[12]

Revolutions "conjure up the spirits of the past" and in doing so borrow the language from the past in order to try to create the future. Marx here makes an interesting comparison to learning a new language. Learning a new language is a matter of constant translation between that language and one's mother tongue. In a more general sense we can say that communication is a translation of the social world, experiences, and ideas of one person or group into the social world, experiences and ideas of another person or group. A can only understand what B communicates to him if the content of communication translates into his own experiences. Communication translates experiences from one context into another and the past into the present and the future.

Debates about Freedom of the Press

Karl Marx worked throughout his life as a journalist. The *Rheinische Zeitung für Politik, Handel und Gewerbe* (*Rhenish Newspaper for Politics, Trade and Commerce*) was a newspaper founded in 1842 that appeared in the Rhineland. It favoured democracy and opposed Prussian absolutism. Marx started to write for the Rhenish Newspaper in 1842 and soon thereafter became its editor in October of the same year. The press in Prussia was censored by the state that did not tolerate criticism. In 1819, the Carlsbad Decrees had resulted in a Press Law that had introduced censorship. The Press Law also governed in paragraph six that the state is allowed to dissolve newspapers in order to "maintain peace and quiet in Germany".[13] Paragraph seven ruled that the editor of a banned newspaper was not allowed to work for another German publisher over a five-year-long period following the ban. As a consequence of the Press Law, the state checked and censored newspapers before publication and had the power to dissolve them.

Karl Marx opposed press censorship. In his articles in the *Rhenish Newspaper*, he argued vehemently for the freedom of the press and against censorship:

> The press is the most general way by which individuals can communicate their intellectual being. It knows no respect for persons, but only respect for intelligence. Do you want ability for intellectual

> communication to be determined officially by special external signs? What I cannot be for others, I am not and cannot be for myself. If I am not allowed to be a spiritual force for others, then I have no right to be a spiritual force for myself; and do you want to give certain individuals the privilege of being spiritual forces? Just as everyone learns to read and write, so everyone must *have the right* to read and write.[14]

Marx here argues that censorship destroys the human right to read and write and installs an official "external sign" – the state authorities – that control intellectual communication.

Marx argues that a press that worships the repressive state contradicts its own nature. He argues for a critical press:

> A free press that is bad does not correspond to its essence. The censored press with its hypocrisy, its lack of character, its eunuch's language, its dog-like tail-wagging, merely realises the inner conditions of its essential nature. The censored press remains bad even when it turns out good products, for these products are good only insofar as they represent the free press within the censored press, and insofar as it is not in their character to be products of the censored press.[15]

But Marx didn't just question the state control of the press and the lack of freedom of speech and freedom of the press. He also questioned the idea that the press should be carried out as a commercial operation yielding profit: "The primary freedom of the press lies in not being a trade".[16] In the 18th and 19th century, newspapers were intellectual and political projects. From the middle of the 19th century onwards, newspapers more and more turned into advertising-financed businesses and into commercial operations controlled by press barons such as Lord Beaverbrook, Lord Camrose, Lord Kemsley, Lord Northcliffe, and Lord Rothermere in the UK; James Gordon Bennett junior, William Randolph Hearst, Frank A. Munsey, and Joseph Pulitzer in the USA; Alfred Hugenberg, Rudolf Mosse, Leopold Ullstein, and August Scherl in Germany. In the 20th century, press barons turned into owners of large media corporations ("media moguls"), often operating in various sectors and exerting huge political power in the public sphere. Examples are Rupert Murdoch, Silvio Berlusconi, Axel Springer, Ted Turner, Mark Zuckerberg, Jack Dorsey, Jeff Bezos, Robert Maxwell, Michael Bloomberg, Hans Dichand, Andrej Babiš, David and Frederick Barclay, and Richard Desmond, etc.

The Prussian state saw the *Rhenish Newspaper* as directed against the monarchy and Christianity and arguing for democracy, which is why the newspaper was banned on 1 April 1843. Not being able to continue to work in Germany, Marx moved to Paris, where he continued work as a critical journalist. But the Prussian government enforced his ban from France in 1845 so that he moved first to Brussels and then in 1849 to London. In the revolutionary period of 1848, when press censorship was abolished in Germany, Marx returned to his country of origin and published *Neue Rheinische Zeitung: Organ der Demokratie* (*New Rhenish Newspaper. Organ of Democracy*). After the defeat of the revolution, it was no longer possible to continue publishing the newspaper because state repression increased. Marx was banned from Prussia and from then on lived in London. The last issue of the *New Rhenish Newspaper* was published in red letters on 19 May 1849. Its title page said: "In bidding you farewell the editors of the *Neue Rheinische Zeitung* thank you for the sympathy you have shown them. Their last word everywhere and always will be: emancipation of the working class!"[17]

The Public Sphere

Marx struggled for the freedom of the press. His understanding of the freedom of speech and the press was political-economic: He saw state control and censorship, capitalist and market control, and bourgeois ideology as forces destroying the freedom of the media. Marx anticipated discussions about the freedom of the public sphere that have taken place in the 20th and 21st centuries. In his famous book, *The Structural Transformation of the Public Sphere*, the German philosopher and communication theorist Jürgen Habermas argues that inequalities limit freedom of the public sphere. If individuals lack education and material resources, then the freedoms of speech and public opinion are violated.[18] If large economic or political organisations "enjoy an oligopoly of the publicistically effective and politically relevant formation of assemblies and associations",[19] then the freedoms of association and assembly are limited. The logic of advertising, consumerism, and capitalism turns the public sphere into "a sphere of culture consumption" that is only a "pseudo-public sphere".[20] Economic, political and ideological control results in a "manufactured public sphere".[21]

8.3 THE MEANS OF COMMUNICATION

Means of Communication as Means of Exploitation and Domination

Marx uses the term "the means of communication" for communication technologies. He considers such technologies to be an important infrastructure of capitalism that is part of the means of production and is therefore interested in analysing the role of the means of communication in capitalism.

Means of communication are fixed constant capital, a means of production that is not immediately used up in the production process, but endures for a longer time. But Marx says the means of communication are different from machines that form another type of fixed capital:

> Regarded as a means of production, it [the means of communication and transport] distinguishes itself from machinery, etc. here in that it is used up by various capitals at the same time, as a common condition for their production and circulation.[22]

For Marx, the means of communication are part of the means of domination and exploitation:

> Every development of new productive forces is at the same time a weapon against the workers. All improvements in the means of communication, for example, facilitate the competition of workers in different localities and turn local competition into national, etc.[23]

> [N]o improvement of machinery, no appliance of science to production, no contrivances of communication, no new colonies, no emigration, no opening of markets, no free trade, nor all these things put together, will do away with the miseries of the industrious masses; but that, on the present false base, every fresh development of the productive powers of labour must tend to deepen social contrasts and point social antagonisms.[24]

Communication, Global Capitalism, Accelerated Capitalism

Capital's search for cheap labour, cheap resources, and commodity markets necessitates the development of means of communication and transport that allow the organisation of capitalist production, circulation and consumption, colonialism, and imperialism on an international and global scale. The development of new means of communication is the outcome of capitalism's political economy.

Capital drives beyond national boundaries and organises itself on a transnational scale in order to find:

1. Cheap(er) labour
2. Cheap(er) means of production
3. Commodity markets
4. Investment opportunities.

"On the other hand, the cheapness of the articles produced by machinery and the revolution in the means of transport and communication provide the weapons for the conquest of foreign markets".[25]

> Capital by its nature drives beyond every spatial barrier. Thus the creation of the physical conditions of exchange – of the means of communication and transport – the annihilation of space by time – becomes an extraordinary necessity for it. Only in so far as the direct product can be realized in distant markets in mass quantities in proportion to reductions in the transport costs, and only in so far as at the same time the means of communication and transport

> themselves can yield spheres of realization for labour, driven by capital; only in so far as commercial traffic takes place in massive volume – in which more than necessary labour is replaced – only to that extent is the production of cheap means of communication and transport a condition for production based on capital, and promoted by it for that reason.[26]

New means of communication and transport are used to speed up the production, circulation, and consumption of commodities:

> the development of the means of communication and transport, in the double sense of determining not only the sphere of those who are in exchange, in contact, but also the speed with which the raw material reaches the producer and the product the consumer.[27]

"The main means of cutting circulation time has been improved communications".[28]

Acceleration and globalisation, the "shortening of time and space by means of communication and transport",[29] are linked to each other. Globalisation means to transport information, goods, commodities, people, and capital over long distances. The use of means of communication and transport allows overcoming such distances in less time. The acceleration of the circuit of capital enables possibilities for interlinking production and consumption that takes place in different parts of the world. In accelerated and globalised manufacturing, parts of a car are produced in different global locations in order to save costs. The speed up of production and transport allows saving production and transport costs because time is money. As a result, companies can produce in places where certain steps can be achieved at low costs. Fast production and transportation saves costs and allows the outsourcing of production in space without losing money, but by reducing the production costs. At the same time, there are negative environmental and social impacts of global capitalism: nature is destroyed by carbon dioxide emissions generated by industry and fossil fuel-based transport.

In the following passage, Marx points out the connection of globalisation and the acceleration of capitalism with the role of the means of communication:

> If the progress of capitalist production and the consequent development of the means of transport and communication shortens the circulation time for a given quantity of commodities, the same progress and the opportunity provided by the development of the means of transport and communication conversely introduces the necessity of working for ever more distant markets, in a word, for the world market. The mass of commodities in transit grows enormously, and hence so does the part of the social capital that stays for long periods in the stage of commodity capital, in circulation time – both absolutely and relatively. A simultaneous and associated growth occurs in the portion of social wealth that, instead of serving as direct means of production, is laid out on means of transport and communication, and on the fixed and circulating capital required to keep these in operation.[30]

The Marxist geographer and theorist David Harvey argues that the reorganisation of capitalism towards a flexible, global regime of accumulation has, since the 1970s, resulted in the development and use of new communication and transport technologies for globalising and accelerating accumulation:

> Capital accumulation has always been about speed-up (consider the history of technological innovations in production processes, marketing, money exchanges) and revolutions in transport and communications (the railroad and telegraph, radio and automobile, jet transport and telecommunications), which have the effect of reducing spatial barriers. The experience of time and space has periodically been radically transformed. We see a particularly strong example of this kind of radical transformation since around 1970: the impact of telecommunications, jet cargo transport, containerization of road, rail and ocean transport, the development of futures markets, electronic banking and computerized production systems. We have recently been going through a strong phase of what I call 'time-space compression': the world suddenly feels much smaller, and the time-horizons over which we can think about social action become much shorter.[31]

The Means of Communication and the Antagonism of the Productive Forces and the Relations of Production

Marx argues that capitalist development requires new methods of production in order to increase its productivity and guarantee profitability. The development of new productive forces on the one hand increases productivity, but on the other hand it also increases the exploitation of labour, the fixed capital costs, the complexity of the production process, the need for human co-operation in production, and it reduces the role of humans in production, which under capitalist conditions can increase unemployment, precarious labour, precarious life, and the unequal distribution of labour-time (some work overtime, others are unemployed). The development of new methods of capitalist production at the same time affirms and undermines capitalism and comes into contradiction with class relations. Marx calls this process the antagonism between the forces of production and the relations of production. The development of the productive forces socialises labour, but at the same time undermines labour as the foundation of capital, which at the same time creates communist potentials for a society built on free time, but in capitalism it advances the potential of crises. For Marx, the means of communication are, in capitalist society, embedded into the antagonism between the productive forces and the relations of production:

> Even within the framework of an earlier mode of production certain needs and certain means of communication and production must have developed which go beyond the old relations of production and coerce them into the capitalist mould. But for the time being they need to be developed only to the point that permits the formal subsumption of labour under capital. On the basis of that change, however, specific changes in the mode of production are introduced which create new forces of production, and these in turn influence the mode of production so that new real conditions come into being. Thus a complete economic revolution is brought about. On the one hand, it creates the real conditions for the domination of labour by capital, perfecting the process and providing it with the appropriate framework. On the other hand, by evolving conditions of production and communication and productive forces of labour antagonistic to

> the workers involved in them, this revolution creates the real premises of a new mode of production, one that abolishes the contradictory form of capitalism. It thereby creates the material basis of a newly shaped social process and hence of a new social formation.[32]

The computer is both a communication and a co-operation tool. It creates new forms of co-operation and communication in the capitalist production process and potential for the reduction of necessary labour-time (the time a society needs to work per year in order for its members to survive) so that foundations of an economy, where free time is the source of wealth and humans only spend a minimum amount of time in necessary labour and most of the time as well-rounded individuals in freely chosen activities. The computer advances communist potentials. At the same time, the computer's embeddedness into class relations creates new forms of automation, phases of structural unemployment, an increase of inequalities and precarious life, etc.

The Telegraph and the Internet

The telegraph was the new information and communication technology that shaped Marx's time. In 1858, the first telegraph cable across the Atlantic Ocean was laid. It connected Western Ireland to the east of Newfoundland and thereby enabled telegraph communication between Europe and North America. The cable worked for only three weeks and it took until 1866 to establish a transatlantic cable that enabled a constant, stable connection. Marx was interested in the role of international communication in capitalism. In the *Grundrisse*, he observed, in the late 1850s:

> Since, 'if you please', the autonomization of the world market (in which the activity of each individual is included), increases with the development of monetary relations (exchange value) and vice versa, since the general bond and all-round interdependence in production and consumption increase together with the independence and indifference of the consumers and producers to one another; since this contradiction leads to crises, etc., hence, together with the development of this alienation, and on the same basis, efforts are made to overcome it:

institutions emerge whereby the individual can acquire information about the activity of all others and attempt to adjust his own accordingly, e.g. lists of current prices, rates of exchange, interconnections between those active in commerce through the mails, telegraphs, etc. (the means of communication of course grow at the same time). This means that, although the total supply and demand are independent of the actions of each individual, everyone attempts to inform himself about them, and this knowledge then reacts back in practice on the total supply and demand. Although on the given standpoint, alienation is not overcome by these means, nevertheless relations and connections are introduced thereby which include the possibility of suspending the old standpoint).[33]

Communication technologies such as the telegraph, and lists of current prices published in newspapers, were important means of communication in the capitalist economy at the time when Marx lived. Marx stresses the need of capital to establish connections in order to accumulate and overcome crisis-provoking tendencies, which contributes to the emergence and use of "new media". Marx was very visionary. When he speaks of the emergence of communication technologies that establish "interconnections" so that "each individual can acquire information about the activity of all others", we are reminded of Internet communication. Marx anticipated the emergence of the Internet. Some say he invented it.

8.4 THE GENERAL INTELLECT

Marx wrote the *Grundrisse* between October 1857 and May 1858. What some Marxist scholars term Marx's "Fragment on Machines" is the section "Capital and the Development of Society's Productive Forces" in the *Grundrisse*'s sixth and seventh notebooks.[34] The "Fragment" was written in the first half of 1858.[35]

Knowledge as Variable Capital and Fixed Constant Capital

In the "Fragment", Marx interprets technology as fixed constant capital that is an "alien power"[36] to the worker. He terms science, knowledge, and technology in production as part of fixed constant capital the "accumulation of knowledge and of skill, of the general productive forces of the social brain" and "general social labour".[37] The "transformation of the production process from the simple labour process into a scientific process [...] appears as a quality of fixed capital in contrast to living labour".[38]

Marx here takes up the issue of knowledge and scientific work as general work that he also discusses in *A Contribution to the Critique of Political Economy*[39] and *Capital Volumes One*[40] and *Three*.[41] General work is general because its results are not just consumed in one specific company or branch of industry, but throughout the entire economy. General work has "a scientific and at the same time general character".[42]

Marx argues that the:

> accumulation of knowledge and of skill, of the general productive forces of the social brain, is thus absorbed into capital, as opposed to labour, and hence appears as an attribute of capital, and more specifically of fixed capital, in so far as it enters into the production process as a means of production proper.[43]

The rise of the importance of knowledge and information in production has not only led to the widespread use of computer technologies and databases in the economy, but also to significant roles for the education system and knowledge labour, i.e. labour that produces knowledge, for the capitalist economy. Knowledge has become an important commodity. In a more general sense, qualifications, skills, and the knowledge of the workforce are today crucial factors of production. Knowledge and skills are acquired through education and in economic production itself. They are part of labour-power and therefore of variable capital. But the knowledge of experts, engineers, and the general workforce is also fixed in the production process and enters into the production of each commodity. In this context, Christian Marazzi points out that "in post-Fordist capitalism, the living body of labour-power simultaneously carries aspects of fixed and variable capital in it".[44] Marx predicted this tendency when arguing, as mentioned at the start of this paragraph, that knowledge and skills are absorbed into fixed capital. The rise of informational capitalism means both the importance of computing as fixed constant capital and human knowledge as aspects of both variable and fixed constant capital. Marazzi argues that the valorisation of education, health care and culture constitutes the rise of an anthropogenic paradigm, where human subjectivity plays a key role in capital accumulation.[45]

Radovan Richta: The Scientific-Technological Revolution

Radovan Richta (1924–1983) was a Czech philosopher. Based on Marx, he termed general labour the scientific and technological revolution. "Science is now penetrating all phases of production and gradually assuming the role of the central productive force of human society and, indeed, the 'decisive factor' in the growth of the productive forces".[46] "Logically, then – from the standpoint of the deeper linkages of the model – the chances of carrying out the scientific and technological revolution to the full lie with a society advancing towards communism".[47] Richta coined the notion of the scientific and technological revolution in the context of hopes for a democratic form of communism in light of the Prague Spring. The rise of the important role of science and the computer in production would constitute a scientific-technological foundation for the transition of capitalism to communism and the transition from authoritarian to human-centred communism.

The idea of the scientific and technological revolution can already be found in the *Grundrisse*:

> But to the degree that large industry develops, the creation of real wealth comes to depend less on labour-time and on the amount of labour employed than on the power of the agencies set in motion during labour-time, whose 'powerful effectiveness' is itself in turn out of all proportion to the direct labour-time spent on their production, but depends rather on the general state of science and on the progress of technology, or the application of this science to production.[48]

As a consequence of technological development, "the entire production process" becomes "the technological application of science".[49]

Marx Anticipated the Emergence of an Information Economy

Marx anticipated the emergence of the important role of knowledge, science, and highly productive technologies, such as the computer, in production by arguing that capital's inherent need to develop the productive forces not only makes technology in production ever more important, but also results in a scientification of production and an increasing importance of knowledge labour: "machinery develops with the accumulation of society's science, of productive force generally".[50]

The General Intellect

The *general intellect* is the "Fragment"'s crucial concept:

> Nature builds no machines, no locomotives, railways, electric telegraphs, self-acting mules, etc. These are products of human industry; natural material transformed into organs of the human will over nature, or of human participation in nature. They are organs of the human brain, created by the human hand; the power of knowledge, objectified. The development of fixed capital indicates to what degree general social knowledge has become a direct force of production, and to what degree, hence, the conditions of the process of social life itself have come under the control of the general intellect and been transformed in accordance with it. To what degree the powers of social production have been produced, not only in the form of knowledge, but also as immediate organs of social practice, of the real life process.[51]

Roman Rosdolsky (1898–1967) was a Marxist economist and theorist. He wrote an outstanding study of the *Grundrisse*, the book titled *The Making of Marx's "Capital"*. Rosdolsky argues that the general intellect passage shows that:

> the development of machinery – although leading under capitalism only to the oppression of workers – offers, in fact, the surest prospect for their future liberation, by facilitating that radical reduction of working time, without which the abolition of class society would remain mere words.[52]

In this passage, Marx's basic idea is that the capitalist development of the productive forces requires that more and more technologies are used in production, which at the same time brings about the growth of scientific and knowledge labour and the role of knowledge in production. At a certain point in time, the growth of the quantity of science and knowledge in production turns into a new quality and the information and knowledge paradigm emerges as a new technological paradigm of capitalism. As a consequence, capitalism's dimension of digital and informational capitalism emerges.

The political philosophers Michael Hardt and Antoni Negri associate with Marx's concept of general intellect the rise of informational capitalism and connect it to the rise of what they term "immaterial labour",[53] a term first introduced by Maurizio Lazzarato, who defines it as "labor that produces the informational and cultural content of the commodity".[54] "General intellect is a collective, social intelligence created by accumulated knowledges, techniques, and know-how. The value of labor is thus realized by a universal and concrete labor force through the appropriation and free usage of the new productive forces".[55]

New Industries

Marx argues that capitalist development results in the emergence of new industries, including technology-producing industries, where machines are used to manufacture machines and means of communication.

> The increase in means of production and subsistence, accompanied by a relative diminution in the number of workers, provides the impulse for an extension of work that can only bear fruit in the distant future, such as the construction of canals, docks, tunnels, bridges, and so on. Entirely new branches of production, creating new fields of labour, are also formed as the direct result either of machinery or of the general industrial changes brought about by it. But the place occupied by these branches in total production is far from important, even in the most developed countries. The number of workers they employ is directly proportional to the demand created by these industries for the crudest form of manual

> labour. The chief industries of this kind are, at present, gas-works, telegraphy, photography, steam navigation and railways.[56]

Marx writes that the "communication industry" focuses on "moving commodities and people, and the transmission of mere information – letters, telegrams, etc".[57] He argues that there are capitalists who "draw the greatest profit from all new development of the universal labour of the human spirit".[58] Today, capitalists drawing profits from the means of communications are the owners, shareholders, directors and managers of large communications/cultural companies such as Apple, AT&T, Samsung, Microsoft, Alphabet/Google, Verizon, China Mobile, Amazon, Comcast, Softbank, Intel, Nippon, Alibaba, IBM, Facebook, Walt Disney, Sony, Cisco, Tencent, and Oracle. Table 8.1 shows that in 2019 these 20 information corporations were among the world's largest 100 companies.

The World's 20 Largest Information Corporations

Table 8.1 shows all the information companies that in 2019 were among the world's 100 largest transnational corporations. They comprise 20 percent, or a total of 20 of the 100 largest capitalist businesses operated in the communication/culture/digital industry. Thirteen of them had their headquarters in the USA and seven in Asian countries. It is notable that none of these companies were located in Africa, Latin America, or Europe, which shows that the information economy is characterised by uneven geographical development. Five of the 20 companies operate in telecommunications, five are Internet service companies, four sell hardware, two sell software, one is focused on semiconductors, and one on both hardware and software. Table 8.2 shows the single branches shares of the total profits and sales of these information companies.

Hardware is the largest branch of these 20 corporations, measured in respect to the share of revenues and profits. Using the same measure, telecommunications and Internet services are the second and third largest branches.

In Marxist theory, the rate of profit is defined as "the ratio of the surplus-value to the total capital advanced".[59] It is calculated

Table 8.1 The world's largest information corporations in 2019 (data source: Forbes 2000 List of the World's Largest 2,000 Companies for 2019) www.forbes.com/global2000/list, accessed on 17 May 2019

Rank	*Corporation*	*Economic branch*	*Headquarter*	*Revenues 2018*	*Profits 2018*
6	Apple	Hardware	USA	US$261.7 bn	US$59.4 bn
12	AT&T	Telecommunications	USA	US$170.8 bn	US$19.4 bn
13	Samsung Electronics	Hardware	South Korea	US$221.5 bn	US$39.9 bn
16	Microsoft	Software	USA	US$118.2 bn	US$33.5 bn
17	Alphabet/Google	Internet services	USA	US$137 bn	US$30.7 bn
20	Verizon	Telecommunications	USA	US$130.9 bn	US$15.5 bn
27	China Mobile	Telecommunications	Hong Kong	US$111.8 bn	US$18.9 bn
28	Amazon	Internet services	USA	US$232.9 bn	US$10.1 bn
33	Comcast	Media content and networks	USA	US$94.5 bn	US$11.7 bn
36	Softbank	Telecommunications	Japan	US$86.2 bn	US$13.9 bn
44	Intel	Semiconductors	USA	US$70.8 bn	US$21.1 bn
51	Nippon	Telecommunications	Japan	US$107.5 bn	US$8.7 bn
59	Alibaba	Internet services	China	US$51.9 bn	US$10.3 bn
60	IBM	Software, hardware	USA	US$78.7 bn	US$8.6 bn
63	Facebook	Internet services	USA	US$55.8 bn	US$22.1 bn
70	Walt Disney	Media content and networks	USA	US$59.4 bn	US$11 bn
73	Sony	Hardware	Japan	US$76.9 bn	US$7.3 bn
74	Cisco	Hardware	USA	US$50.8 bn	US$12.9 bn
74	Tencent	Internet services	China	US$47.2 bn	US$11.9 bn
92	Oracle	Software	USA	US$39.6 bn	US$10.8 bn
			Total:	US$ 2,204.1 bn	US$ 376.7 bn

Table 8.2 Branches' shares of the 20 largest transnational information corporations' profits and sales (calculations based on the data in Table 8.1)

Branch	*Number of companies*	*Share of revenues*	*Share of profits*
Hardware	4	27.7%	31.7%
Telecommunications	5	27.5%	20.0%
Internet services	5	23.8%	22.6%
Software	2	7.2%	11.8%
Media content and networks	2	7.0%	6.0%
Software & hardware	1	3.6%	2.3%
Semiconductors	1	3.2%	5.6%

as profit divided by invested capital: rp = $rp = \frac{p}{c+v}$. Profit is monetary surplus-value. Constant capital c is the total value of the utilised means of production during the full financial year. Given that fixed constant capital stays in the production process over a longer period of time and is not immediately consumed fully in production, the share of the value of fixed constant capital that is used up and depreciates during the one year in question needs to be taken into account in the calculation of the profit rate. Variable capital c is the value of the labour-power used during the financial year (= wages). The profit rate is a measure of how profitable a company is. The higher the profit rate, the more profitable a company is. High profitability can be achieved by high productivity, a high level of exploitation of labour (achieved by, for example, long working hours, low wages, a high share of unpaid labour-time, etc.), or low constant capital costs. Profit rates can be calculated for single companies, economic branches, industries, national economies, or the global economy.

In 2019, Facebook, with 39.6 percent, had the highest profit rate of the world's largest 20 information corporations. It virtually derives all of its revenues from targeted advertising. On 31 December 2018, Facebook had 35,587 employees,[60] which is a relatively small number for a global corporation. Its main

Table 8.3 Profit rates of the world's largest information corporations (2019) (calculations based on data from Table 8.1)

Rank	*Corporation*	*Economic branch*	*Rate of profit*
6	Apple	Hardware	22.7%
12	AT&T	Telecommunications	11.4%
13	Samsung Electronics	Hardware	18.0%
16	Microsoft	Software	28.3%
17	Alphabet/Google	Internet services	22.4%
20	Verizon	Telecommunications	11.8%
27	China Mobile	Telecommunications	16.0%
28	Amazon	Internet services	4.3%
33	Comcast	Media content and networks	12.4%
36	Softbank	Telecommunications	16.1%
44	Intel	Semiconductors	29.8%
51	Nippon	Telecommunications	8.1%
59	Alibaba	Internet services	19.8%
60	IBM	Software, hardware	10.9%
63	Facebook	Internet services	39.6%
70	Walt Disney	Media content and networks	18.5%
73	Sony	Hardware	9.5%
74	Cisco	Hardware	25.4%
74	Tencent	Internet services	25.2%
92	Oracle	Software	27.3%
		All Companies: Average Rate of Profit	18.9%
		All Companies: Combined Rate of Profit	17.1%
		Hardware Branch ROP	19.6%
		Telecommunications ROP	12.4%
		Internet services ROP	16.2%
		Software ROP	28.1%
		Media content and networks ROP	14.7%
		Software & hardware ROP	10.9%
		Semiconductors ROP	29.8%

workers are the users, who generate value by responding to ads and using the platform, which generates data, content, metadata that allows targeting ads, and generates the time needed for presenting ads. Facebook's extraordinarily high profit rate can be explained by the fact that the share of unpaid labour the company exploits is extremely high. The combined profit rate of all 20 companies was 17.1 percent, which is a high value.

Rich Corporations, Poor People

Table 8.4 shows data on the world's least developed countries. The United Nation's Human Development Indicator is a composite indicator calculated and based on data for life expectancy, education, and per capita income. The table shows all countries that the UN considered as having low human development in 2018. These are the world's poorest countries. The gross domestic product measures the monetary value of all goods and services produced during one year in a particular country. It is an indicator for the total economy activity in that state. As such, Table 8.4 shows the GDP for the world's poorest countries.

Table 8.4 The gross domestic product of the world's least developed countries (data sources: HDI: *UNDP Human Development Indices and Indicators 2018 Statistical Update* (New York: UNDP, 2018), GDP (at current prices, in billion US$): World Bank World Development Indicators Data) https://data.worldbank.org, accessed on 17 May 2019[61]

Least developed countries (UNHDR)		
Human Development Index (HDI) rank 2018	*Country*	*GDP 2017 (bn US$)*
189	Niger	8.1
188	Central African Republic	1.9
187	South Sudan	2.9
186	Chad	9.9

(Continued)

Table 8.4 (Cont.)

Least developed countries (UNHDR)		
Human Development Index (HDI) rank 2018	*Country*	*GDP 2017 (bn US$)*
185	Burundi	3.2
184	Sierra Leone	3.8
183	Burkina Faso	12.3
182	Mali	15.3
181	Liberia	3.3
180	Mozambique	12.6
179	Eritrea	5
178	Yemen	31.3
177	Guinea-Bissau	1.3
176	DRC	37.6
175	Guinea	10.5
174	Gambia	1.5
173	Ethiopia	80.6
171	Malawi	6.3
170	Côte d'Ivoire	37.4
169	Haiti	8.4
168	Afghanistan	19.5
167	Sudan	117.5
165	Togo	4.8
165	Comoros	1.1
164	Senegal	21.1
163	Benin	9.2
162	Uganda	26
161	Madagascar	11.5
159	Mauritania	5
159	Lesotho	2.6
158	Rwanda	9.1
157	Nigeria	375.7
156	Zimbabwe	22
155	Syria	15.2
154	Tanzania	53.3
153	Papua New Guinea	20.5
152	Solomon Islands	1.3
	Total:	US$ 1,008.6

In 2018, the combined GDP of the world's 38 least developed countries was US$1,008.6 billion (US$ 1 trillion). In comparison, the total economic activity of the world's 20 largest information corporations, measured as their combined revenues, was in the same year US$2,204.1 billion (US$2.2 trillion; see Table 8.1). The annual revenues of the world's 20 largest corporations in the culture/digital industry are 2.2 times larger than the combined GDP of the world's poorest 20 countries. This circumstance shows the tremendous economic size and power of transnational corporations.

According to the latest data available in 2019, 783 million people – around 10 percent of the world's population – lived below the international poverty line of US$1.90.[62] This means that 10 percent of the world's population live on a total of less than US$543 billion per year, whereas the world's largest information corporations make more than four times that amount per year in revenues. In 2018, 26.5% of the world population in employment lived on less than US$3.10 (purchasing power parity, or PPP).[63] The United Nations considers them as working poor. According to the International Labour Organization (ILO) estimates, in the year 2018 there were 3.3 billion employed persons in the world.[64] The absolute number of poor employees was around 875 million. Together, these workers earned less than US$990 billion per year, whereas the total revenues of just 20 of the world's largest corporations – the largest information corporations – were 2.2 times as large as the total sum of these poverty wages. Whereas a small number of companies yield huge profits, billions of humans have to live in poverty. Digital capitalism is first and foremost a global class society.

8.5 CONCLUSION

This chapter shows that the claims of bourgeois thinkers, such as McLuhan and Baudrillard, that Marx has nothing to say on communication(s) is false. In his works, Marx provides an analysis of communication and language in society and capitalism.

Humans started communicating because there was a material need for it. For Marx, humans are material, social, communicating, sensuous beings. Marx participated in struggles for press freedom and the freedom of speech. He anticipated the contemporary theory of the public sphere by stressing that economic, political, and ideological control of the press and the media destroys the democratic character of the public sphere.

For Marx, the means of communication are part of the means of domination and exploitation. They are means for the acceleration and globalisation of capitalism and are part of the capitalist antagonism between productive forces and relations of production that at the same time constitutes and undermines capitalism.

Marx anticipated the emergence of the Internet. With his concept of the general intellect, he also anticipated the emergence of informational capitalism.

Recommended Further Readings About the Means of Communication and the General Intellect

Raymond Williams. 1977. *Marxism and Literature*. Chapters I.2: Language; III.3: From Medium to Social Practice; III.4: Signs and Notations. Oxford: Oxford University Press.

In these chapters of his seminal book Marxism and Literature, Raymond Williams discusses the notions of language and media from a cultural materialist perspective.

Christian Fuchs. 2018. Towards A Critical Theory of Communication with Georg Lukács and Lucien Goldmann. *Javnost – The Public* 25 (3): 265–281.

Christian Fuchs. 2019. Henri Lefebvre's Theory of the Production of Space and the Critical Theory of Communication. *Communication Theory* 29 (2): 129–150.

Christian Fuchs. 2019. Revisiting the Althusser/E. P. Thompson-Controversy: Towards a Marxist Theory of Communication. *Communication and the Public* 4 (1): 3–20.

These essays discuss some of the theoretical foundations of a critical, dialectical, Marxist-humanist theory of communication. They do so by on the one hand building on Marx's works and on the other hand engaging with aspects of communication in humanist-Marxist approaches, especially the ones by the philosopher Georg Lukács (1885–1971), the sociologist Lucien Goldmann (1913–1970), the philosopher Henri Lefebvre (1901–1991), and the historian Edward P. Thompson (1924–1993). Hegel's dialectical philosophy, Marx's works, and humanism influenced all of these thinkers. Furthermore, the articles are critical of the approach taken by structuralist Marxism that has been heavily influenced by the works of Louis Althusser.

Karl Marx. 1857/1858. *Grundrisse: Foundations of the Critique of Political* Economy. London: Penguin. pp. 690–714

This section in Marx's *Grundrisse* is also called "The Fragment on Machines". In it, Marx introduces the notion of the general intellect and discusses the role and contradictions of technology as fixed constant capital in capitalism.

Michael Hardt and Antonio Negri. 2000. *Empire.* Cambridge, MA: Harvard University Press.

Section 1.2: Biopolitical Production (pp. 22–41).

Section 3.4: Postmodernization, or The Informatization of Production (pp. 280–303).

At the start of the second millennium, Hardt and Negri's *Empire* was the most widely discussed Marxist book. They argue that capitalism has transformed itself into a global, knowledge-based capitalism they call Empire, in which immaterial labour (their term for knowledge labour) plays an important role and the working class is a social worker they term the multitude. Whereas many Marxist approaches ignore issues of communication, culture, and the digital, Hardt and Negri have consistently paid attention to these phenomena's roles in capitalism, which makes their approach a fascinating read for those interested in Marxism, communication, and culture.

Radovan Richta. 1969. *Civilization at the Crossroads. Social and Human Implications of the Scientific and Technological Revolution.* White Plains, NY: International Arts and Sciences Press Inc.

Introduction: The Purpose of Change (pp. 13–21)

Chapter 1: The Nature of the Scientific and Technological Revolution (pp. 23–103).

Radovan Richta (1924–1983) was a Czech Marxist philosopher who was part of, and influenced by, the Prague Spring's attempts to establish a humanist, democratic form of communism. In this context, he led a research team that published "Civilization at the Crossroads", a work also known as the Richta Report that has shamefully been largely ignored in discussions of the information society. From a Marxist theory approach, Richta and his colleagues discuss the role of technology and knowledge in capitalism and communism. In this context they coin the notion of the scientific and technological revolution.

Notes

1 Jean Baudrillard. 1981. *For A Critique of the Political Economy of the Sign*. St. Louis, MI: Telos Press. p. 165.
2 Marshall McLuhan. 1964/2001. *Understanding Media: The Extensions of Man*. New York: Routledge. p. 41.
3 Friedrich Engels. 1876. The Part Played by Labour in the Transition from Ape to Man. In *MECW Volume 25*. London: Lawrence & Wishart. pp. 452–464.
4 Karl Marx and Friedrich Engels. 1845/1846. The German Ideology. In *Marx & Engels Collected Works (MECW) Volume 5*. London: Lawrence & Wishart. pp. 19–539.
5 Ibid., pp. 43–44.
6 Ibid., p. 44.
7 Karl Marx. 1857/1858. *Grundrisse: Foundations of the Critique of Political* Economy. London: Penguin. p. 84.
8 Ibid., p. 490.
9 Karl Marx. 1844. Economic and Philosophic Manuscripts of 1844. In *MECW Volume 3*. London: Lawrence & Wishart. p. 229–346.
10 Karl Marx. 1867. *Capital Volume 1*. London: Penguin. p. 144, footnote 19.
11 Marx, *Grundrisse*, pp. 162–163.
12 Karl Marx. 1852. The Eighteenth Brumaire of Louis Bonaparte. In *MECW Volume 1*. London: Lawrence & Wishart. pp. 99–197.
13 Translation from German: www.heinrich-heine-denkmal.de/dokumente/karlsbad2.shtml, accessed on 16 May 2019.
14 Karl Marx. 1842. Proceedings of the Sixth Rhine Province Assembly. First Article. Debates on Freedom of the Press and Publication of the Proceedings of the Assembly of the Estates. In *MECW Volume 1*. London: Lawrence & Wishart. p. 133–181.
15 Ibid., p. 158.

16 Ibid., p. 175.
17 To the Workers of Cologne. In *MECW Volume* 9. London: Lawrence & Wishart. p. 467.
18 Jürgen Habermas. 1991. *The Structural Transformation of the Public Sphere. An Inquiry into a Category of Bourgeois Society*. Cambridge, MA: MIT Press. p. 227.
19 p. 228.
20 p. 162.
21 p. 217.
22 Marx, *Grundrisse*, p. 725.
23 Marx, Karl. 1847. Wages. In *MECW Volume 6*. London: Lawrence & Wishart. pp. 415–437.
24 Marx, Karl. 1865. Value, Price and Profit. In *MECW Volume 20*. London: Lawrence & Wishart. pp. 101–149.
25 Marx, *Capital Volume 1*, p. 579.
26 Marx, *Grundrisse*, pp. 524–525.
27 Ibid., p. 187.
28 Karl Marx. 1894. *Capital Volume 3*. London: Penguin. p. 164.
29 Marx, Value, Price and Profit, p. 125.
30 Karl Marx. 1885. *Capital Volume 2*. London: Penguin. p. 329.
31 David Harvey. 2001. *Spaces of Capital. Towards a Critical Geography*. New York: Routledge. p. 123.
32 Karl Marx, *Capital Volume 1*, pp. 1064–1065.
33 Marx, *Grundrisse*, pp. 160–161.
34 Ibid., pp. 690–714.
35 Ibid., p. 697 & 555.
36 Ibid., p. 693.
37 Ibid., p. 694.
38 Ibid., p. 700.
39 Karl Marx. 1859. A Contribution to the Critique of Political Economy. In *MECW Volume 29*. New York: International Publishers. pp. 257–417.
40 Marx, *Capital Volume 1*, p. 667.
41 Marx, *Capital Volume 3*, p. 199.
42 Marx, *Grundrisse*, p. 612.
43 Ibid., p. 694.
44 Translation from German: Christian Marazzi. 2012. *Sozialismus des Kapitals*. Zürich: diaphanes. p. 18.
45 Ibid., p. 39.
46 Radovan Richta. 1969. *Civilization at the Crossroads. Social and Human Implications of the Scientific and Technological Revolution*. White Plains, NY: International Arts and Sciences Press Inc. p. 28.

47 Ibid., pp. 53–54.
48 Ibid., pp. 704–705.
49 Ibid., p. 699.
50 Ibid., p. 694.
51 Ibid., p. 706.
52 Roman Rosdolsky. 1977. *The Making of Marx's "Capital"*. London: Pluto Press. p. 243.
53 Michael Hardt and Antonio Negri. 2000. *Empire*. Cambridge, MA: Harvard University Press. pp. 29–30, 364–367.
54 Maurizio Lazzarato. 1996. Immaterial Labor. In *Radical Thought in Italy*, eds. Paolo Virno and Michael Hardt. Minneapolis, MN: University of Minnesota Press. pp. 132–146.
55 Hardt and Negri, *Empire*, p. 364.
56 Marx, *Capital Volume 1*, p. 573.
57 Marx, *Capital Volume 2*, p. 134.
58 Marx, *Capital Volume 3*, p. 199.
59 Marx, *Capital Volume 1*, p. 660.
60 Data source: Facebook SEC-filings 10-K, financial year 2018, available on https://investor.fb.com/financials, accessed on 17 May 2019, p. 23.
61 The 2017 GDP data for Eritrea was obtained from, available on https://tradingeconomics.com; for Syria from https://countryeconomy.com, accessed on 18 May 2019. The data for South Sudan are for 2016 because no newer data was available.
62 www.un.org/en/sections/issues-depth/poverty, accessed on 18 May 2019.
63 Data source: UNDP. 2018. *UNDP Human Development Indices and Indicators 2018 Statistical Update*. New York: UNDP.
64 Data source: ILO Statistics, available on www.ilo.org/ilostat, accessed on 18 May 2019.

9

IDEOLOGY

9.1 INTRODUCTION

The French philosopher Destutt de Tracy (1754–1836) is credited as having introduced the notion of ideology as a form of study.[1] He defined ideology as the science of ideas.

Karl Marx gave a particular meaning to the notion of ideology. Together with Friedrich Engels, in 1845 and 1846 he authored a lengthy manuscript titled *The German Ideology*. This chapter discusses Marx's notion of ideology. Given that ideology has to do with a particular form of the communication of particular ideas, it is evident that the notion of ideology is important for a Marxist theory of communication and culture.

Section 9.2 discusses Marx's concept of ideology. Section 9.3 focuses on his notion of fetishism. Section 9.4 gives attention to Georg Lukács's concept of reified consciousness. Section 9.5 deals with the communication of ideology.

9.2 MARX'S IDEOLOGY CRITIQUE

Different Ways of How to Define Ideology

Ideology has several meanings. Raymond Williams points out three of them:

> The concept of 'ideology' did not originate in Marxism and is still in no way confined to it. Yet it is evidently an important concept in almost all Marxist thinking about culture, and especially about literature and ideas. The difficulty then is that we have to distinguish three common versions of the concept, which are all common in Marxist writing. These are, broadly:
>
> (i) a system of beliefs characteristic of a particular class or group;
> (ii) a system of illusory beliefs – false ideas or false consciousness – which can be contrasted with true or scientific knowledge;
> (iii) the general process of the production of meanings and ideas.[2]

Terry Eagleton further complicates the picture by arguing that there are six meanings of ideology:

> 1 We can mean by it, firstly, the general material process of production of ideas, beliefs and values in social life. [...]
> 2 A second, slightly less general meaning of ideology turns on ideas and beliefs (whether true or false) which symbolize the conditions and life experiences of a specific, socially significant group or class. [...]
> 3 A third definition of the term [...] attends to the *promotion* and *legitimation* of the interests of such social groups in the face of opposing interests. [...]
> 4 A fourth meaning of ideology would retain this emphasis on the promotion and legitimation of sectoral interests, but confine it to the activities of a dominant social power. [...]
> 5 A fifth definition, in which ideology signifies ideas and beliefs which help to legitimate the interests of a ruling group or class specifically by distortion and dissimulation. [...]

6 There is, finally, the possibility of a sixth meaning of ideology, which retains an emphasis on false or deceptive beliefs but regards such beliefs as arising not from the interests of a dominant class but from the material structure of society as a whole. The term ideology remains pejorative, but a class-genetic account of it is avoided. The most celebrated instance of this sense of ideology, as we shall see, is Marx's theory of the fetishism of commodities.[3]

Definitions of ideology range from worldviews and ideas on the one end, to the process of the production of false consciousness on the other end of the spectrum. Williams's third level corresponds to Eagleton's first one. Williams's first understanding is similar to Eagleton's second one. Williams's second definition matches Eagleton's fifth and sixth understandings. Eagleton's fourth definition is situated at an intermediate level.

Lenin and Lukács: General and Critical Concepts of Ideology

Disagreements about ideology among Marxists boil down to the question of whether or not socialism is an ideology. For example, Lenin writes that "the only choice is – either bourgeois or socialist ideology".[4] In contrast, Georg Lukács sees ideology as a feature of class societies, which implies that socialism is not an ideology: "The emergence and diffusion of ideologies appears as the general characteristic of class societies".[5] What is clear is that the general concept of ideology is not a method of critique because it conceives of ideology as a general feature of society. It is part of a theory of ideology. The concept of ideology that Lukács advances and that is represented by Williams's second and Eagleton's sixth definition is, in contrast, part of the critique of ideology.

Max Horkheimer criticises general theories of ideology. He writes that they "thoroughly purge from the ideology concept the remains of its accusatory meaning".[6] Theodor W. Adorno in a comparable manner says that such general theories utilise "the terminology of social criticism while removing its sting".[7]

How did Marx use the term ideology? One can find passages where he uses the general understanding of ideology. The most well-known one can be found in the *Preface to A Contribution to the Critique of Political Economy*, where he speaks of "natural science, and the legal, political, religious, artistic or philosophic" forms as "ideological forms in which men become conscious of this conflict and fight it out".[8] By far the most frequent usage of the notion of ideology in the works of Marx and Engels corresponds to Williams's second and Eagleton's sixth level. Friedrich Engels summarises this understanding in the following words:

> Ideology is a process which is, it is true, carried out consciously by what we call a thinker, but with a false consciousness. The actual motives by which he is impelled remain hidden from him, for otherwise it would not be an ideological process. Hence the motives he supposes himself to have are either false or illusory.[9]

Marx on Religion

In his early philosophical works, Marx engaged with critiques of religion, which resulted in his famous dictum that religion is the opium of the people, which he formulated in the *Introduction to the Critique of Hegel's Philosophy of Law*:

> *Religious* suffering is, at one and the same time, the *expression* of real suffering and a *protest* against real suffering. Religion is the sigh of the oppressed creature, the heart of a heartless world, just as it is the spirit of spiritless conditions. It is the *opium* of the people. To abolish religion as the *illusory* happiness of the people is to demand their *real* happiness. The demand to give up illusions about the existing state of affairs is the *demand to give up a state of affairs which needs illusions*.[10]

Marx argues that religions create artificial, illusionary claims about the existence of a metaphysical, extra-worldly being (God) that dominates the world, and thereby deceive and manipulate humans. The critique of religion was a starting point for

Marx's critique of ideology. But he did not stop there; rather, he started there. For Marx, religion is not pure false consciousness. He stresses that it is also an expression of "real suffering" and a protest against such suffering in a "heartless world". Religion also contains worldly elements having to do with solidarity, care, and compassion.

Marx argues that the abolition of religion requires the abolition of the conditions that create unhappiness, the abolition of society as the "vale of tears":

> The abolition of religion as the *illusory* happiness of the people is the demand for their *real* happiness. To call on them to give up their illusions about their condition is to call on them to *give up a condition that requires illusions*. The criticism of religion is, therefore, *in embryo, the criticism of that vale of tears* of which religion is the *halo*.[11]

In the critique of religion, Marx arrives at a description of features of the general critique of ideology:

> Criticism has plucked the imaginary flowers on the chain not in order that man shall continue to bear that chain without fantasy or consolation, but so that he shall throw off the chain and pluck the living flower. The criticism of religion disillusions man, so that he will think, act, and fashion his reality like a man who has discarded his illusions and regained his senses, so that he will move around himself as his own true Sun. Religion is only the illusory Sun which revolves around man as long as he does not revolve around himself.[12]

Marx here describes ideology as a chain of "imaginary flowers". Critique of ideology throws off and breaks the ideology's chain and plucks the "living flower". It becomes evident here that ideology tries to alienate humans from their own interests so that they act in the interests of their oppressors and exploiters. Critique of ideology aims at strengthening humans' critical and independent thinking so that they unmask domination and exploitation and become their "own true Sun" so that they see their own interests and act according to them.

Marx already, in the *Contribution to the Critique of Hegel's Philosophy of Law*, that he wrote in 1843 abstracts the critique of ideology from religion and argues that ideology often tries to present particularistic interests as general interests: "[It is] the illusion that the *matters of general concern* are matters of general concern, public matters".[13]

Marx and Engels's The German Ideology

In 1845 and 1846, Karl Marx and Friedrich Engels wrote the manuscript *The German Ideology* that criticises some of the most important philosophers of the time in Germany, especially Bruno Bauer, Ludwig Feuerbach, and Max Stirner. Marx and Engels argue that these thinkers focus their critique on religion and ideas and do not advance to the critique of political economy and therefore to the critique of capitalism. "It has not occurred to any one of these philosophers to inquire into the connection of German philosophy with German reality, the relation of their criticism to their own material surroundings".[14]

In a key passage in *The German Ideology*'s Feuerbach chapter, Marx writes:

> Consciousness [*das Bewusstsein*] can never be anything else than conscious being [*das bewusste Sein*], and the being of men is their actual life-process. If in all ideology men and their relations appear upside-down as in a *camera obscura*, this phenomenon arises just as much from their historical life-process as the inversion of objects on the retina does from their physical life-process. [...] The phantoms formed in the brains of men are also, necessarily, sublimates of their material life-process, which is empirically verifiable and bound to material premises. Morality, religion, metaphysics, and all the rest of ideology as well as the forms of consciousness corresponding to these, thus no longer retain the semblance of independence. They have no history, no development; but men, developing their material production and their material intercourse, alter, along with this their actual world, also their thinking and the products of their thinking.[15]

Features of Ideology

In this excerpt, several important features of ideology become evident:

- *Ideology is a form of consciousness*: Ideology has to do with human consciousness.
- *Ideology is material*: Ideology is not immaterial, but emerges from material processes. It is a reflection of structures of domination and exploitation.
- *Illusion and distortion in order to try to manipulate consciousness*: In ideology, there are attempts to manipulate human consciousness. Ideology operates like a *camera obscura*. It tries to portray parts of the world "upside-down", which means in a distorted and manipulative way. Ideology inverts reality and claims that something that is illusionary, invented, made-up is real. Marx therefore speaks of "phantoms formed in the brains" of humans.
- *Ideology is a false appearance that conceals the world's essence*: Marx bases his understanding of ideology on Hegel's dialectic of essence and appearance: Ideologies make something appear as something that does not exist. Thereby, reality appears in manners that do not correspond to their essence. Ideology tries to install a false consciousness about reality. It tries to conceal reality as it truly is behind illusionary appearances. When discussing appearance, Hegel says that the "immediate being of things is [...] represented as a sort of rind or curtain behind which the essence is concealed". [16] The hiding of truth is for Hegel an aspect of logic, whereas for Marx the processes of the concealment and hiding of the truth are typical for class societies, where the ruling class wants to hide its true interests.

There is a danger in separating ideology from the economy. Not only does ideology stand in a relationship with political economy because it distorts reality in order to justify particularistic political economic interests, but there is an economic aspect operating within ideology, namely ideological labour. Marx argues in this context that:

> The division of labour [...] manifests itself also in the ruling class as the division of mental and material labour, so that inside this class one part appears as the thinkers of the class (its active, conceptive ideologists, who make the formation of the illusions of the class about itself their chief source of livelihood), while the others' attitude towards these ideas and illusions is more passive and receptive, because they are in reality the active members of this class and have less time to make up illusions and ideas about themselves.[17]

The ruling class requires a consciousness and tries to "sell" this consciousness to others as the only true view of the world according to which politics should operate and society should be organised. Marx argues that there is a division of labour in the ruling class between ideological workers on the one side and capitalists and bourgeois politicians on the other. Ideologues plan the content of an ideology and strategies to enforce ideology. Ideologues include, for example, think tanks, consultants, advisors, speechwriters, academics, journalists, and other intellectuals who devise the worldviews and strategies of the ruling class and "make up illusions" about the ruling class. Ideologues are ideological workers who are paid for practising the production and reproduction of ideology as their profession in order to try to reproduce class society. Ideological labour is the economic foundation of ideology. At the same time, ideology is not restricted to the economy but has emergent meanings that ideological labour produces and that shape society in ways not determined by the economy.

Friedrich Hayek (1899–1992) was an economist and the godfather of neoliberalism. He believed that state intervention in the economy is harmful and he propagated that markets be left to themselves (he called a society ruled by the market a "spontaneous order"); a wide-ranging rule of the commodity form and markets in many realms of society; and the curbing of trade unions. Hayek heavily influenced Margaret Thatcher (1925–2013), who was

Britain's Prime Minister from 1979 until 1990. "Thatcherism" is the British version of neoliberalism. In a letter to Hayek dated 13 May 1980, Thatcher wrote that "we are indebted to your economic ideas and philosophy".[18] In another letter, Thatcher wrote to Hayek about how "instructive and rewarding" it was "to hear your views on the great issues of our time"[19] at a dinner. Thatcher executed the politics and ideology of Thatcherism, but she did not do so alone, she did so based on the ideological labour of think tanks, consultants, and advisors, etc. who were, like her, deeply influenced by the neoliberal ideology that Hayek had devised in opposition to Keynes and Marx.

9.3 COMMODITY FETISHISM

What Is Commodity Fetishism?

In *Capital Volume One* (1867), Marx wrote a section titled "The Fetishism of the Commodity and Its Secret".[20] He here applies his earlier critique of religion to the commodity form and argues that in capitalism, the commodity takes on an ideological, quasi-religious form. He argues that the commodity form itself is ideological by hiding and concealing social relations in which humans produce commodities. The commodity is "mysterious"; it is "a very strange thing"[21]:

> The mysterious character of the commodity-form consists therefore simply in the fact that the commodity reflects the social characteristics of men's own labour as objective characteristics of the products of labour themselves, as the socio-natural properties of these things. Hence it also reflects the social relation of the producers to the sum total of labour as a social relation between objects, a relation which exists apart from and outside the producers. Through this substitution, the products of labour become commodities, sensuous things which are at the same time supra-sensible or social.[22]

Capitalism's commodity form makes things such as commodities, money, and capital appear as if they were natural features of the social world. In class societies there is a division of labour, which is why no individual can directly experience the labour and class relations that others are involved in and that result in commodities. They are only confronted with commodities as dead labour in their everyday life. Commodities and money as exchange-value conceal the social relations of production, i.e. class relations. Capitalism's fetishism of commodities, money, and capital is inherently ideological, which means that ideology is built into the structures of capitalism. The philosopher Slavoj Žižek argues in this context that the ideological is a form of social reality: "*'ideological' is a social reality whose very existence implies the non-knowledge of its participants as to its essence*".[23]

Commodity fetishism is ideology. But, vice versa, ideology is also fetishist: Ideology is a process by which humans present historical and transformable social relations of domination as natural, eternal, and unchangeable. They reduce the dynamic social world to a static world. Ideology makes domination and exploitation appear like a thing; as something immoveable. Ideologies present phenomena such as commodities as eternal and absolutely necessary for human existence. They discard the fact that social phenomena are made by humans in social relations and can therefore be changed.

9.4 GEORG LUKÁCS'S CONCEPT OF REIFIED CONSCIOUSNESS

History and Class Consciousness

Georg Lukács (1885–1971) was one of the 20th century's most influential Marxist philosophers. His book *History and Class Consciousness* established the foundations of a Marxist critical theory of ideology. Reification is *History and Class Consciousness*'s key category. With it, Lukács describes and analyses capitalism's structural effects on human subjectivity and, especially, consciousness. The notion of reification derives from Marx's concept of commodity fetishism.

"The essence of commodity-structure" is that "a relation between people takes on the character of a thing and thus acquires a 'phantom objectivity', an autonomy that seems so strictly rational and all-embracing as to conceal every trace of its fundamental nature: the relation between people".[24] A phantom is schizophrenic. It is visible and invisible at the same time. With the metaphor of the commodity as phantom or ghost, Lukács and Marx tell us that the immediacy of the commodity as thing hides its true essence, which is not visible to us, namely the abstract labour of workers and the class relations they are forced to enter and which they produce.

Reified Consciousness

Ideology is a necessary aspect of capitalism because the latter needs legitimatisation. The "veil drawn over the nature of bourgeois society is indispensable to the bourgeoisie itself. [...] the need to deceive the other classes and to ensure that their class consciousness remain amorphous is inescapable for a bourgeois regime".[25]

"Reification and the Consciousness of the Proletariat" is *History and Class Consciousness*'s longest chapter.[26] In this chapter, Lukács shows that the capitalist class has a necessary false consciousness. The proletarians have a revolutionary potential, but they can also be blinded by ideology and reified structures: "The danger to which the proletariat has been exposed since its appearance on the historical stage was that it might remain imprisoned in its immediacy together with the bourgeoisie".[27] Lukács argues that there are three basic foundations of the "bourgeoisification of the proletariat":[28] elite sections of the working class,[29] the reification of consciousness by capitalism's structures and ideology,[30] and reformist, right-wing social democracy.[31]

Reified consciousness is false consciousness, consciousness that "by-passes the essence of the evolution of society and fails to pinpoint it and express it adequately".[32] Bourgeois consciousness is an ideology that favours, justifies, and legitimates capitalism. Bourgeois ideology tries to present capitalism as a natural, thing-like entity that is the best possible or the only possible form of society. Although most individuals who have a bourgeois existence because they are capitalists or work as managers have bourgeois, reified consciousness, some of them can see through ideology and support socialist causes. Conversely, not everyone who is part of the working class and the exploited has non-reified, socialist consciousness. There are ideologies such as entrepreneurialism, neoliberalism, racism, nationalism, and fascism, etc., that aim at reifying all members of society's consciousness, which can also affect workers and those coming from a working-class background. A typical example is blue-collar workers who support and vote for racist parties.

Lukács's critical theory has had a wide influence. For example, Theodor W. Adorno sees ideology, like Lukács, as "a consciousness which is objectively necessary and yet at the same time false, as the intertwining of truth and falsehood".[33]

Ideology first exists on the side of production, i.e. it is produced and communicated. There are various ways in which individuals react to ideological content. They do not necessarily and do not automatically "buy into" ideology. But they also do not necessarily and do not automatically "resist" ideology. How can one explain why someone follows a certain ideology? The belief in ideology is grounded in political economy, but cannot be reduced to it. Psychological factors play a role too.

Erich Fromm: Psychological Aspects of Ideology

Erich Fromm (1900–1980) was a Marxist psychologist and philosopher. He introduced the notion of the social character as "the matrix of the character structure *common to a group*".[34] The social character is the totality of the common psychological features of a social group. Fromm argues that "*the social character is the intermediary between the socio-economic structure and the ideas and ideals prevalent in a society*".[35] For Fromm, the authoritarian and the humanistic character are the two main types of the social character. Socialisation in certain social relations and education shape and create the character structure of an individual. Marx's sixth Feuerbach thesis that the individual and the human being's essence are "the ensemble of the social relations"[36] implies that the totality of our social relations and the totality of the history of the totality of our social relations shape our psychological structure and make us what we are. For Fromm, humanism is in opposition to authoritarianism. As a consequence, he distinguishes between the authoritarian and the humanistic character. In authoritarianism, "an authority states what is good for man and lays down the laws and norms of conduct", whereas in humanism the human being is "both the norm giver and the subject of the norms".[37] Individuals with an authoritarian personality who believe in the need for hierarchy, domination, dictatorship, and violence are particularly susceptible to following ideologies.

9.5 THE COMMUNICATION OF IDEOLOGY

In capitalist society, media are spaces where ideologies are produced, reproduced, communicated, but sometimes also contested. In this section, we will have a look at some forms of how ideology is communicated.

Advertising

In the sale of a commodity, the commodity and capital "speaks to" humans through advertisements and prices. In an indirect manner, companies tell consumers that, and why, they should buy commodities. Marx in this context argues that value and price form "the language of commodities".[38] Commodities' "universal language is price and their common bond is money"[39]. Capitalist communication is alienated, de-humanised communication. Capital speaks to consumers in an instrumental form and with the sole purpose of doing everything possible to make them buy commodities. Through price and advertisements, the commodity only *appears* to speak to us. In reality the messages communicated are designed by corporations that tell us "Buy me!", "I am cheap!", "I will make your life better!", "I am worth the investment!", etc. The advertisement speaks to us as if the commodity were a human being that can act on our lives and make our lives better. Advertisements make false promises.

Marx argues that the logic of commodities and communication through commodity-exchange has so deeply shaped humans' subjectivity in capitalism that direct communication often seems alien to us and communication through commodity logic seems natural, although in reality the communication through exchange-value is alienated:

> We are to such an extent estranged from man's essential nature that the direct language of this essential nature seems to us a *violation of human dignity*, whereas the estranged language of material values seems to be the well-justified assertion of human dignity that is self-confident and conscious of itself.[40]

Example: A Coca-Cola Advertisement

A Coca-Cola advertisement, run by the US beverage company in 2019, speaks to the consumer in the following way:

> A Coke is a Coke. It's the same for everyone. You can get one if you want it no matter where you're from. He drinks Coke and she drinks Coke. Even though they disagree. And while the bottles look alike, you aren't the same as me. Stars drink it. Chefs drink it. Farmers want one when it's hot. There's a Coke here if you are thirsty. But that's cool if you're not. We all have different hearts and hands, heads holding various views. Don't you see: different is beautiful. And together is beautiful too.

The ad ends with the appearance of the Coca-Cola logo and the slogan "Together Is Beautiful" next to it.[41]

Section 9.2 argued that we can learn from Marx and Engels's *The German Ideology* that there are several features of ideology:

- Ideology is a form of consciousness
- Ideology is material
- Illusion and distortion in order to try to manipulate consciousness
- Ideology is a false appearance that conceals the world's essence.

All of these dimensions matter for the analysis of an advertisement such as the one by Coca-Cola. The Coca-Cola ad is a *form of consciousness*: Ad workers and filmmakers paid by Coca-Cola produced this content that has been broadcast on television and spread on social media. In May 2019, Coca-Cola's YouTube channel had 3.1 million followers. The ad in question had been online for three months and had reached 1.1 million views, with 266 comments. Social media is a major means of communicating ideological consciousness.

The advert is one of the ways in which Coca-Cola tries to advance its *material interest* of capital accumulation. In 2019, Coca-Cola was the world's 133rd largest company.[42] In 2018, it achieved revenues of US$31.7 billion and made profits of US$6.4 billion.

The advert *creates illusions* that try to manipulate humans, i.e. to try to make them buy Coca-Cola. The basic message that the ad communicates is: "Buying, drinking and enjoying a Coke makes everyone equal. Coke transcends gender differences, class differences and cultural differences". The ad claims that Coke is "the same for everyone". It uses the idea of unity in diversity as a marketing slogan. The dialectic of difference and togetherness is expresses by stressing that difference "is beautiful" and togetherness "is beautiful too". The advertisement appeals to humans' desire for fairness, democracy, equality, beauty, togetherness, and difference. A soft drink is presented as helping to achieve these desires for humans. The promises the ad makes reflects commodity fetishism: A drink is said to change the life of humans for the better and to bring about positive qualities such as togetherness and equality. The ad abstracts from the political and economic relations that enable or hinder togetherness and equality and promises that the purchase of a commodity-thing is enough to create a good life for everyone. The overall aim is to make consumers buy and consume Coke frequently in order to increase Coca-Cola's profits.

Lifestyle Branding

Coca-Cola conducts lifestyle branding. It doesn't just sell soft drinks but the promise that this commodity will bring about a better life for its consumers. Coca-Cola and other brands do not just sell their primary commodity but along with it they sell a culture in the form of a lifestyle ideology. They try to sell cultural promises that appeal to human desires and dreams.

The critical writer and filmmaker Naomi Klein argues in her book *No Logo* that lifestyle branding has become a dominant form of advertising in cultural capitalism:

> This is the true meaning of a lifestyle brand: you can live your whole life inside it. [...] Savvy ad agencies have all moved away from the idea that they are flogging a product made by someone else, and have come to think of themselves instead as brand factories, hammering out what is of true value: the idea, the lifestyle, the attitude. Brand builders are the new primary producers in our so-called knowledge economy.[43]

Global corporations such as Coca-Cola increasingly have started to sell multiculturalism as commodity ideology. The ad just analysed is a good example of this trend. Coca-Cola is not so much interested in using the "American way of life" as a marketing slogan, it tries to sell multiculturalism as a commodity ideology:

> Today the buzzword in global marketing isn't selling America to the world, but bringing a kind of market masala to everyone in the world. In the late nineties, the pitch is less Marlboro Man, more Ricky Martin: a bilingual mix of North and South, some Latin, some R&B, all couched in global party lyrics. This ethnic-food-court approach creates a One World placelessness, a global mall in which corporations are able to sell a single product in numerous countries without triggering the old cries of 'Coca-Colonization'.[44]

Sut Jhally and Raymond Williams on Advertising as Ideology

Advertisements such as the Coke ad are examples of product propaganda that *conceal the world's essence*. They only portray commodities in a positive light and invent imaginaries that are present in the world in a false and deceptive way. Ads conceal negative aspects of commodities and capitalism because they want consumers to buy and buy more commodities. The necessary positivist character of advertising conceals the negative aspects of the world of commodities. It hides and denies the way the world truly is. The critical communication studies scholar Sut Jhally argues in this context that "The social relations of production embedded in goods are systematically hidden from our eyes. The real meaning of goods, in fact, is *emptied* out in capitalist production and consumption".[45]

Meanings are produced by humans in social relations. Commodity fetishism, as expressed in advertisements and the everyday reality of capitalism in general, destroys the meaning of goods; it empties meaning out of goods by hiding the social relations that underpin them. Given that workers cannot speak through the commodities they produce, a silence is created in production in the commodity form. Advertising is the ideological way that the commodity's void of meaning is filled. "Production empties. Advertising fills".[46] Advertising invents illusionary meanings as commodity ideologies. It fills commodities with artificial meanings that are distant from the world of the workers who produce them.

The cultural theorist Raymond Williams wrote an important critical essay about advertising. In "Advertising: The Magic System",[47] Williams argues that advertising is a capitalist form of magic, an ideology that promises to bring about magic transformations of the lives of individuals. Advertising is "a major form of modern social communication", "an institutionalized system of commercial information and persuasion",[48] and "a highly organized and professional system of magical inducements and satisfactions, functionally very similar to magical systems in simpler societies, but rather strangely coexistent with a highly developed scientific technology".[49] Advertising obscures "the real sources of general satisfaction".[50] Ads are a type of "organized fantasy" that tries to portray what corporations want as "your choice".[51]

Advertising is a type of social form where ideological communication operates in the economy. But ideological communication is not limited to the economic system. It also takes place in the political and cultural spheres when the state, the nation, bureaucracy, nationalism, wars, racism, and xenophobia, etc. are presented as natural features of society and humanity. Advertising is a consumption- and commodity-realisation ideology. It tries to advance the sale and consumption of commodities. Ideology in general, as political and cultural strategy beyond the economy, aims at a legitimation of the interests of the exploiting class and groups that want to dominate humans.

Horkheimer and Adorno: the Culture Industry as Ideology and Deception

In their book *Dialectic of Enlightenment*, Max Horkheimer and Theodor W. Adorno introduce the notion of the culture industry. They argue that the sale and consumption of commodities creates a culture focused on entertainment that diverts attention from society's problems and its causes and makes humans uncritical:

> Today the culture industry has taken over the civilizing inheritance of the frontier and entrepreneurial democracy, whose receptivity to intellectual deviations was never too highly developed. All are free to dance and amuse themselves, just as, since the historical neutralization of religion, they have been free to join any of the countless sects. But freedom to choose an ideology, which always reflects economic coercion, everywhere proves to be freedom to be the same. [...] The most intimate reactions of human beings have become so entirely reified, even to themselves, that the idea of anything peculiar to them survives only in extreme abstraction: personality means hardly more than dazzling white teeth and freedom from body odor and emotions. That is the triumph of advertising in the culture industry: the compulsive imitation by consumers of cultural commodities which, at the same time, they recognize as false.[52]

Nationalism and Xenophobia

Nationalism and xenophobia are examples of a political ideology – a political fetishisation of the nation. Let us look at an example. In the years from 2006 to 2009 and from 2010 to 2016, Nigel Farage led the far-right UK Independence Party (UKIP). In 2019, he founded a new party, The Brexit Party, and became its leader. He sent the following tweet, shown in Figure 9.1, a couple of days before the British referendum on staying in or leaving the European Union.

We can analyse the tweet by again having a look at the four dimension of ideology that Marx analyses in the Feuerbach chapter of *The German Ideology*:

- Ideology is a form of consciousness
- Ideology is material

Figure 9.1 Tweet by Nigel Farage in the context of the Brexit referendum (data source: Twitter @NigelFarage) posted on 16 June 2016, https://twitter.com/nigel_farage/status/743403318232244225, accessed on 18 May 2019

- Illusion and distortion in order to try to manipulate consciousness
- Ideology is a false appearance that conceals the world's essence.

First, there is the aspect of *ideology as consciousness*. Twitter is a popular Internet service that allows the publishing of short messages that can be accompanied by a video or an image. At the end of March 2019, Twitter had an average of 330 million users per month.[53] Farage posted this tweet exactly one week before the British EU referendum. At this point in time, 321,000 accounts followed his Twitter handle.[54] The tweet displays a BBC report, in which Nigel Farage comments on a UKIP poster campaign. The posters show a crowd of refugees accompanied by the slogan "BREAKING POINT. The EU has failed us all. We must break free of the EU and take back control of our borders. Leave EU". Farage posted on Twitter alongside this video: "We must break free of the EU and take back control of our borders".

Second, ideology is *material*. Such tweets are a form of communication that wants to advance specific *material interests*. In this case, UKIP and Farage aimed at convincing as many British citizens as possible to vote for the British exit from the European Union. In UKIP's 2016 Local Election Manifesto, the party's political interest was clearly formulated in the following manner: "UKIP will bring back control of our borders and end the government's policy of open-door immigration".[55] UKIP blames the EU and migration for social problems and sees immigration as harmful to society.

Third, ideology works with *distortions and illusions*. The UKIP poster portrays refugees and immigrants as crowd, flood, and mass. The audience is reminded of "a water-course/current/flood that has to be 'dammed'".[56] Describing fleeing and migrating humans as constituting a "breaking point" is a combination of two linguistic ideological strategies: the strategy of large numbers and the strategy of burdening.[57] Membership of the EU and immigration are presented as having "specific dangerous, threatening consequences"[58] for British society. Furthermore, refugees and migrants are presented as a burden on the British social system. The tweet uses the friend/enemy scheme, which is a common ideological strategy. It constructs a nationalist narrative that separates "us" British citizens from "them" and constructs an illusionary social antagonism between individuals who hold a British passport on the one side and migrants without British passport on the other side.

Farage also opposes the British nation to the EU ("We must break free of the EU"). Borders are presented as a national property of which the British nation has lost control, which in Farage's logic has spurred immigration ("We must [...] take back control of our borders"). Nationalism is a form of ideology that opposes the nation as cultural homogeneity to groups that are presented as aliens and enemies that threaten the nation.

Nationalism distracts attention from the class antagonism. In Britain, neoliberal politics have continued to exist since Margaret Thatcher resigned in November 1990. Both the Conservative Party under John Major, David Cameron, Theresa May, and Boris Johnson as well as New Labour under Tony Blair and Gordon Brown advanced Thatcherite politics. More than four decades of neoliberalism created large inequalities and political discontent. Farage and UKIP claim that it's not the antagonisms of capitalism that are the cause of inequality, but, rather, refugees, immigrants and the EU. He turns the EU and migrants into political fetish objects. Farage communicates the existence of political scapegoats in order to distract attention from class inequality.

Nationalism is a political ideology. It constructs and communicates an illusory political and national interest of capital and labour in the form of the nation. The German Marxist theorist and politician Rosa Luxemburg (1871–1919) argues that nationalism is a "misty veil" that "conceals in every case a definite historical content",[59] namely the historical content of class society. Nationalist communication argues and publicly claims that there is a national people ("we") that is under attack by foreigners (other nations, immigrants, and refugees, etc.). Marx writes that nationalism makes workers hate each other and is "the secret of the [...] *working class's impotence* [...] and the secret of the maintenance of power by the capitalist class".[60] Marx also points out the ideological role that the bourgeois media play: Nationalism "is kept artificially alive and [is] intensified by the press [...] [and] all the means at the disposal of the ruling class".[61]

Fourth, ideology *conceals the world's essence*. Often, racists and nationalists do not communicate with facts, but by stoking fears, negative emotions, and prejudices. Ideology ignores, denies, and conceals facts. Nigel Farage's tweet ignores the reality of immigration in Britain: In 2018, a share of 26 percent of all British doctors did not hold a British passport, almost 10 percent of them were EU citizens, and 16 percent of the nurses working in the National Health Service did not have a UK passport.[62] Without immigrants, the NHS would come to a "breaking point". Immigration sustains British society. In 2020, 28 percent of the individuals living in Britain had reached the pension age. According to projections, this share will amount to 37 percent in 2040.[63] In 2016, 83 percent of those seeking asylum in one of the EU's 28 countries were younger than 35. Fifty-one percent of these first-time asylum seekers were in the age range of 18 to 34.[64] Many contemporary modern societies are ageing, and life expectancy continues to grow. This is a positive result of medical and human progress that requires policy responses. Immigration is a way of preventing pension systems from reaching a "breaking point".

9.6 CONCLUSION

How to define ideology has been contested among Marxists. Whereas some prefer to define ideology in a general sense as worldview, Marx saw ideology as a particular phenomenon of class societies. Ideology has to do with the material interests of the ruling class, illusion and distortion, false appearances, the concealment of the world's essence, and false consciousness.

Marx's notion of ideology is interconnected with the concept of commodity fetishism. The commodity's structure is ideological, just like ideology operates in a fetishist manner. Based on Marx's concept of commodity fetishism, Georg Lukács introduced the notions of reified consciousness and reification.

In capitalist society, media are spaces where ideologies are produced, reproduced, communicated, and contested. A world without ideology requires a post-capitalist framework and post-capitalist media.

Recommended Further Readings about Ideology

Terry Eagleton. 1991. *Ideology: An Introduction*. London: Verso. Chapter 1: What Is Ideology? (pp. 1–31).

This chapter provides an introduction to questions that Marxists ask about ideology.

Raymond Williams. 1977. *Marxism and Literature*. Oxford: Oxford University Press.
Chapter 4: Ideology (pp. 55–71).

In this chapter, Williams discusses some important aspects of Marx's understanding of ideology.

Karl Marx. 1867. The Fetishism of the Commodity and Its Secret. In *Capital Volume 1*. London: Penguin. pp. 163–177.

In this chapter, Marx introduces the notion of the fetishism of the commodity. It makes for difficult reading, but is very important for everyone who wants to understand Marx's concept of ideology.

Georg Lukács. 1971. Reification and the Consciousness of the Proletariat. In *History and Class Consciousness*. London: Merlin. pp. 83–222.

In this work, Georg Lukács builds on Marx's notion of fetishism and introduces the concept of reified consciousness. This chapter is a must-read for everyone who wants to understand what false consciousness is.

Raymond Williams. 1960/2005. Advertising: the Magic System. In *Culture and Materialism*, London: Verso. pp. 170–195.

Sut Jhally. 2006. Advertising as Religion: The Dialectic of Technology and Magic. In *The Spectacle of Accumulation*. New York: Peter Lang. pp. 85–97.

These two readings provide an introduction to the Marxist analysis of advertising as commodity ideology.

Max Horkheimer and Theodor W. Adorno. 1947/2002. *Dialectic of Enlightenment: Philosophical Fragments*. Stanford, CA: Stanford University Press.

Chapter 2: The Culture Industry: Enlightenment as Mass Deception (pp. 94–136).

In this seminal chapter, Horkheimer and Adorno introduce the notion of the culture industry. They argue that entertainment and the culture industry operate as ideology that deceives humans and tries to make them uncritically accept domination.

Christian Fuchs. 2018. *Digital Demagogue: Authoritarian Capitalism in the Age of Trump and Twitter.* London: Pluto Press.
Chapter 2: Ideology, Nationalism and Fascism (pp. 9–45)
Chapter 6: Trump and Twitter: Authoritarian-Capitalist Ideology on Social Media (pp. 197–257)

These two readings together provide an introduction to the Marxist understanding of ideology, nationalism, and fascism. They show how ideology can be critically analysed on social media such as Twitter. For doing so, Donald Trump's use of Twitter is presented as a case study.

Notes

1 Destutt de Tracy. 1817/1970. *A Treatise on Political Economy.* Translated by Thomas Jefferson. New York: August M. Kelley Publishers.
2 Raymond Williams. 1977. *Marxism and Literature.* Oxford: Oxford University Press. p. 55
3 Terry Eagleton. 1991. *Ideology: An Introduction.* London: Verso. pp. 28, 29, 30.
4 Lenin. 1902. What Is To Be Done? In *Lenin Collected Works* 5, 347–529. Moscow: Progress Publishers. p. 384.
5 Translation from German: "Entstehen und Verbreitung von Ideologien erscheint als das allgemeine Kennzeichen der Klassengesellschaften". In Georg Lukács. 1986. *Zur Ontologie des gesellschaftlichen Seins. Zweiter Halbband. Georg Lukács Werke Band 14.* Darmstadt: Luchterhand. p. 405.
6 Translation from German: Max Horkheimer. 1972. *Sozialphilosophische Studien.* Frankfurt am Main: Fischer. p. 28.
7 Theodor W. Adorno. 1981. *Prisms.* Cambridge, MA: MIT Press. p. 38.
8 Karl Marx. 1859. Preface to a Contribution to the Critique of Political Economy. In *MECW Volume 29.* London: Lawrence & Wishart. pp. 261–265.

9 Letter from Engels to Franz Mehring, 14 July 1893. In *MECW Volume 50*, London: Lawrence & Wishart. pp. 163–167. p. 164. I twice substitued the term "spurious" here with "false" because in the original German letter Engels writes about "falsches Bewußtsein" (MEW Band 39, 97), which should be translated as "false consciousness" and not as "spurious consciousness" as is the case in the MECW edition.
10 Marx, Karl. 1844b. Contribution to the Critique of Hegel's Philosophy of Law. Introduction. In *MECW Volume 3*. London: Lawrence & Wishart. pp. 175–187.
11 Ibid., p. 176.
12 Ibid., p. 176.
13 Karl Marx. 1843. Contribution to the Critique of Hegel's Philosophy of Law, 3–129. In *MECW Volume 3*, London: Lawrence & Wishart. p. 62.
14 Karl Marx and Friedrich Engels. 1845/46. The German Ideology. Critique of Modern German Philosophy According to Its Representatives Feuerbach, B. Bauer and Stirner, and of German Socialism According to Its Various Prophets. In *MECW Volume 5*. London: Lawrence & Wishart. pp. 15–539.
15 Ibid., pp. 36–37.
16 Georg Wilhelm Friedrich Hegel. 1830/1991. *The Encyclopaedia Logic (with the Zusätze). Part I of the Encyclopaedia of the Philosophical Sciences with the Zusätze.* Indianapolis, IN: Hackett. Addition to §112.
17 Ibid., pp. 59–60.
18 Letter from Margaret Thatcher to Friedrich Hayek, 13 May 1980. Thatcher Digital Archive (Thatcher MSS), THCR 3/2/26 f47, available on https://c59574e9047e61130f13-3f71d0fe2b653c4f00f32175760e96e7.ssl.cf1.rackcdn.com/DD10E6A929394708870606AE68B05C93.pdf, accessed on 19 May 2019.
19 Letter from Margaret Thatcher to Friedrich Hayek, 17 February 1982. Thatcher Digital Archive (Thatcher MSS), available on https://c59574e9047e61130f13-3f71d0fe2b653c4f00f32175760e96e7.ssl.cf1.rackcdn.com/3D5798D9C38443C6BD10B1AB166D3CBF.pdf, accessed on 19 May 2019.
20 Karl Marx. 1867. *Capital Volume 1*. London: Penguin. pp. 163–177.
21 Ibid., p. 163.
22 Ibid., pp. 164–165.
23 Slavoj Žižek. 1989/2008. *The Sublime Object of Ideology*. London: Verso. New edition. pp. 15–16, emphasis in the original.
24 Georg Lukács. 1971. *History and Class Consciousness*. London: Merlin. p. 83.

25 Ibid., 66.
26 Ibid., pp. 83–222.
27 Ibid., p. 196.
28 Ibid., p. 310.
29 Ibid., pp. 304–305.
30 Ibid., p. 310.
31 Ibid., p. 310.
32 Ibid., p. 50.
33 Theodor W. Adorno. 1954: Ideology. In Theodor W. Adorno: *Aspects of Sociology*, ed. Frankfurt Institute for Social Research. Boston, MA: Beacon Press. p. 182–205
34 Erich Fromm. 1965. The Application of Humanist Psychoanalysis to Marx's Theory. In *Socialist Humanism: An International Symposium*, ed. Erich Fromm, 207–222. Garden City, NY: Doubleday. p. 210.
35 Ibid., p. 212.
36 Karl Marx. 1845. Theses on Feuerbach. In *MECW Volume* 5, 3–8. London: Lawrence & Wishart. p. 7
37 Erich Fromm. 1947/2003. *Man for Himself. An Inquiry into the Psychology of Ethics.* Abingdon: Routledge. P. 6
38 Marx, *Capital Volume 1*, p. 144.
39 Karl Marx. 1859. A Contribution to the Critique of Political Economy. In *MECW Volume 29*. London: Lawrence & Wishart. pp. 257–507.
40 Karl Marx. 1844. Comments on James Mill, Éléments d'économie Politique. In *MECW Volume* 3, 211–228. London: Lawrence & Wishart. p. 227.
41 Coca-Cola advertisement, "A Coke is a Coke", 2019, source: Coca-Cola YouTube channel, available on www.youtube.com/watch?v=CiEcW_YEs3E, accessed on 22 October 2019.
42 Forbes 2000 List of the World's Largest Public Companies, 2019, available on www.forbes.com/global2000/list, accessed on 21 May 2019.
43 Naomi Klein. 2000. *No Logo*. New York: Picador. pp. 148, 195–196
44 Ibid., p. 117.
45 Sut Jhally. 2006. *The Spectacle of Accumulation*. New York: Peter Lang. p. 88.
46 Ibid., p. 89.
47 Raymond Williams. 1960/2005. Advertising: the Magic System. In Raymond Williams: *Culture and Materialism*. London: Verso. pp. 170–195.
48 Ibid., p. 170.
49 Ibid., p. 185.
50 Ibid., p. 189.

51 Ibid., p. 193.
52 Max Horkheimer and Theodor W. Adorno. 1947/2002. *Dialectic of Enlightenment: Philosophical Fragments*. Stanford, CA: Stanford University Press. pp. 135–136.
53 Twitter Investor Relations, SEC filings form 10-Q for the first quarter of financial year 2019. Available on https://investor.twitterinc.com, accessed on 21 May 2019, p. 27
54 Data source: available on https://web.archive.org/web/20160616163225/http://twitter.com/nigel_farage, accessed on 8 May 2019.
55 UKIP Local Election Manifesto 2016, available on https://web.archive.org/web/20160720115512/https://d3n8a8pro7vhmx.cloudfront.net/ukipdev/pages/3440/attachments/original/1459984864/UKIP_Local_Manifesto_2016.pdf?1459984864, accessed on 21 May 2019.
56 Martin Reisigl and Ruth Wodak. 2001. *Discourse and Discrimination. Rhetorics of Racism and Antisemitism*. London: Routledge. p. 59.
57 Ibid., pp. 77–79.
58 Ibid., p. 77.
59 Rosa Luxemburg. 1976. *The National Question: Selected Writings*. New York: Monthly Review Press. p. 135.
60 Karl Marx. 1870. Letter of Marx to Sigfrid Meyer and August Vogt, 9 April 1870. In *MECW Volume 43*. London: Lawrence & Wishart. pp. 471–476.
61 Ibid., p. 475.
62 UK Parliament. 2018. NHS Staff from Overseas: Statistics. House of Commons Library, available on https://researchbriefings.parliament.uk/ResearchBriefing/Summary/CBP-7783, accessed on 22 May 2019. Benjamin Kentish. 2018. How Reliant is the NHS on Foreign Doctors? *The Independent Online*. 4 June 2018. Available on www.independent.co.uk/news/uk/politics/nhs-foreign-doctors-how-many-reliant-immigration-theresa-may-brexit-explained-visa-a8383306.html.
63 Pensions Policy Institute. 2019. Demographics. www.pensionspolicyinstitute.org.uk/research/pension-facts/table-1/, accessed on 21 May 2019.
64 Data source: Eurostat, available on https://ec.europa.eu/eurostat, accessed on 21 May 2019.

10

SOCIALISM AND COMMUNISM

10.1 INTRODUCTION

This chapter asks: What is communism? What is socialism? What is the connection between communism and communication?[1]

When we hear the term "communism", many of us are immediately reminded of Stalin, Mao, dictatorship, terror against political opponents, mass surveillance of citizens, a controlled and censored press, etc. But the likes of Stalin and Mao are not the same as Marx. Marx's vision of communism is in fact incompatible with the regimes that Stalin, Mao, etc. established and that were communist in name only. Marx and Engels argue that communism is the "struggle for democracy".[2] Stalinist states are forms of state capitalism, where the state bureaucracy acts as a combined, collective capitalist that exploits workers and enforces this exploitation by coercive state power.[3]

This chapter introduces the notion of communism (Section 10.2), discusses the role of technology in the establishment in a communist society (Section 10.3), and focuses on the relationship of communism and communication (Section 10.4).

10.2 COMMUNISM

10.2.1 *Socialism and Communism*

Lenin argues that "the first phase of communist society" is "usually called socialism".[4] Marx spoke of a first and a second phase of communism. In the first phase, private property and capital cease to exist and the ownership of the means of production is socialised, but wage-labour, money, the state, and exchange continue to exist. In the second phase, wages, wage-labour, money, the state, exchange-value, and all forms of alienation cease to exist.[5] But Marx did not call the first phase socialism and the second phase communism. Rather, he spoke of two stages or phases of communism. Communism is not just a type of society, but also a political movement.

In *The Manifesto of the Communist Party*,[6] Marx and Engels speak of communism as a type of socialist movement. Besides communism, they identify reactionary socialism, bourgeois socialism, critical-utopian socialism as types of socialism. When one speaks of communism, one therefore means a type of socialism that aims at the abolition of class society and a democratic, worker-controlled economy within a participatory democracy. Given that Marx and Engels saw communism as a type of socialism, Marxists often use socialism interchangeably with the term communism. Strictly speaking, socialism is broader than communism.

10.2.2 *Rosa Luxemburg on Socialism and Communism*

Rosa Luxemburg clarifies the difference between socialism and communism:

> Socialism goes back for thousands of years, as the ideal of a social order based on equality and the brotherhood of man, the ideal of a communistic society. With the first apostles of Christianity, various religious sects of the Middle Ages, and in the German peasants' war, the socialist idea always glistened as the most radical expression of rage against the existing society. [...] It was in the late eighteenth and

> early nineteenth century that the socialist idea first appeared with vigor and force, freed from religious enthusiasm, but rather as an opposition to the terror and devastation that emerging capitalism wreaked on society. Yet this socialism too was basically nothing but a dream, the invention of individual bold minds. [...] The socialist ideas represented by the three great thinkers: [Claude Henri] Saint-Simon and [Charles] Fourier in France, [Robert] Owen in England, in the 1820s and 30s, with far greater genius and brilliance, relied on quite different methods, but essentially rested on the same foundation. [...] A new generation of socialist leaders emerged in the 1840s: [Wilhelm] Weitling in Germany, [Pierre Joseph] Proudhon, Louis Blanc and Blanqui in France. The working class, for its part, had already embarked on struggle against the rule of capital, it had given the signal for class struggle in the elemental insurrections of the Lyons silk weavers in France, and in the Chartist movement in England. But there was no direct connection between these spontaneous stirrings of exploited masses and the various socialist theories. [...] the socialist idea was placed on a completely new footing by Marx and Engels. These two sought the basis for socialism not in moral repugnance towards the existing social order nor in cooking up all kinds of possible attractive and seductive projects, designed to smuggle in social equality within the present state. They turned to the investigation of the *economic* relationships of present-day society. [7]

Marx and Engels grounded socialism and the potentials of communism in the antagonistic class structure of capitalism that pits workers against capitalists. Marx saw the proletariat as the class that has the potential for "a revolutionary seizure of power for the realization of socialism".[8]

10.2.3 The Split of the Second International as Split between Communism and Socialism

In the 19th century, the socialist movement experienced a split between reformist revisionists and revolutionary socialists. On the one side, the revisionist believed in the evolutionary transition to socialism through victories in elections and an automatic breakdown of capitalism. On the other side, revolutionaries stressed the importance of class struggle, street action, mass political strikes, and fundamental transformations of society in order to establish a free society. In the Second International (1889–1916), the various factions of socialism were part of one organisation. The Second International collapsed during the First World War. Socialists were split between those who supported the war and those who radically opposed it.

After the First World War, the Communist International and the Labour and Socialist International were created. The latter was the forerunner of the Socialist International. After the collapse of the Second International, there was an institutional distinction between socialists and communists. Whereas reformism dominated the Socialist International, Stalinism became dominant in the Communist International. The notion of "socialism" became associated with social democratic parties and the notion of "communism" with communist parties. From a historical point of view, both Stalinism and revisionist social democracy have failed. It is today time to no longer strictly separate between communism and socialism. One can, rather, argue for a communist socialism as radical, democratic socialism that aims at substituting capitalism by the democratic control of society. Such a participatory democracy includes worker control of the economy, citizens' control of the political system, and human control of culture and everyday life.. Marx saw communism as a radical, democratic socialist movement.

10.2.4 Class-Struggle Social Democracy

With the rise of neoliberalism, social democracy turned towards the right and increasingly adopted neoliberal policies. When Tony Blair became British Prime Minster in 1997, his neoliberal version of social democracy influenced social democracy around the world. The consequence was that social democracy became in many respects indistinguishable from conservative parties, especially in respect to class politics. We need a left-leaning social democracy that struggles for democratic socialism. Rosa Luxemburg practised a class-struggle-based social democracy that struggled for radical reforms and combined mass strikes and parliamentary action.[9] Luxemburg practised dialectics of party/movements, organisation/spontaneity, and intellectual leadership/masses.

Bhaskar Sunkara[10] argues for a new class-struggle-based social democracy that aims at winning elections and taking power, combines social movements, trade unions and the party, and realises transitional policies that move society "quickly from social democracy to democratic socialism",[11] acknowledges the changes of the working class, embeds itself in working-class struggles, struggles for "dignity, respect, and a fair shot at the good life" through universalist, "democratic class politics" that unites individuals "against our common opponent and win[s] the type of change that will help the most marginalized, all while engaging in a far longer campaign against oppression rooted in race, gender, sexuality, and more".[12]

Michael Hardt and Antonio Negri term the convergence of unions and social movements "social unionism" (social movements + unions). Social unionism organises social strikes that take place in society, which has become a factory at large.[13] Social unions entail "organizing new social combinations, inventing new forms of social cooperation, generating democratic mechanisms for our access to, use of, and participation in decision-making about the common".[14] Hardt and Negri argue for the complementarity of the three political strategies:

> The taking of power, by electoral or other means, must serve to open space for autonomous and prefigurative practices on an ever-larger scale and nourish the slow transformation of institutions, which must continue over the long term. Similarly practices of exodus must find ways to complement and further projects of both antagonistic reform and taking power.[15]

Examples of projects that such a complementary left-wing politics could struggle for include guaranteed basic income as "a money of the common" and "open access to and democratic management of the common".[16]

Class-struggle social democracy struggles for communism as a democratic socialist society by practising dialectics of reform/revolution (radical reformism), party/movement (movement parties), organisation/spontaneity (organised spontaneity), and working-class politics/societal politics (social working-class politics).

We will discuss aspects of democratic communism along three lines: the economy (10.2.4.1), politics (10.2.4.2), and culture (10.2.4.3). Section 10.2.4.4 introduces a summary framework.

10.2.4.1 The Communist Economy

10.2.4.1.1 COMMON OWNERSHIP

A key characteristic of a communist society is that the means of production are the common property of the producers:

> In this sense, the theory of the Communists may be summed up in the single sentence: Abolition of private property. [...] When, therefore, capital is converted into common property, into the property of all members of society, personal property is not thereby transformed into social property. It is only the social character of the property that is changed. It loses its class character.[17]

For Marx, "communism is humanism mediated with itself through the supersession of private property".[18]

10.2.4.1.2 PRODUCTION AND LABOUR

Toil is for Marx and Engels incompatible with a communist society. They see the reduction of necessary labour and the abolition of hard labour as an important aspect of communism. "The realm of freedom really begins only where labour determined by necessity and external expediency ends; [...] The reduction of the working day is the basic prerequisite"[19]. Therefore, a communist society is only possible as a high-tech society that has a high level of productivity.

> *What is the aim of the Communists?* Answer: To organise society in such a way that every member of it can develop and use all his capabilities and powers in complete freedom and without thereby infringing the basic conditions of this society.[20]

> In communism, "nobody has one exclusive sphere of activity but each can become accomplished in any branch he wishes, society regulates the general production and thus makes it possible for me to do one thing today and another tomorrow, to hunt in the morning, fish in the afternoon, rear cattle in the evening, criticise after dinner, just as I have a mind, without ever becoming hunter, fisherman, shepherd or critic".[21]

In a high-tech communist society, where the division of labour is abolished, humans are enabled to freely choose their work activities and to be active as well-rounded individuals who have many different activities. This means that humans can freely use their capabilities. Labour turns into free activity without a struggle for survival and coercion by the market.

In communist society, production takes place based on the principle of human need and not based on the principle of profit (the need of capital). This requires some form of planning for production:

> In communist society, where the interests of individuals are not opposed to one another but, on the contrary, are united, competition is eliminated. [...] In communist society it will be easy to be informed about both production and consumption. Since we know how much, on the average, a person needs, it is easy to calculate how much is needed by a given number of individuals, and since production is no longer in the hands of private producers but in those of the community and its administrative bodies, it is a trifling matter *to regulate production according to needs.*[22]

Part of the reason why state communism failed was that the central planning of human needs and the economy failed. Economies are complex and have unpredictable features. Economic planning needs to be decentralised, which in a networked and computerised society can take on the form of a decentralised collection of the goods that individuals and households require. This information can then be sent to production units that thereby know how many goods are required during a certain period of time. Networking of production within industrial sectors enables the comparison of the available production capacities and productivity levels, which enables the production of the right amount of goods.

For Marx and Engels, communism includes a democratic economy, in which the workers own the means production in common. In such self-managed companies, decisions are taken in common:

> Above all, it will have to take the running of industry and all branches of production in general out of the hands of separate individuals competing with each other and instead will have to ensure that all these branches of production are run by society as a whole, i.e., for the social good, according to a social plan and with the participation of all members of society. It will therefore do away with competition and replace it by association. [...] private ownership will also have to be abolished, and in its stead there will be common use of all the instruments of production and the distribution of all products by common agreement, or the so-called community of property. The abolition of private ownership is indeed the most succinct and characteristic summary of the transformation of the entire social system necessarily following from the development of industry, and it is therefore rightly put forward by the Communists as their main demand.[23]

10.2.4.1.3 CIRCULATION, DISTRIBUTION AND CONSUMPTION

Marx argues that a communist society must reuse parts of the social product as means of production, whereas the other parts are means of consumption that need to be distributed among the individuals:

> Let us finally imagine, for a change, an association of free men, working with the means of production held in common, and expending their many different forms of labour-power in full self-awareness as one single social labour force. [...] The total product of our

> imagined association is a social product. One part of this product serves as fresh means of production and remains social. But another part is consumed by the members of the association as means of subsistence. This part must therefore be divided amongst them.[24]

Marx and Engels distinguish between two phases of society: crude communism that is sometimes also called a socialist society as the first stage, and fully developed communism as the second stage. In the first stage, there is the elimination of capital, profit, and the private property of the means of production but not necessarily the abolition of wage-labour, money, exchange, and commodities. The means of production are collectively owned, but the productive forces are not yet developed to the stage that allows the abolishment of necessary labour.

The first stage of communism has not "*developed* on its own foundations", it develops "just as it *emerges* from capitalist society, which is thus in every respect, economically, morally and intellectually, still stamped with the birth-marks of the old society from whose womb it emerges".[25] In the first stage of communism, "the community is simply a community of *labour,* and equality of *wages* paid out by communal capital – by the *community* as universal capitalist".[26]

> a given amount of labour in one form is exchanged for an equal amount of labour in another form. [...] The right of the producers is *proportional* to the labour they supply; [...] It recognises no class distinctions, because everyone is only a worker like everyone else.[27]

Marx writes elsewhere that, in communism, money would immediately disappear: "If we were to consider a communist society in place of a capitalist one, then money capital would immediately be done away with, and so too the disguises that transactions acquire through it".[28] The implication is that there might be versions of lower-stage communism with and without money.

In the higher, fully developed form of communism, the means of production are highly developed, so that necessary labour and exchange are abolished:

> In a higher phase of communist society, after the enslaving subordination of the individual to the division of labour, and thereby also the antithesis between mental and physical labour, has vanished; after labour has become not only a means of life but life's prime want; after the productive forces have also increased with the all-round development of the individual, and all the springs of common wealth flow more abundantly – only then can the narrow horizon of bourgeois right be crossed in its entirety and society inscribe on its banners: From each according to his abilities, to each according to his needs![29]

"From each according to their abilities, to each according to their needs" is a central communist principle. In a fully developed communist society, there is no wage-labour and no compulsion to work. Everyone works as far as he can and work is largely self-fulfilment. Goods are not sold or exchanged, but given to humans freely as gifts. There is distribution not according to the possession of money, but according to human needs.

10.2.4.2 Communist Politics

> *Communism* as the *positive* transcendence of *private property* as *human self-estrangement*, and therefore as the real *appropriation* of the *human* essence by and for man; communism therefore as the complete return of man to himself as a *social* (i. e., human) being – a return accomplished consciously and embracing the entire wealth of previous development.[30]

Freedom is an important principle of democratic societies. For Marx, communism means the abolition of alienation and the realisation of true freedom that allows humans to fully develop their potentials. Communism is a democracy and a humanism, in which the freedom of all interacts with individual freedom. "In place of the old bourgeois society, with its classes and class antagonisms, we shall have an association, in which the free development of each is the condition for the free development of all".[31]

It has often been argued that communism is totalitarian but for Marx and Engels, democracy is a precondition of communism. This circumstance becomes, for example, very clear in the following two passages: "*Question 18*: What will be the course of this revolution? *Answer:* In the first place it will inaugurate a *democratic constitution* and thereby, directly or indirectly, the political rule of the proletariat".[32]

> *Democracy nowadays is communism.* [...] Democracy has become the proletarian principle, the principle of the masses. The masses may be more or less clear about this, the only correct meaning of democracy, but all have at least an obscure feeling that social equality of rights is implicit in democracy. The democratic masses can be safely included in any calculation of the strength of the communist forces. And if the proletarian parties of the different nations unite they will be quite right to inscribe the word 'Democracy' on their banners, since, except for those who do not count, all European democrats in 1846 are more or less Communists at heart.[33]

Marx and Engels argue that communists do not oppose reforms, but argue for progressive and radical reforms that reduce the power of capital and forces that support domination:

> Democracy would be quite useless to the proletariat if it were not immediately used as a means of carrying through further measures directly attacking private ownership and securing the means of subsistence of the proletariat. [...] Once the first radical onslaught upon private ownership has been made, the proletariat will see itself compelled to go always further, to concentrate all capital, all agriculture, all industry, all transport, and all exchange more and more in the hands of the State. [...] Finally, when all capital, all production, and all exchange are concentrated in the hands of the nation, private ownership will automatically have ceased to exist, money will have

> become superfluous, and production will have so increased and men will be so much changed that the last forms of the old social relations will also be able to fall away.[34]

Progressive politics that communists support include, for example, a "heavy progressive or graduated income tax", the "[e]xtension of factories and instruments of production owned by the State", the "[c]ombination of agriculture with manufacturing industries"; the "gradual abolition of all the distinction between town and country by a more equable distribution of the populace over the country", or the "[f]ree education for all children in public schools".[35]

10.2.4.3 Communist Culture

10.2.4.3.1 TOGETHERNESS

Communism also changes social relations in the realm of culture. Whereas capitalist culture, through the logic of commodity consumption, advances a culture of isolation and individualisation focused on the individual consumption of commodities and the competition for reputation, communist culture means the development of a common culture, where humans associate and produce and consume culture together:

> When communist *artisans* associate with one another, theory and propaganda, etc., is their first end. But at the same time, as a result of this association, they acquire a new need – the need for society – and what appears as a means becomes an end. In this practical process the most splendid results are to be observed whenever French socialist workers are seen together. Such things as smoking, drinking, and eating, etc., are no longer means of contact or means that bring them together. Association, society and conversation, which again has association as its end, are enough for them; the brotherhood of man is no mere phrase with them, but a fact of life, and the nobility of man shines upon us from their work-hardened bodies.[36]

10.2.4.3.2 THE FAMILY

Communism also changes personal relations and the family. It reduces the dependence and power relations within the family and thereby advances equality:

> What influence will the communist order of society have upon the family? Answer: It will make the relation between the sexes a purely private relation which concerns only the persons involved, and in which society has no call to interfere. It is able to do this because it abolishes private property and educates children communally, thus destroying the twin foundation of hitherto existing marriage – the dependence through private property of the wife upon the husband and of the children upon the parents.[37]

10.2.4.3.3 INTERNATIONALISM

Communist culture is inherently internationalist. All humans are seen as members of the global family of humanity. There is no place for the nation and nationalism in a communist society. Humans have commonalities and differences. Communism advances a culture that is based on global unity in diversity, a dialectic of common culture and differentiated lifestyles and norms:

> The working men have no country. We cannot take from them what they have not got. Since the proletariat must first of all acquire political supremacy, must rise to be the leading class of the nation, must constitute itself *the* nation, it is so far, itself national, though not in the bourgeois sense of the word.[38]

> *Will nationalities continue to exist under communism?* Answer: The nationalities of the peoples who join together according to the principle of community will be just as much compelled by this union to merge with one another and thereby supersede themselves as the various differences between estates and classes disappear through the superseding of their basis – private property.[39]

10.2.4.4 Alienation vs. Communism

10.2.4.4.1 A MODEL OF COMMUNISM

In Chapter 7, I identified three dimensions of alienation (see Tables 7.1 and 7.2). In communism, there are three dimensions: the communist economy, communist politics, and communist culture. Whereas in an alienated, dominative, heteronomous class society, the three spheres of society are ruled by instrumental reason and particularistic interests, the three realms are, in communism, shaped by co-operative reason and the common interest. Communist society is organised in ways that benefit all. In class society, society only benefits some at the expense at others. Table 10.1 opposes alienated society to communist society. It shows three dimensions of communism that are sublations of alienation.

The common, socialist economy is the sublation of class society. The common politics of participatory democracy is the sublation of dictatorship. Common culture is the sublation of ideology and disrespect. We saw in Chapter 5 that production in society is a dialectic of objects and human subjects that results in

Table 10.1 Three dimensions of the communist society and their opposition to alienated society

	Alienated society	*Communist society*
Economy	Class	Common, socialist economy: collective ownership of the means of production, abolition of toil and unnecessary labour, well-rounded individuality with free work, self-managed companies, production from each according to their abilities, distribution to each according to their needs, wealth for all
Politics	Dictatorship	Common politics: participatory democracy
Culture	Ideology, disrespect	Common culture: internationalism, culture of unity in diversity

the creation of products. Table 10.2 shows what these three dimensions look like in a communist society in respect to the three dimensions of society.

10.2.4.4.2 THE COMMONS

Discussions about communism in the 21st century have foregrounded the commons. The basic argument is that neoliberal capitalism has resulted in the commodification and privatisation of common goods that are either produced by all humans or that all humans need in order to exist.[40]

Slavoj Žižek distinguishes between the cultural commons (language, means of communication, education, infrastructures), the commons of external nature (the natural environment), and the commons of internal nature (human subjectivity, our bodies and minds).[41]

Michael Hardt and Antonio Negri argue that there are two major forms of the commons: the social and the natural commons.[42] These forms are divided into five subtypes: the earth and its ecosystems; the "immaterial" common of ideas,

Table 10.2 Subjects, objects, and products in three realms of communism

Type	*Subjects*	*Object*	*Products*
Economic communism	Commoners, well-rounded individuals	Collectively owned means of production, self-managed companies	Common goods, wealth for all, self-fulfilment for all
Political communism	Democrats	Participatory democracy	Common decisions and rights
Cultural communism	Friends	Shared meanings and knowledge	Common, internationalist culture of unity in diversity, recognition and voice for all

codes, images, and cultural products; physical goods produced by co-operative work; metropolitan and rural spaces that are realms of communication, cultural interaction and co-operation; and social institutions and services that organise housing, welfare, health, and education.[43] For Hardt and Negri, contemporary capitalism's class structure features the extraction of the commons, which includes the extraction of natural resources; data mining/data extraction; the extraction of the social from the urban spaces on real estate markets; and finance as an extractive industry.[44]

The advantage of such understandings of the commons is that they allow a popular critique of neoliberal capitalism and neoliberalism's undermination of the welfare state, nature, and cultural institutions such as the education system and hospitals. The radical notion of the commons also stresses that the commons advance communist potentials from within the contradictions of capitalism, a "communism of capital".[45] This perspective allows one to reinvent communism in the 21st century as "commonism", a politics that struggles against the dispossession, privatisation, commodification, and financialisation of the commons. But, at the same time, the discussed definitions of the commons are not fully in line with Marx and Engels's understanding of the commons as "common property, [...] the property of all members of society"[46] that is governed by "common agreement".[47] All economic, political and cultural goods and structures can be turned into common goods that are controlled by all those who are affected by them. Tables 10.1 and 10.2 are based on this understanding of the commons as common economy, common politics, and common culture.

10.3 COMMUNISM AND TECHNOLOGY

10.3.1 The Antagonism of Productive Forces and Relations of Production

Capitalism is based on an antagonism between the productive forces and the relations of production. Capitalist technology socialises labour, i.e. it brings about new forms of co-operation and potential for collective ownership, new common goods (such as the digital commons) and the reduction of necessary labour-time, that are communist potentials, or, what some term the communism of capital. Digital capitalism creates new forms and technologies of co-operation that are the foundations of new common goods. Within class relations and capitalism, such forms and technologies are also means of exploitation and domination. In capitalism common goods are often subsumed under the commodity form and class relations under the commodity form, class relations, and capital. In capitalism, the new communist potentials cannot fully develop and technological development advances social antagonisms, such as the rise of precarious labour and life. Marx and Engels describe this antagonism in the following manner:

> The productive forces at the disposal of society no longer tend to further the development of the conditions of bourgeois property; on the contrary, they have become too powerful for these conditions, by which they are fettered, and so soon as they overcome these fetters, they bring disorder into the whole of bourgeois society, endanger the existence of bourgeois property. The conditions of bourgeois society are too narrow to comprise the wealth created by them. And how does the bourgeoisie get over these crises? On the one hand by enforced destruction of a mass of productive forces; on the other, by the conquest of new markets, and by the more thorough exploitation of the old ones. That is to say, by paving the way for more extensive and more destructive crises, and by diminishing the means whereby crises are prevented.[48]

In Chapter 32 of *Capital Volume 1*, Marx formulates the antagonism between productive forces and relations of production in the following way:

> "At a certain stage of development, it [the capitalist mode of production] brings into the world the material means of its own destruction. From that moment, new forces and new passions spring up in the bosom of society, forces and passions which feel themselves to be fettered by that society".[49]

In the 21st century, information technology and the Internet are founded on an antagonism between class relations and the now-networked productive forces. A good example is that the Internet allows the free sharing of information via peer-to-peer platforms and other technologies, which on the one hand questions the capitalist character of culture – and so makes the music and film industry nervous – but on the other hand within capitalism can also constitute problems for artists who depend on deriving income from cultural commodities. Informational networks aggravate the capitalist antagonism between the collective production and the individual appropriation of goods, and the antagonism between productive forces and relations of production. Productive forces that are tied up by existing relations do not necessarily or automatically develop fully. It is in no way assured that they can be freed from these relations. They can remain enchained and will remain enchained as long as individuals let themselves be enchained. Networks are a material condition of a free association, but the co-operative networking of the relations of production is not an automatic result of networked productive forces.

10.3.2 The Antagonism between Productive Forces and Relations of Production in the Grundrisse's "Fragment on Machines"

In the *Grundrisse*'s "Fragment on Machines", Marx shows how modern technology reduces necessary labour-time – the annual labour-time a society needs in order to survive – and thereby creates conditions for communism, free individuality, and a life based on free time as source of wealth. But at the same time it is embedded into capitalist class relations that have to set labour-time as the source of wealth so that the antagonism between the ever more socialised productive forces and the relations of production deepens the crisis-prone nature of capitalism, the enslavement of labour, unemployment, and precarity. The capitalist antagonism between productive forces and relations of production is an antagonism between necessary labour (which technology reduces more and more) and surplus labour (which capital tries to increase more and more). Under the conditions of capitalist technology, the worker:

> steps to the side of the production process instead of being its chief actor. [...] as the great foundation-stone of production and of wealth. The theft of alien labour-time, on which the present wealth is based, appears a miserable foundation in face of this new one, created by large-scale industry itself. As soon as labour in the direct form has ceased to be the great well-spring of wealth, labour-time ceases and must cease to be its measure, and hence exchange value [must cease to be the measure] of use-value. The surplus labour of the mass has ceased to be the condition for the development of general wealth, just as the non-labour of the few, for the development of the general powers of the human head. With that, production based on exchange value breaks down, and the direct, material production process is stripped of the form of penury and antithesis. The free development of individualities, and hence not the reduction of necessary labour-time so as to posit surplus labour, but rather the general reduction of the necessary labour of society to a minimum, which then corresponds to the artistic, scientific etc. development of the individuals in the time set free, and with the means created, for all of them.[50]

10.3.3 Technology and Time in Capitalism and Communism

Marx ascertains that a capitalist antagonism exists between the tendency of technology to reduce necessary labour-time and the capitalist tendency to turn all labour-time into surplus labour, and he argues that modern technology creates the foundation of a communist society, in which free time and free activity beyond necessity is maximised and the source of wealth. Capital:

> increases the surplus labour time of the mass by all the means of art and science [...] It is thus, despite itself, instrumental in creating the means of social disposable time, in order to reduce labour time for the whole society to a diminishing minimum, and thus to free everyone's time for their own development. But its tendency always, on the one side, to create disposable time, on the other, to convert it into surplus labour. If it succeeds too well at first, then it suffers from

> surplus production, and then necessary labour is interrupted, because no surplus labour can be realized by capital. The more this contradiction develops, the more does it become evident that the growth of the forces of production can no longer be bound up with the appropriation of alien labour, but that the mass of workers must themselves appropriate their own surplus labour. Once they have done so – and disposable time thereby ceases to have an antithetical existence – then, on one side, necessary labour time will be measured by the needs of the social individual, and, on the other, the development of the power of social production will grow so rapidly that, even though production is now calculated for the wealth of all, disposable time will grow for all. For real wealth is the developed productive power of all individuals. The measure of wealth is then not any longer, in any way, labour time, but rather disposable time.[51]

Marx adds that "[r]eal economy [...] consists of the saving of labour time" so that there can be "an increase of free time, i.e. time for the full development of the individual".[52] Marx ascertains in the *Grundrisse* that communism requires a technological foundation so that society can be based on the communist principle, "From each according to his abilities, to each according to his needs!". Communism is only possible as a computerised, high-technology, post-scarcity society that creates wealth and luxury for all,

In his study of the *Grundrisse*, Roman Rosdolsky comments on the importance of the technological foundations of communism:

> It is hardly necessary today – in the course of a new industrial revolution – to emphasise the prophetic significance of this enormously dynamic and essentially optimistic conception. For the dreams of the isolated German revolutionary in his exile in London in 1858 have now, for the first time, entered the realm of what is immediately possible. Today, for the first time in history, thanks to the developments of modern technology, the preconditions for a final and complete abolition of the 'theft of alien labour-time' actually exist; furthermore, the present period is the first in which the development of the productive forces can be carried so far forward that, in fact, in the not too distant future it will be not labour-time, but rather disposable time, by which social wealth is measured.[53]

10.3.4 Fully Automated Luxury Communism?

Aaron Bastani argues in his book *Fully Automated Luxury Communism*[54] that new technologies such as information technology ("the defining feature of the Third Disruption" – by which he means a third technological revolution in the history of humankind – "is ever-greater abundance in information"[55]), AI-based automation, green energy technologies, space travel, 3D printing, gene therapy and editing, and synthetic food, such as cultured meat, will soon enable humans to overcome scarcity and to thereby create an abundance of free time, energy, space, health, and sustainable artificial food. He sees these technologies as the foundation of fully automated luxury communism, where "work is eliminated, scarcity replaced by abundance and where labour and leisure blend into one another".[56] Fully automated luxury communism is a "realm of plenty"[57] with "luxury for all"[58] and everything for all.

Bastani rightly reiterates Marx's insight that communism requires material and technological foundations and can therefore only be a high-tech communism. His version of technological analysis avoids technological determinism because he is aware that communism does not automatically emerge from technology, but rather requires political-economic transformations. The book's analysis is a techno-optimism without technological determinism. But such optimism is a new, 21st-century form of utopian socialism because it underestimates how capitalism results in the design of negative and destructive potentials into contemporary technologies. For Bastani, there are only positive potentials of technology and he seems to think that, when communism comes, the same technologies can be used without humans having to transform and redesign many of them and having to abolish at least some of them. He also underestimates that technologies are complex systems that can, in any society, have unpredictable, negative consequences. Bastani's technological analysis confers the image of a perfectly controllable technology. When he writes that "resources, energy, health, labour and food – just like information – want to be free",[59] he overlooks that only humans and not resources act and have interests.

Freedom as want is a human want and interest that cannot be reduced to technology.

Automated technologies can involve programming or system errors that result in serious accidents and disasters. Space exploration is part of geopolitical and military rivalries. Even in a communist society that is relatively peaceful, massive resource investments into space exploration may result in a lack of resources available for welfare. 3D home printing could result in the production of a massive amount of non-recyclable consumer goods that pose an environmental problem. Genetic engineering can cause new diseases and risks to health and life. The mass production of cultured meat could create unforeseen risks that do not make it clean meat, but rather dirty meat. Operating a vast number of labs for producing cultured meat could increase the world's energy use. If a transition to renewable energy has at the same time not been achieved, total carbon dioxide emissions could increase.

Communism is likely to reduce the risks of technologies that stem from cost cutting and profit imperatives, but collective ownership and non-profit production oriented on use-value is no panacea for the potential risks that new technologies pose. A communist society requires prospective, critical technology assessments and communist tech ethics and tech policies that regulate new technologies. Technology is not just an economic issue but also has political and cultural dimensions that are based on, but not reducible to, the economy.

It is questionable that there can be "full" automation. Automation will always have to remain under human control and can never fully replace humans. For society to exist, technologies and societies need to be built, repaired, morally judged and assessed, which only humans can do. And there are forms of human work, such as social care and education, whose automation is morally undesirable if we want to exist in a humane society built on the principle of communist love. A posthuman technology without any human work would result in the technologically induced breakdown of society because once robots that repair robots encounter a system error or a power outage, humans have to step in. Posthuman ideology overestimates the capacities of technologies to automate human subjectivity. No robot will ever understand what love is. It can therefore not practice love. You cannot automate love. And artificial imitations of love are nothing more than cheap fakes. Communism requires technological foundations, but high-tech alone is not enough. Communism's guiding principle is neither technology nor love of technology, but love. Bastani advances a form of posthumanist communism.

Bastani does not give much attention to Marx's concept of well-rounded individuality in a communist society. One reason why work, understood as the creation of use-values, will not stop is that humans have a desire for self-fulfilment and creativity whose potential cannot be fully realised in a class society. In a communist society, humans would be too bored if they sat all day on the couch watching television. They will engage in a multitude of social and productive activities free from necessity and compulsion. For Bastani, luxury populism is the opposite of neoliberal politics.[60] But he leaves open the question of if, in his view, the nation continues to exist in communist society. He argues for internationalism and not for an alternative form of globalisation. The nation is an artificial, ideological construct. Populism does not appeal only to the working class, but to a people. It is therefore mostly based on nationalism.[61] But Marx and Engels knew that communism requires, as its political foundation, global solidarity. Communism needs a working-class politics that liberates humanity from class, capital, labour, toil, pollution, destruction, war, and necessity, etc.

It is encouraging that there is a new interest in the role of technology in communism and an understanding of communism as wealth and luxury for all. But such discoveries are nothing new.

In his 1892 manifesto, *The Conquest of Bread*, Peter Kropotkin wrote about wealth and luxury for all in a communist society: "What is now the privilege of an insignificant minority would be accessible to all. Luxury, ceasing to be a foolish and ostentatious display of the bourgeois class, would become an artistic pleasure".[62] Kropotkin clearly built on Marx's insights and therefore argued that luxury and wealth for all requires a high-tech communist society:

> It now remains for society, first, to extend this greater productivity, which is limited to certain industries, and to apply it to the general good. But it is evident that to utilize this high productivity of labour, so as to guarantee well-being to all, society must itself take possession of all means of production.[63]

Murray Bookchin in the 1960s argued that we "of this century have finally opened the prospect of material abundance for all to enjoy – a sufficiency in the means of life without the need for grinding, day-to-day toil".[64] Liberatory technologies enable a "post-scarcity society", where "we can begin to provide food, shelter, garments, and a broad spectrum of luxuries without devouring the precious time of humanity and without dissipating its invaluable reservoir of creative energy in mindless labor".[65] Bookchin reminds us that not all technologies are liberating. Technologies need to be combined with and shaped by environmentalism and communalism. Bookchin argues for an "ecological approach to technology that takes the form of *ensembles* of productive units, energized by solar and wind power units".[66]

The list of theorists of socialist technology could be continued, with names such as Herbert Marcuse (post-technology), Erich Fromm (humanised technology), Ivan Illich (convivial technologies), André Gorz (post-industrial socialism), and Ernst Bloch (alliance technology), etc. Luxury communism is a new discovery for, but not by, Aaron Bastani, but is relatively old hat in the history of the radical theory of technology and society. Communist theory needs proper engagement with this history.

Fully Automated Luxury Communism is, despite its tendencies towards idealist utopianism and historical blindness, good food for thought about the foundations of communism.

10.4 COMMUNISM AND COMMUNICATION

10.4.1 *Alienated and Communist Culture*

Given that communist society sublates the economy, politics, and culture, new relations of communication also emerge in such a society. The way humans think, work, live, and communicate changes in such a society. Table 10.3 opposes knowledge and communication's roles in alienated societies to their roles in communist society.

In a class society, knowledge and communication are privately controlled and owned by the few as private property, whereas in a communist society knowledge and communication technologies are gifts and common goods that are collectively produced and owned. If one looks at the way that contemporary media corporations are run, then one sees that the decisions are made by a small class of CEOs and managers who control these companies' decision-making processes in a dictatorial manner. Privately owned companies are economic dictatorships. In contrast, communist politics implies that organisations in the culture and communication industries should not only be owned by their workers, but should also have democratic decision-making structures, where everyone working in the organisation or affected by it can participate. While alienated cultural systems produce

Table 10.3 Alienated and communist forms of knowledge and communication

	Alienated society	*Communist society*
Economic system	Knowledge and communication as commodities, exploitation of knowledge labour, means of communication as private property	Knowledge and communication(s) as commons, co-ownership, and co-production in self-managed knowledge-creating companies
Political system	Dictatorial control of knowledge and communication processes	Participatory knowledge and democratic communication
Cultural system	Ideological knowledge and communication	Humanist knowledge and communication that advances togetherness, unity in diversity, and recognition of all

ideologies and reputational hierarchies, communist culture creates togetherness, respect for all, recognition of all, and unity in diversity of identities and lifestyles.

10.4.2 Public Service Media and Community Media

Already in contemporary capitalism, we find forms of media and culture that operate outside of and in opposition to capital accumulation. The two most important social communication forms operating outside of capital are public service media and community media. Both operate on a not-for-profit basis. The difference is that public service media are organised and financed with the help of state legislation. They are independent from capital and the state, but are organised based on laws that regulate their remit (such as creating public service content) and their funding (e.g. in the form of a licence fee). Community media are citizen media that are run and operated by citizens who act as citizen journalists and citizen media producers.

The political economist of communication Graham Murdock argues that the three political-economic possibilities in the media and cultural sector are ownership by capital (the commodity form of communications), the state (public service form of communications) and civil society (communications as gifts/commons).[67]

Public service media such as the BBC tend to reject the logic of the commodity. They make use of state power for collecting licence fees or parts of taxes in order to fund their operations. Alternative, citizen and community media such as open channels, free radio stations, the alternative press, or alternative Internet platforms are run by civil society groups. They do not embrace, but reject, the commodity logic. They tend not to want to sell content, technologies, and audiences. Given that they reject exchange-value, they have to look for other sources of funding if they want to exist within capitalism. Such sources are, for example, voluntary unpaid labour, state funding, donations, and endowments from foundations, etc. Table 10.4 presents a distinction between: (a) capitalist media, (b) community media, and (c) public service media. These media are respectively

Table 10.4 Three political economies of information

	Capitalist media	*Public service media*	*Community media*
Economy (ownership)	Corporations	State institutions	Citizen-controlled
Culture (public circulation of ideas)	Content that addresses humans in various social roles and results in meaning-making	Content that addresses humans in various social roles and results in meaning-making	Content that addresses humans in various social roles and results in meaning-making

based on: (a) information commodities, (b) information commons, and (c) information as public good. Information is owned in specific ways and has a specific cultural role, in which it allows humans to inform themselves, communicate, and organise social systems.

The Slovenian critical media and communication scholar Slavko Splichal provides a concise definition of public service media:

> In normative terms, public service media must be a service *of* the public, *by* the public, and *for* the public. It is a service *of* the public because it is financed by it and should be owned by it. It ought to be a service *by* the public – not only financed and controlled, but also produced by it. It must be a service *for* the public – but also for the government and other powers acting in the public sphere. In sum, public service media ought to become 'a cornerstone of democracy'.[68]

Ellie Rennie argues that "Community media is usually run on a not-for-profit basis and provides community members with an opportunity to participate in the production process" and has democratic governance structures.[69]

There is a tension and contradiction between public service and community media on the one hand and capitalist media on the other hand. Capitalism is expansive, imperialist, and colonising – it tries to subsume everything under the commodity form and to destroy realms of life that do not adhere to the commodity logic. It can therefore be difficult for public service media and community media to exist in capitalism. Community media are, in capitalism, often based on voluntary, self-exploitative, unpaid, or low-paid labour. The history of alternative and community media is a history of self-determination, but precarious labour and resource precarity. Such media tend to lack resources. Although alternative media represent common communications that transcend capitalism they lack the capital of the common needed for effectively challenging capitalist communication corporations. Culture, information, and other goods and services can also be de-commodified by social struggles and thereby turned into public or common goods. The more the logic of the commodity asserts itself, the more difficult is the existence and survival of public service media and community media. The more this logic is constricted, the more these alternative forms of organisation can flourish. In a communist society, there are no capitalist media, and information and culture have no commodity form.

Marx spoke about the importance of alternative, non-capitalist ways of organising the media. He wrote that "*primary freedom*" of the media "*lies in not being a trade*".[70] Marx feared that capitalist control of communications limits the freedom of speech and expression and colonises the public sphere. In *The Manifesto of the Communist Party*, Marx and Engels say that one of the political measures that communists aim at implementing is the "[c]entralisation of the means of communication and transport in the hands of the State".[71]

In the 20th century, many states held monopolies over telecommunications, broadcasting networks, railways, and the postal service. These are large infrastructures of communication. Organising them as public services enables fair, universal, affordable access. Today, there is a need for public service Internet platforms, such as a public service YouTube run by a network of public service companies, in order to challenge the monopolies of the digital giants Google, Facebook, and Twitter, etc. Alternatives to communication services that store and process lots of personal data, such as Facebook, should be better organised as self-managed community platforms because too much involvement by the state poses potential dangers of the state surveillance of citizens. The same can be said of the press: Self-managed newspapers are preferable to newspapers owned and operated as public services by institutions that are located close to the state. Public service media should also have news departments where independent journalists work. It is therefore important that public service media are truly independent from the state, economic forces, and ideological forces.

10.4.3 Rosa Luxemburg: The Freedom of the Press in Communist Society

Immediately after the 1917 October Revolution, the Bolsheviks set up the Revolutionary Press Tribunal that had the power to censor or suspend publications, to deprive those responsible for them of their liberties, and deport them from Russia in cases where the Tribunal found that "crimes and offences [...] against the national through the use of the press" were committed.[72] The freedom of the press was abolished.

Rosa Luxemburg on the one hand supported the need to replace the Czarist regime with a socialist society and on the other hand stressed the need for the democratic character of such a society. She commented:

> Freedom only for the supporters of the government, only for the members of one party – however numerous they may be – is no freedom at all. Freedom is always and exclusively freedom for the one who thinks differently. Not because of any fanatical concept of 'justice' but because all that is instructive, wholesome and purifying in political freedom depends on this essential characteristic, and its effectiveness vanishes when 'freedom' becomes a special privilege.[73]

Luxemburg criticised the curtailment of the freedom of expression in Russia under Lenin. She stressed that "universal suffrage, freedom of press and assemblage" and "the whole apparatus of the basic democratic liberties of the people" constitute the "right of self-determination".[74] Luxemburg spoke of "freedom of the press, the rights of association and assembly" as "the most important democratic guarantees of a healthy public".[75] Without "a free and untrammelled press, without the unlimited right of association and assemblage, the rule of the broad mass of the people is entirely unthinkable".[76]

A democratic communist society needs to guarantee the freedom of expression, assembly, association, and the press. Corporate media monopolies have to be dissolved by expropriating the capital of the owners and handing over the ownership of these organisations (including publishing technologies) to workers and citizens. In such a society, groups of citizens need to have the right and the technological and organisational possibility to create their own media that are collectively owned and operated as self-managed companies that are not operated for profit and which pursue the goals of informing and educating. The communist public does not consist of state-controlled media, but is a vivid public sphere that operates as a multitude of public service media organisations and self-managed media organisations.

10.4.4 Democratic Communications

In his book *Communications*, Raymond Williams distinguishes between authoritarian, paternal, commercial and democratic communication systems (communications).[77] The first three communication systems are political, cultural, and commercial expressions of instrumental reason. Authoritarian communications involve state control, manipulation, and censorship of the media. The "purpose of communication is to protect, maintain, or advance a social order based on minority power".[78] Paternal communications are authoritarian communications "with a conscience: that is to say, with values and purposes beyond the maintenance of its own power".[79] In such communication systems, there is ideological control that aims to impose certain moral values on audiences. The controllers of paternal communication systems assume that specific morals are good for citizens and that the latter are too silly to understand the world. In commercial communications, there is commercial control: "Anything can be said, provided that you can afford to say it and that you can say it profitably".[80] All three forms are instrumental: They instrumentalise communications as tools for control and domination.

In contrast, democratic communications are for Williams based on co-operative rationality. Such media systems are based on the freedom to speak and the free choice of what to receive. Such communications are "means of participation and of common discussion".[81] Williams argues for a cultural democracy that combines public service media, cultural co-operatives, and local media.[82] Such a democracy establishes "new kinds of communal, cooperative and collective institutions".[83] The core of Williams's proposal is

> "that public ownership of the basic means of production [the means of communication and cultural production] should be combined with leasing their use to self-managing groups, to secure maximum variety of style and political opinion and to ensure against any bureaucratic control".[84]

"The idea of public service must be detached from the idea of public monopoly, yet remain public service in the true sense"[85] of public service content. Instrumental and co-operative media are contradictory forces. Only cultural forms of class struggle can drive back the capitalist colonisation of communications. Democratic communications are the dominant form of communication in a socialist society, in which "the basic cultural skills are made widely available, and the channels of communication widened and cleared, as much as possible".[86]

10.4.5 Communist Journalism

Béla Fogarasi (1891–1959) was a Hungarian philosopher. In his essay, "The Tasks of the Communist Press", Fogarasi distinguishes between the capitalist and the communist press. He argues that the capitalist press is "an ideological weapon in the class struggle"[87] utilised by the bourgeoisie in order to "dominate the ideology of the ensemble of classes":[88]

> What the capitalist press seeks is to shape the structure of the reader's consciousness in such a way that he will be perpetually unable to distinguish between true and false, to relate causes and effects, to place individual facts in their total context, to rationally integrate new knowledge into his perspective.[89]

Fogarasi implicitly applies Georg Lukács's critique of reified consciousness[90] to the capitalist press. In the capitalist press, the focus is often not on the dialectic of totality, particularity, and individuality, but merely on individual, isolated pieces of news. According to Fogarasi, strategies of the capitalist press include reporting a multitude of isolated facts that shall quench the readers' thirst for knowledge, de-politicisation, and sensationalism that work "systematically in the service of such diversion",[91] and pseudo-objectivity. In contrast, the communist press tries to advance the consciousness of society as a totality, and of the relation of single events with each other and broader contexts, the unmasking of the capitalist press, and the participation of readers as producers of reports.[92]

Fogarasi not only applied Lukács's concepts of reification and the totality to journalism, but in 1921 he also anticipated Walter Benjamin's idea of turning "consumers [...] into producers" and "readers or spectators into collaborators"[93] as well as Bertolt Brecht's idea of a radio that lets "the listener speak as well as hear".[94] Fogarasi's essay also anticipates some elements of Edward Herman and Noam Chomsky's propaganda model.[95] Herman and Chomsky identified some dimensions of how bourgeois journalism creates reified presentations of reality. Corporate media use five filters that limit the freedom of the media: corporate ownership and monopolies, advertising, selective sources, the effects of lobbying, and ideology.[96]

10.4.6 Digital Commons

Computers and computer networks enable new ways of organising information, communication, and co-operation. Given that computing has become a central resource in modern society, the use of computers for organising cognition, communication, and co-operation has become part of human needs. Humans have certain cognitive needs (such as being loved and recognised), communicative needs (such as friendships and community) and co-operative needs (such as working together with others in order to achieve common goals) in all types of society. In a digital and information society, computers are vital means for realising such needs. But given that computers are always used in societal contexts, computer use as such does not necessarily foster the good life, but can also contribute to damaging human lives

Digital capitalism at the same time deepens exploitation and creates new foundations for autonomous realms that transcend the logic of capitalism. There is an antagonism between the networked productive forces and the class relations of digital production. This antagonism is also an antagonism between digital labour and digital capital and between digital gifts and digital commodities.

Table 10.5 provides a summary overview of the dimensions of the digital commons.

The typology presented in Table 10.5 is structured along the three realms of society (economy, politics, culture), which allows distinguishing between three types of commons and three types of digital commons. The commons are the Aristotelian-Marxian vision of a good society. They form the essence of society, which means that the digital commons are part of digital society's essence. For Hegel and Marx, the essence is often hidden behind false appearances and that actuality means the correspondence of essence and appearance. One needs to distinguish between the essence of digital society and the false appearance and existence of digital society as digital class society and digital capitalism. Class society is the false condition of society-in-general. Digital class society is the false condition of digital society. A critical theory of the digital commons needs to not just have a vision of a good digital society, but also to critique digital capitalism and digital alienation. Table 10.5 therefore also features two columns that outline dimensions of alienation-in-general and digital alienation.

Table 10.5 Three dimensions of the digital commons

	Commons in society	*Digital commons*	*Lack of common control in society (alienation)*	*Lack of common control of digital society (digital alienation)*
Economy	Economic commons: wealth and self-fulfilment for all	Economic digital commons: network access for everyone, community is in control of technology, digital resources as common goods	Private property	Digital commodities, digital resources as private property
Politics	Political commons: participation and democracy in decision-making	Political digital commons: common decision-making /governance of information and communication technologies (ICTs)	Dictatorship	Dictatorial governance and control of ICTs
Culture	Cultural commons: voice and recognition of all	Cultural digital commons: use of ICTs for fostering learning, recognition, and community activities	Ideology	Digital ideology: ideologies of and on the Internet

10.5 CONCLUSION

Communism is often associated with Stalin and Mao, whose ideas and societies had little to do with Marx and Engels's democratic vision of communism. Communism is a framework for society and a movement towards a good society for all.

Common property, a computerised, high-technology, post-scarcity society that creates wealth and luxury for all, well-rounded individuals, distribution according to human needs, participatory governance, a common culture, and internationalism are some of the aspects of a communist society.

Capitalism is shaped by the antagonism between productive forces and relations of production that takes on new relevance in the age of networked productive forces.

Commons-based communication is an alternative to alienated communication. Public service media and community media are two not-for-profit models. They face specific contradictions in capitalist society. In a communist society, communication and culture take on a common character. Communist means of communication feature common control, common decision-making, and a common culture. Communist communications are truly democratic communications.

Recommended Further Readings about Socialism and Communism

Karl Marx and Friedrich Engels. 1848. The Manifesto of the Communist Party. In *MECW Volume 6*. London: Lawrence & Wishart. pp. 477–519.
In this classical political pamphlet written on the eve of the 1848 uprisings in Europe, Marx and Engels formulate foundations of communist politics.

Friedrich Engels. 1847. Principles of Communism. In *MECW Volume 6*. London: Lawrence & Wishart. pp. 341–357.
This text is written in the format of questions and answers. Using this style, Engels outlines the foundations of communist politics.

Bhaskar Sunkara. 2019. *The Socialist Manifesto: The Case for Radical Politics in An Era of Extreme Inequality*. London: Verso.
Chapter One: A Day in the Life of a Socialist Citizen (pp. 5–31)

In *The Socialist Manifesto*, the editor of *Jacobin* magazine Bhaskar Sunkara argues for a renewal of democratic socialism. In Chapter One, he describes what a socialist society – the first stage of communism "just as it *emerges* from capitalist society"[97] – could look like.

P.M. 1983/2011. *Bolo'Bolo*. Brooklyn, NY: Autonomedia.

Peter Kropotkin. 1892/2012. The Conquest of Bread. In *The Conquest of Bread and Other Writings*, ed. Marshall S. Shatz. Cambridge: Cambridge University Press. pp. 1–199.

The two books *Bolo'Bolo* and *The Conquest of Bread* show that organising a communist society is possible and feasible and outline what such a society could look like.

Murray Bookchin. 1963/1986. Towards a Liberatory Technology. In *Post-Scarcity Anarchism*. Montreal: Black Rose Books. pp. 105–161.

In this essay, Murray Bookchin discusses what role technology can play in a communist society in order to create a good life for all and a post-scarcity society free of toil.

Slavoj Žižek. 2010. How to Begin From the Beginning. In *The Idea of Communism*, ed. Costas Douzinas and Slavoj Žižek. London: Verso. pp. 209–226.

Slavoj Žižek. 2013. No Way Out? Communism in the New Century. In *The Idea of Communism 3*, ed. Slavoj Žižek and Alex Taek-Gwang Lee, London: Verso. Chapter 11.

In these essays, Slavoj Žižek discusses aspects of communist politics, including how the commons can be a foundation of such a politics.

Nick Dyer-Witheford. 2007. Commonism. *Turbulence* 1. http://turbulence.org.uk/turbulence-1/commonism

Jodi Dean. 2012. *The Communist Horizon*. London: Verso. Chapter 4: Common and Commons (pp. 119–156).

In these texts, Nick Dyer-Witheford and Jodi Dean discuss aspects of the commons, including the communicative commons and the digital commons.

Michael Hardt. 2010. The Common in Communism. In *The Idea of Communism*, ed. Costas Douzinas and Slavoj Žižek. London: Verso. pp. 131–144.
Antonio Negri. 2010. Communism: Some Thoughts on the Concept of Practice. In *The Idea of Communism*, ed. Costas Douzinas and Slavoj Žižek. London: Verso. pp. 155–165.
These two texts discuss the foundations of autonomist communist politics in the 21st century and the role of the common in communism.

Adalbert Fogarasi. 1921/1983. The Tasks of the Communist Press. In *Communication and Class Struggle 2: Liberation, Socialism*, ed. Armand Mattelart and Seth Siegelaub. New York: IMMRC. pp. 149–153.
In this text, Fogarasi discusses differences between the capitalist press and the communist press.

Raymond Williams. 1976. *Communications*. Harmondsworth: Penguin.
In this short book, Williams gives an introduction to the analysis of the means of communication. He introduces four forms of communications: authoritarian, paternal, commercial, and democratic communications.

Notes

1 Parts of this chapter were first published in: Christian Fuchs. 2020. Communicative Socialism/Digital Socialism. *tripleC: Communication, Capitalism & Critique* 18 (1). www.triple-c.at. Reproduced with permission of the journal *tripleC*.
2 Translation from German: "Wir sahen schon oben, dass der erste Schritt in der Arbeiterrevolution die Erhebung des Proletariats zur herrschenden Klasse, die Erkämpfung der Demokratie ist"; Karl Marx and Friedrich Engels. 1848. Manifest der Kommunistischen Partei. In *MEW Band* 4, 459–493. p. 481.
3 Compare: C. L. R. James. 1986. *State Capitalism & World Revolution*. Chicago, IL: Charles H. Kerr. Fourth edition. Herbert Marcuse. 1958. *Soviet Marxism: A Critical Analysis*. New York: Columbia University Press.
4 Vladimir I. Lenin. 1917. The State and Revolution. The Marxist Theory of the State and the Tasks of the Proletariat in the

Revolution. In *Lenin Collected Works Volume* 25, 385–497. Moscow: Progress. p. 472.

5 See: Karl Marx. 1875. Critique of the Gotha Programme. In *MECW Volume* 24, 75–99. London: Lawrence & Wishart.

6 Karl Marx and Friedrich Engels. 1848. The Manifesto of the Communist Party. In *MECW Volume* 6, 477–519. London: Lawrence & Wishart.

7 Rosa Luxemburg. 1925. Introduction to Political Economy. In *The Complete Works of Rosa Luxemburg. Volume I: Economic Writings* 1, ed. Peter Hudis, 89–300. London: Verso. pp. 141–144.

8 Ibid., p. 142.

9 See: Rosa Luxemburg. 2008. *The Essential Rosa Luxemburg*. Chicago, IL: Haymarket Books.

10 Bhaskar Sunkara. 2019. *The Socialist Manifesto: The Case for Radical Politics in An Era of Extreme Inequality*. London: Verso. pp. 215–237.

11 Ibid., p. 221.

12 Ibid., p. 236.

13 Michael Hardt and Antonio Negri. 2017. *Assembly*. Oxford: Oxford University Press.

14 Ibid., p. xix.

15 Ibid., p. 278.

16 Ibid., p. 294.

17 Karl Marx and Friedrich Engels. 1848. The Manifesto of the Communist Party, pp. 498, 499.

18 Karl Marx. 1844. Economic and Philosophic Manuscripts of 1844. In *MECW Volume* 3, 229–346. London: Lawrence & Wishart. p. 341

19 Karl Marx. 1894. *Capital Volume* 3. London: Penguin. pp. 958–959

20 Friedrich Engels. 1847. Draft of a Communist Confession of Faith. In *MECW Volume* 6, 96–103. London: Lawrence & Wishart. p. 96.

21 Karl Marx and Friedrich Engels. 1845/1846. The German Ideology. Critique of Modern German Philosophy According to Its Representatives Feuerbach, B. Bauer and Stirner, and of German Socialism According to Its Various Prophets. In *MECW Volume* 5, 15–539. London: Lawrence & Wishart. p. 47.

22 Friedrich Engels. 1845. Speeches in Elberfeld. In *MECW Volume* 4, 243–255 London: Lawrence & Wishart. p. 96.

23 Friedrich Engels. 1847. Principles of Communism. In *MECW Volume* 6, 341–357. London: Lawrence & Wishart. p. 348.

24 Karl Marx. 1867. *Capital Volume* 1. London: Penguin. pp. 172–173.

25 Karl Marx. 1875. Critique of the Gotha Programme. In *MECW Volume* 24, 75–99. London: Lawrence & Wishart. p. 85.

26 Marx, Economic and Philosophic Manuscripts of 1844, p. 295
27 Marx, Critique of the Gotha Programme, p. 86.
28 Karl Marx. 1885. *Capital Volume 2*. London: Penguin. p. 390.
29 Marx, Critique of the Gotha Programme, p. 87.
30 Marx, Economic and Philosophic Manuscripts of 1844, p. 296.
31 Marx and Engels, The Manifesto of the Communist Party, p. 506.
32 Engels, Principles of Communism, p. 350.
33 Friedrich Engels. 1845. The Festival of Nations in London (To Celebrate the Establishment of the French Republic, 22 September 1792). In *MECW Volume 6*, 3–14. London: Lawrence & Wishart. p. 5.
34 Engels. Principles of Communism, p. 351.
35 Marx and Engels, The Manifesto of the Communist Party, p. 505.
36 Marx, Economic and Philosophic Manuscripts of 1844, p. 313.
37 Engels, Principles of Communism, p. 354.
38 Marx and Engels, The Manifesto of the Communist Party, pp. 503–504.
39 Engels, Draft of a Communist Confession of Faith, p. 103.
40 See: Costas Douzinas and Slavoj Žižek, eds. 2010. *The Idea of Communism*. London: Verso. Slavoj Žižek, ed. 2013. *The Idea of Communism 2*. London: Verso. Slavoj Žižek and Alex Taek-Gwang Lee, eds. 2016. *The Idea of Communism 3*. London: Verso. Tariq Ali. 2009. *The Idea of Communism*. Alain Badiou. 2015. *The Communist Hypothesis*. London: Seagull Books. Jodi Dean. 2012. *The Communist Horizon*. London: Verso. Michael Hardt and Antonio Negri. 2009. *Commonwealth*. Cambridge, MA: Harvard University Press.
41 Slavoj Žižek. 2010. How to Begin From the Beginning. In *The Idea of Communism*, pp. 212–213.
42 Michael Hardt and Antonio Negri. 2017. *Assembly*. Oxford: Oxford University Press. p. 166.
43 Ibid., p. 166.
44 Ibid., pp. 166–171.
45 Paolo Virno. 2004. *Grammar of the Multitude*. Los Angeles, CA: Semiotext(e). pp. 110–111. Christian Marazzi. 2010. *Il comunismo del capitale*. Ombre Corte. Michel Bauwens and Vasilis Kostakis. 2014. From the Communism of Capital to Capital for the Commons: Towards Open Co-Operativism. *tripleC: Communication, Capitalism & Critique* 12 (1): 356–361. Armin Beverungen, Anna-Maria Murtola and Gregory Schwartz. 2013. The Communism of Capital? *Ephemera* 13 (3): 483–495. Nick Dyer-Witheford. 2014. The Global Worker and the Digital Front. In *Critique, Social Media and the Information Society*, ed.

Christian Fuchs and Marisol Sandoval, 165–178. New York: Routledge. Arwid Lund. 2017. *Wikipedia, Work and Capitalism. A Realm of Freedom?* Cham: Palgrave Macmillan. pp. 76–81, 298–328.

46 Marx and Engels, The Manifesto of the Communist Party, p. 499.

47 Engels, Principles of Communism, p. 348.

48 Marx and Engels, The Manifesto of the Communist Party, p. 490.

49 Marx, *Capital Volume 1*, p. 928.

50 Karl Marx. 1857/1858. *Grundrisse: Foundations of the Critique of Political* Economy. London: Penguin. pp. 705–706.

51 Ibid., p. 708.

52 Ibid., p. 711.

53 Roman Rosdolsky. 1977. *The Making of Marx's "Capital"*. London: Pluto Press. pp. 427–428.

54 Aaron Bastani. 2019. *Fully Automated Luxury Communism*. London: Verso.

55 Ibid., p. 37.

56 Ibid., p. 50.

57 Ibid., p. 54.

58 Ibid., p. 192.

59 Ibid., p. 216.

60 Ibid., 185–200.

61 Christian Fuchs. 2019. *Nationalism on the Internet: Critical Theory and Ideology in the Age of Social Media and Fake News.* New York: Routledge.

62 Peter Kropotkin. 1892/2012. The Conquest of Bread. In *The Conquest of Bread and Other Writings*, ed. Marshall S. Shatz, 1–199. Cambridge: Cambridge University Press. p. 106.

63 Ibid., p. 88.

64 Murray Bookchin. 1986. *Post-Scarcity Anarchism*. Montreal: Black Rose Books. p. 12.

65 Ibid., p. 12.

66 Ibid., p. 46.

67 Graham Murdock. 2011. Political Economies as Moral Economies: Commodities, Gifts, and Public Goods. In *The Handbook of Political Economy of Communications*, ed. Janet Wasko, Graham Murdock, and Helena Sousa, 13–40. Malden, MA: Wiley-Blackwell. p. 18.

68 Slavko Splichal. 2007. Does History Matter? Grasping the Idea of Public Service at its Roots. n *From Public Service Broadcasting to Public Service Media. RIPE@2007*, ed. Gregory Ferrell Lowe and Jo Bardoel, 237–256. Gothenburg: Nordicom. p. 255.

69 Ellie Rennie. 2006. *Community Media: A Global Introduction*. Lanham, MD: Rowman & Littlefield. p. 3

70 Karl Marx. 1842. Proceedings of the Sixth Rhine Province Assembly. First Article. Debates on Freedom of the Press and Publication of the Proceedings of the Assembly of the Estates. In *MECW Volume 1*, 132–181. London: Lawrence & Wishart. p. 175.
71 Marx and Engels, The Manifesto of the Communist Party, p. 505.
72 Vladimir I. Lenin. 1917. On the Revolutionary Press Tribunal. In *Lenin About the Press*, 206–207. London: Journeyman Press. p. 206.
73 Rosa Luxemburg. 1918. The Russian Revolution. In *The Russian Revolution and Leninism or Marxism?*, 25–80. Ann Arbor, MI: The University of Michigan Press. p. 69.
74 Ibid., p. 48.
75 Ibid., p. 66.
76 Ibid., p. 67.
77 Raymond Williams. 1976. *Communications*. Harmondsworth: Penguin. pp. 130–137.
78 Ibid., p. 131.
79 Ibid., 131.
80 Ibid., p. 133.
81 Ibid., p. 134.
82 See also: Raymond Williams. 1983. *Towards 2000*. London: Chatto & Windus. pp. 65–72.
83 Ibid., p. 123.
84 Raymond Williams. 1979. *Politics and Letters: Interviews with New Left Review*. London: Verso. 370.
85 Williams, *Communications*, p. 134.
86 Raymond Williams. 1958/1983. *Culture & Society: 1780–1950*. New York: Columbia University Press. p. 283.
87 Adalbert Fogarasi. 1921/1983. The Tasks of the Communist Press. In *Communication and Class Struggle 2: Liberation, Socialism*, ed. Armand Mattelart and Seth Siegelaub, 149–153. New York: IMMRC. p. 149.
88 Ibid., 149.
89 Ibid., 150.
90 Georg Lukács. 1971. *History and Class Consciousness*. London: Merlin.
91 Ibid., 150.
92 Ibid., 151–153.
93 Walter Benjamin. 1934. The Author as Producer. In *Walter Benjamin: Selected Writings Volume 2, Part 2, 1931–1934*, 768–782. Cambridge, MA: Belknap Press. p. 777.
94 Bertolt Brecht. 1932. The Radio as a Communications Apparatus. In *Bertolt Brecht on Film & Radio*, ed. Marc Silberman, 41–46. London: Bloomsbury. p. 42

95 Edward S. Herman and Noam Chomsky. 1988. *Manufacturing Consent: The Political Economy of the Mass Media*. London: Vintage.
96 For discussions of the relevance of this propaganda model today, see the contributions in: Joan Pedro-Carañana, Daniel Broudy and Jeffery Klaehn, eds. 2018. *The Propaganda Model Today: Filtering Perception and Awareness*. London: University of Westminster Press.
97 Marx, Critique of the Gotha Programme, p. 85.

11

CLASS STRUGGLES

11.1 INTRODUCTION

This chapter builds on Chapters 5 and 6 of this book, which focus on outlining the class structure of capitalist society. It asks: What are working-class struggles? What is the role of communication in class struggles? What do working-class struggles look like in the age of digital capitalism?

Section 11.2 describes how Marx conceived of class struggles. Section 11.3 deals with the question of what protest movements are and in what relation the working class and communism stand to other protest movements. Section 11.4 looks at class struggles in the age of digital capitalism.

11.2 CLASS STRUGGLES

Marx and Engels on Class Struggles

For Marx and Engels, communism is not only a societal formation, but also the movement that leads from capitalism to communism:

> Communism is for us not a *state of affairs* which is to be established, an *ideal* to which reality [will] have to adjust itself. We call communism the *real* movement which abolishes the present state of things. The conditions of this movement result from the premises now in existence.[1]

The communist movement includes on the one hand objective factors such as the productive forces and crises, and on the other hand, as a key aspect, the subjective factor, namely class struggles against capital's power. The difference in the way Marx uses the terms communism and socialism is that he considers communism as one type of socialist movement, whereas socialism is a broad umbrella movement that, besides communism, also contains movements that Marx does not see as revolutionary or considers as idealist.[2] Communism is a type of socialist movement that aims at the radical transformation of capitalism and class society.

Working-class struggles and radical transformations of capitalism do not occur automatically as the result of crises or inequalities, but only come about when masses of workers see the need for transformations and organise collectively. Working-class struggles require the emergence of:

> communist consciousness, which may, of course, arise among the other classes too through the contemplation of the situation of this class. [...] Both for the production on a mass scale of this communist consciousness, and for the success of the cause itself, the alteration of men on a mass scale is, necessary, an alteration which can only take place in a practical movement.[3]

Only the oppressed groups' collective human action – praxis – can abolish a class society. Class and power structures and economic, political, or ideological crises merely condition, but do not determine, the possibilities for struggles. Marx and Engels say that "the history of all hitherto existing society is the history of class struggles", but stress at the same time that class struggles and their success are not an automatism of history. Revolutionary struggles end "either in a revolutionary reconstitution of society at large, or in the common ruin of the contending classes".[4] Marx says that humans "make their own history, but they do not make it just as they please; they do not make it under circumstances chosen by themselves, but under circumstances directly encountered, given and transmitted from the past".[5] He stresses the role of praxis as class struggle: the self-organisation of the working class for humanising society. But given that class struggle depends on societal circumstances, its emergence, and that results are always uncertain.

Repression and Ideology

Two factors that play a role in the formation of class struggles are repression and left-wing organisations. State repression (e.g. censorship, surveillance, prison sentences, lack of freedom of speech and assembly, etc), repression by economic forces that leave humans no time to think critically, and ideological repression can dampen, undermine, weaken, prevent, or destroy class struggles. If left-wing organisations are able to have a large presence in the public sphere, then this can have a positive influence on the development of class struggles. Structures (such as capital, the market, the state, and ideologies, etc.) condition human practices through which structures are produced and reproduced. Situations of crises open up historical opportunities for fundamental social change that are, however, not determined, but dependent on the question of whether the oppressed class's critical collective consciousness arises and can be politically organised, mobilised in class struggles, and prevail against countervailing forces (such as ideological and state violence). A historically novel type of society arises out of crises in which revolutionary praxis succeeds against conservative forces.

Georg Lukács argues in *History and Class Consciousness* that the ideological reification of the working class's consciousness is a factor that supports the conservation of capitalism: "The danger to which the proletariat has been exposed since its appearance on the historical stage was that it might remain imprisoned in its immediacy together with the bourgeoisie".[6] The proletariat can fail "to take this step" of becoming "the identical subject-object of history whose praxis will change reality".[7] Capitalism constitutes at the same time the potential for the "quantitative increase of the forms of reification" and the "undermining of the forms of reification".[8] Revolutionary consciousness is not automatism; the proletariat "can be transformed and liberated only by its own actions".[9] "History is at its least automatic when it is the consciousness of the proletariat that is at issue".[10] "Above all the worker can only become conscious of his existence in society when he becomes aware of himself as a commodity".[11] Ideologies that can divert workers' attentions from the real causes of social problems and can thereby forestall or prevent the formation of critical class consciousness and working-class protest include racism/xenophobia, nationalism, neoliberal entrepreneurialism, individualism, fascism, consumerism, etc.

The Development of Class Struggles

A structural crisis of capitalism opens up a space of possibilities in which the future is relatively undetermined and is shaped by the question of whether the oppressed classes can organise themselves in a revolutionary manner, or remain rather passive, or follow bourgeois or fascist ideology. Lenin pinpoints this matter by writing that it:

> is only when the '*lower classes*' *do not want* to live in the old way and the 'upper classes' *cannot carry on in the old way* that the revolution can triumph. This truth can be expressed in other words: revolution is impossible without a nation-wide crisis (affecting both the exploited and the exploiters).[12]

Structural crises condition political practices: There will inevitably be some response to the crisis, but whether or not it will have an emancipatory character, i.e. whether or not critical consciousness and social struggles from below will arise, is not determined. Crisis *has to force the need for change* onto the political agenda (one "cannot carry on in the old way") and in this situation, the oppressed have to *want* fundamental change as a precondition for emancipatory practice (praxis). Lukács pinpoints this fact by arguing that a crisis opens up possibilities for both revolution and reaction:

> The deeper the crisis, the better the prospects for the revolution. But also, the deeper the crisis, the more strata of society it involves, the more varied are the instinctive movements which criss-cross in it, and the more confused and changeable will be the relationship of forces between the two classes upon whose struggle the whole outcome ultimately depends: the bourgeoisie and the proletariat.[13]

Party and Movements

Strong left-wing organisations can positively influence class struggles. Communist movements try to:

> instil into the working class the clearest possible recognition of the hostile antagonism between bourgeoisie and proletariat. [...] In all these movements, they bring to the front, as the leading question in each, the property question, no matter what its degree of development at the time. Finally, they labour everywhere for the union and agreement of the democratic parties of all countries.[14]

Left-wing movements/parties should avoid two severe pitfalls: On the one hand, anti-democratic, authoritarian leadership as in Stalinist parties, are one of the seeds and roots of the authoritarian and anti-democratic organisation of society after a radical transformation. On the other hand, horizontal grassroots movements without delegation often face a tyranny of structurelessness[15] that limits the collective capacity to action, consumes everyone's energy, and installs new hierarchies where those with the best endurance, loudest voice, most time, etc. become quasi-leaders dominating the movement. The best way is a dialectic of party and movement (movement parties), representation and participation (representative participatory democracy), organisation and spontaneity (organised spontaneity), reform and revolution (radical reformism).

Reform and Revolution

Another important question of left-wing politics is whether it should be reformist or revolutionary. Reformist politics assumes that elections in a liberal democratic system and legal changes are the path towards a socialist society. Revolutionary politics opposes parliamentary politics and argues for extra-parliamentary, collective, mass political action in the form of strikes, demonstrations, campaigns, etc. that should result in the overthrow of capitalism. For Marx and Engels, reformist and radical politics were not two opposed, but two complementary strategies. They argued for radical reformist politics, i.e. the struggle for reforms that weaken the power of capital and create better conditions for class struggles. They saw parliamentary democracy, elections, and state power "as a means of carrying through further measures directly attacking private ownership and securing the means of subsistence of the proletariat".[16] They recommend "that everywhere workers' candidates are put up alongside the bourgeois-democratic candidates".[17] Elections and parliamentary democracy are for Marx and Engels part of the proletariat's "battle cry [...]: The Revolution in Permanence".[18] Marx and Engels describe the dialectical politics of reform and revolution (radial reformism) in the following manner:

> They must carry to the extreme the proposals of the democrats, who in any case will not act in a revolutionary but in a merely reformist manner, and transform them into direct attacks upon private property; thus, for example, if the petty bourgeois propose purchase of the railways and factories, the workers must demand that these railways and factories should be simply confiscated by the state without compensation as being the property of reactionaries. If the democrats propose proportional taxation, the workers must demand progressive taxation; if the democrats themselves put forward a moderately progressive taxation, the workers must insist on a taxation with rates that rise so steeply that big capital will be ruined by it; if the democrats demand the regulation of state debts, the workers must demand state bankruptcy. Thus, the demands of the workers must everywhere be governed by the concessions and measures of the democrats.[19]

In the 1890s, there was a debate in the German Social Democratic Party about reformist and revolutionary politics. Eduard

Bernstein argued in favour of a purely reformist politics and claimed that such a politics would constitute an evolutionary transition towards socialism. Rosa Luxemburg opposed this politics and argued for a radical reformism that combined mass strikes and parliamentary action. She affirmed Marx and Engels's understanding of socialist politics.

> The daily struggle for reforms, for the amelioration of the condition of the workers within the framework of the existing social order, and for democratic institutions, offers to the social democracy the only means of engaging in the proletarian class war and working in the direction of the final goal – the conquest of political power and the suppression of wage labor. Between social reforms and revolution there exists for the social democracy an indissoluble tie. The struggle for reforms is its means; the social revolution, its aim.[20]

11.3 PROTEST MOVEMENTS

What Is a Protest Movement?

Marx and Engels saw the communist movement as a protest movement that aims at the emancipation of the working class and the replacement of class society by communist society. Today, there is a wide range of progressive protest movements, including, for example, the working-class movement, the environmental and green movement, feminism, the LGBTQ+ movement, technology reform movements, the human rights movement, the peace movement, youth movements, civil rights movements, anti-racist movements, anti-fascist movements, movements of movements combining many demands and movements (e.g. the movement for democratic globalisation). And there are reactionary movements, such as racist movements, nationalist movements, neo-Nazis, fascist, and right-wing extremist movements, etc.

What is a protest movement? Donatella della Porta and Mario Diani define social movements as: "(1) informal networks, based (2) on shared beliefs and solidarity, which mobilize about (3) conflictual issues, through (4) the frequent use of various forms of protest"[21]. In another definition, Diani says that social movements are "networks of informal interactions between a plurality of individuals, groups and/or organizations, engaged in political or cultural conflicts, on the basis of shared collective identities".[22]

Dieter Rucht gives the following definition:

> A social movement consists of two kinds of components: (1) networks of groups and organizations prepared to mobilize for protest actions to promote (or resist) social change (which is the ultimate goal of social movements); and (2) individuals who attend protest activities or contribute resources without necessarily being attached to movement groups or organizations.[23]

Based on these definitions, we can identify important aspects of social movements: societal problems; the negation of dominant values, institutions, and structures; dissatisfaction; adversaries; shared collective identities; orientation toward social change; triggers of protest, contagion effects; mobilisation, protest practices and collective action, protests methods, and extra-parliamentary politics.[24] Social movements depend on but cannot be reduced to the public communication and organisation of protest. Social movements exist only as long as they move themselves, i.e. as long as they communicate their goals through political practices to the public. Table 11.1 shows dimensions that allow us to characterise social movements.

In respect to each dimension of a protest movement, there are two opposing modes of organisation and a third, dialectical one that combines the two modes and sublates their exclusiveness. For example, there are forms of protest that take place face-to-face, such as demonstrations, marches, occupations, and sit-ins and others that take place at a distance, such as petitions, boycotts, or online communication. The dialectical unity of both combines forms of face-to-face protest and mediated protest and tries to take make both of them overgrasp into each other. An example is that a demonstration in front of a company headquarter is combined with mass protest e-mails that are sent to the company around the same time and make the same demand.

Communication plays a role in protests as: (a) an internal method for the organisation of the movement and particular

Table 11.1 Dimensions of collective protest actions and protest movements

Protest dimension	*Aspect 1*	*Aspect 2*	*Aspect 3*
Protest goal	Single-issue goals: economic, political, cultural, nature/society, technology	Multi-issue goals, societal transformation	Long-term goals and short-term goals
Scale of the goal	Reform of policy, law, rule, distribution, representation	Fundamental change: new organisations, new institutions, new society	Radical reformism
Scope of action	Local, regional, national, transnational, global protests	Combination of various levels	Scope of action
Protest spaces	Face-to-face relations, social spaces with direct encounter of humans	Mediation: co-ordinated action at a distance in symbolic and virtual spaces with indirect encounters	Face-to-face and mediated
Protest time	Synchronous: everyone acts at the same time	Asynchronous: actions are taken at different times over a certain period	Combination of synchronous and asynchronous protests
Protest duration	Limited time period	Unlimited time period	Multiple actions with different time frameworks, repeated single actions
Relationship of protest actors to the state	State organisations (e.g. elected political parties, chambers, administrative units of the state, public services)	Extra-state groups (e.g. extra-parliamentary opposition, trade unions, protest movements, cultural	Network of state organisation and extra-state groups (e.g. Movement party)

(*Continued*)

Table 11.1 (Cont.)

Protest dimension	*Aspect 1*	*Aspect 2*	*Aspect 3*
		organisations, non-government organisations)	
Protest organisation	Planned	Spontaneous	Organised spontaneity
Protest organisation	Grassroots, participatory	Hierarchical, leadership, representation	Participatory representation
Protest organisation	Informal, unstructured	Formal, structured	Network of different organisations and organisational structures
Place of action	Private	Public	Public and private
Utilised forms of public communication	Face-to-face communication: protest slogans, performance of protest songs, speeches at demonstrations, theatre of the oppressed, political performance art, etc. Theatre, concerts, speeches, public debates, artistic live performances	Mediated: manifestos, pamphlets, posters, recorded audio material, recorded audio-visual content, live broadcast of content, user-generated digital content on the Internet, artworks, written communication, oral communication, visual communication, audio-visual communication	Combination of face-to-face and mediated communication
Organisational communication	Face-to-face	Mediated	Combination

events, and as (b) an external method for communicating in various forms the movement's critique and demands to the public and its adversaries.

Marxism and Social Movements

Marxist theory and socialist praxis situate progressive protest movements in the context of capitalism and class.[25] They argue for a dialectical articulation of struggles. This does not mean one should reduce protest to class issues or argue that only working-class issues are politically relevant. There is a multitude of protest themes and movements. What is characteristic for a Marxist analysis of social movements and socialist politics is that they see non-economic issues as articulated with economic issues. For example, they argue that capitalist industry and consumer culture is an important factor in environmental degradation:

> Capitalist economies are geared first and foremost to the growth of profits, and hence to economic growth at virtually any cost – including the exploitation and the misery of the vast majority of the world's population. This rush to grow generally means rapid absorption of energy and materials and the dumping of more and more wastes into the environment – hence widening environmental degradation.[26]

What makes a movement socialist is not just a dialectical materialist analysis, but also a politics that focuses on the transformations of the class structure and wants to abolish classes. It is, for example, not a socialist demand to close all car factories so that auto-workers lose their jobs in order to cut carbon dioxide emissions. It is also not a socialist demand to campaign for everyone to buy electric cars. Rather, socialists demand that workers in car factories who are threatened by job cuts should be seen as a starting point for the environmental movement's campaigns, as this allows building alliances and links between economic and extra-economic issues, demands, and groups. A socialist strategy is to struggle for workers' self-management of car factories and the introduction of green production strategies to these self-managed companies as a way of making their products distinct. Not all environmental politics is socialist; quite a lot of it constitutes liberal and conservative wings in green parties and movements that form an ecological bourgeoisie. Red-green politics, in contrast, thinks about environmental degradation and exploitation together and wants to unite environmental activists with the working-class movement and political struggles with class struggles. Similar socialist-alliance politics are feasible in respect to other themes.

Struggles over Working Conditions

Capital struggles from above to increase the exploitation of labour by reducing wage costs and lengthening the working day and surplus labour-time. It conducts class struggle from above against the working class in order to increase profits and survive in the capitalist market.

Capital "takes no account of the health and the length of life of the worker, unless society forces it to do so".[27] Capitalists think: "Should that pain [of the working class] trouble us, since it increases our pleasure (profit)?"[28] Marx argues that capital has no interest in reducing the working day voluntarily and that, therefore, only state power can force it to do so by law. The length of the working day is subject to class struggle. "The establishment of a normal working day is the result of centuries of struggle between the capitalist and the worker".[29]

Marx points out that the legal system was used from the 14th to the end of the 17th century to forcefully extend the working day. In Britain, the 1349 and the 1496 Statutes of Labourers regulated the working day in such a way that its length was 14 to 15 hours, including 3 hours for meals[30]. Marx says that the five Labour Laws passed in Britain between 1802 and 1833 were not enforced. Therefore they "remained a dead letter".[31]

Factory workers, "especially since 1838, had made the Ten Hours Bill their economic, as they had made the Charter their political, election cry".[32] The Factory Act of 1847 introduced the 10-hour working day. It was therefore also called the Ten Hours Bill. As a result, capitalists reduced wages on average by 25 percent and petitioned against the law. Many of them argued that they would ignore the new regulations, which, as one of the goals, wanted to abolish the relay system. They did everything possible to keep their machines going for 12 to 15 hours a day without interruption. Many workers, because of the relay system, idle time, and the time it took to go from one factory shop to the next, spent 15 hours per day in the factory. The working class felt that capitalist practices turned the Ten Hours Bill into a fraud; this resulted in protests and an intensification of class struggle.

The 1850 Factory Act constituted a compromise between capitalist and working-class interests. Young people's and women's working days were lengthened from 10 to 10.5 hours from Monday to Friday and shortened to 7.5 hours on Saturday. The labour had to be performed between 6 a.m. and 6 p.m. with at least 1.5 hours for meals, which needed to be taken by all workers at the same time. "By this the relay system was ended once and for all".[33] The 10-hour working day was finally fully established after a long time of working-class struggle.

The International Working Men's Association (IWA, 1864–1876) was the first international association of socialists, communists, and anarchists. The Geneva Congress of the International Working Men's Association in 1866 proposed to formulate a demand for "eight hours work as the legal limit of the working day".[34] Karl Marx was a member of the IWA's council.

In 1919, the International Labour Organization passed the Hours of Work (Industry) Convention, which regulates in Article 2 that:

> working hours of persons employed in any public or private industrial undertaking or in any branch thereof, other than an undertaking in which only members of the same family are employed, shall not exceed eight in the day and forty-eight in the week.[35]

In 1930, the Hours of Work (Commerce and Offices) Convention followed. It says in Article 3 that the "hours of work of persons to whom this Convention applies shall not exceed forty-eight hours in the week and eight hours in the day". An international convention for the introduction of the eight-hour day was thereby introduced. In 2019, 52 countries had ratified the 1919 Convention and 30 the 1930 Convention.

Labour-time has always been a highly antagonistic aspect of capitalism. Capitalism advances automation in order to increase productivity, but thereby creates the problem that people are put out of work, which has negative effects on consumption and therefore on demand. There is a tendency that the costs for maintaining technology increase. Capitalism in the 21st century is being shaped by a contradiction between overtime and precarious labour: On the one hand there are professions, such as software engineering, where people work very long hours, whereas on the other hand there are people who work precariously, hardly find employment, have low incomes, or are unemployed. Labour is asymmetrically distributed. The only real solution is to reduce labour-time from the average standard of 40 hours to 30 hours or fewer with full wage compensation. Capital, however, does not welcome such reforms because paying more workers a living wage for fewer standard hours is less profitable than paying fewer workers who work overtime. A 20–25- or 30-hour workweek for the wage of 40 hours is needed in order to mitigate the antagonism between profit maximisation and labour-time.

11.4 CLASS STRUGGLES IN THE AGE OF DIGITAL CAPITALISM

The history of the working day is a history of class struggle and the fundamental antagonisms of capitalism. Classically, struggles for reduction of the working day and wage increases have been limited to wage-labour. Given the complexity of the societal worker, socialist politics' strategies and demands have to be adapted in order to represent workers' interests. Specifically, the situation of low-paid, unpaid, and precarious workers needs to be taken into account. This includes houseworkers, prosumers, consumer labour, crowd labour, audience labour, and digital labour, etc. Unpaid workers cannot demand a reduction of their working hours because they do not receive a wage. They can only demand a wage for their unremunerated labour.

An example of a movement that dealt with unremunerated labour was the International Wages for Housework Campaign in the 1970s. As part of this campaign, Silvia Federici wrote the "Wages Against Housework" manifesto. A short excerpt:

> We must admit that capital has been very successful in hiding our work. It has created a true masterpiece at the expense of women. By denying housework a wage and transforming it into an act of love, capital has killed many birds with one stone. First of all, it has got a hell of a lot of work almost for free, and it has made sure that women, far from struggling against it, would seek that work as the best thing in life [...] Wages for housework, then, is a revolutionary demand not because by itself it destroys capital, but because it attacks capital and forces it to restructure social relations in terms more favourable to us and consequently *more favourable to the unity of the class.* [...] Wages for housework is only the beginning, but its message is clear: *from now on they have to pay us because as females we do not guarantee anything any longer.* We want to call work what is work so that eventually we might rediscover what is love and create what will be our sexuality which we have never known. And from the viewpoint of work we can ask not one wage but many wages, because we have been forced into many jobs at once. [...] From now on we want money for each moment of it, so that we can refuse some of it and eventually all of it.[36]

The artist Laurel Ptak created the "Wages for Facebook" artwork by substituting the term "housework" in Federici's manifesto with "Facebook", "women" with "users", etc. Let us have a look at how the same passage cited above reads in the "Wages for Facebook" manifesto (see http://wagesforfacebook.com):

> We must admit that capital has been very successful in hiding our work. By denying our Facebook time a wage while profiting directly from the data it generates and transforming it into an act of friendship, capital has killed many birds with one stone. First of all, it has got a hell of a lot of work almost for free, and it has made sure that we, far from struggling against it, would seek that work as the best thing online. [...] Wages for Facebook, then, is a revolutionary demand not because by itself it destroys capital,

> but because it attacks capital and forces it to restructure social relations in terms more favorable to us and consequently more favorable to working class solidarity. [...] Wages for Facebook is only the beginning, but its message is clear: from now on they have to pay us because as users we do not guarantee anything any longer. We want to call work what is work so that eventually we might rediscover what friendship is. [...] And from the viewpoint of work we can ask not one wage but many wages, because we have been forced into many jobs at once – we also work for Google, Twitter, Microsoft, YouTube, and countless others. From now on we want money for each moment of it, so that we can refuse some of it and eventually all of it".[37]

The text makes sense as a political demand in respect to Facebook. Given the clear parallels, it becomes evident that there are connections between houseworkers and Facebook users, namely that they produce commodities without any payment. But just like the demand for wages for housework is just a starting point, "Wages for Facebook" is too. If we were suddenly paid by Facebook for our use of it, our exploitation as digital workers would not stop. Facebook would continue to make profits from our data, violate our privacy, conduct mass surveillance, commodify our activities, endanger democracy by allowing targeted advertising of fake news and fascist content, etc. We require alternatives to Facebook, so ultimately class struggle must include the struggle for building and maintaining non-profit social media that are truly social.

It is not sufficient that single parts of the social working-class struggle separately. In order to be successful, and exert larger pressure on capital, different factions of the working class need to unite around particular struggles and demands, such as the demand for a universal basic income (UBI)[38] financed through capital taxation. UBI is a soci(et)al wage for the soci(et)al working class. It can unite the interests and struggles of houseworkers, the unemployed, precarious workers, and Facebook users, etc. UBI is a demand that can advance the networking of the various factions of the social working class.

Universal Basic Income

Progressive universal basic income is an income that:

1. Is paid to all members of a society.
2. Is unconditional (no needs tested, not based on previous employment, no willingness to work, no prohibition of work).
3. Is paid on an individual level.
4. Secures existence (it is not set below the subsistence level).
5. Includes health insurance.
6. Has the effect of the top-down redistribution of wealth from corporations and the rich to the working class and the poor.

Basic income doesn't substitute, but modernises the welfare state. Providing a public infrastructure – in the areas of education, health, care, child care, transport, energy, habitation – shall remain an important function of the state. But why should there be a UBI? There are many reasons:

- *Right to social security, enablement of self-respect and self-determination:* Basic income is a redistribution mechanism that realises and guarantees the human right to social security according to Article 22 of the Universal Declaration of Human Rights. It enables self-respect. Degrading jobs can be refused based on one's own decision. People without wage-labour no longer have to become applicants in a coercive bureaucratic system (employment office). With basic income, human beings can organise their lives in more flexible ways – self-determined and beyond the requests of corporations.
- *Compensation for the utilisation of external collective resources:* There many resources in society that have not been produced by corporations but that are used by them for free in order to achieve profit. Such external resources are, e.g. natural resources, land, inherited

property, labour forces, reproductive labour, social labour, knowledge, and technological progress. Those who consume these resources for free in order to gain economic profit owe something to society, i.e. all individuals. They should pay back something to society, e.g. in the form of a basic income tax for corporations.

- *Compensation for the effects of automation:* With the help of automation and technification, corporations cut labour costs and gain productivity and profit. They are able to produce more profit and commodities in less time with less labour effort. In contemporary society, rising unemployment rates are a direct consequence of technological rationalisation. A basic income that is financed by company taxation is a compensation for the disadvantages caused to society by the advantages gained by corporations.
- *Increased autonomy of reproductive, precarious and unremunerated workers*: Capital accumulation is not only based on the exploitation of wage-labour, but also on the exploitation of humans who work unpaid or very low-paid jobs in areas such as households, care, emotional intelligence, education, parenting, health, prosumption, and the Internet, etc. Basic income makes reproductive workers more independent.
- *Advancement of self-development:* Economic development is based on the evolvement of personal skills. Basic income gives humans more time for self-development or what could be termed self-work.
- *Securing imperilled jobs:* Basic income guarantees the continued existence of activities with no or low economic productivity that don't yield marketable commodities and can't exist under market conditions. Examples are civil society activities, welfare work, art, and philosophy.
- *Immanent economic advantages:* Basic income strengthens purchasing power. If higher demand is generated, more goods have to be produced, and the need for new work

and economic activities could emerge. Basic income supports individual initiative and responsibility in the economy because more free time can enhance individual awareness.

- *Acknowledgement of the networking of labour and the economy*: In contemporary information societies, all activities are networked and depend on each other. It is not exactly clear and measurable where economic value is generated. Hence, individual performance in value production also can't be measured and expressed in a specific wage rate.
- *Freedom and self-determination for all:* Human life shall be something else than the compulsory selling of labour-power, stress, and the struggle for economic survival. Dull economic compulsion manifests itself today as the compulsion for securing existence by estranged and heteronomous wage-labour.
- *Elimination of poverty and economic risks:* Contemporary society is a high-risk society in which more and more people, regardless of their backgrounds, are confronted with the risks of poverty, social degradation, and precarious living and working conditions. Basic income eliminates these risks.
- *Integrative democracy and the advancement of society's capacity for reflection:* A democratic society needs members who are critical, politically aware, and politically and socially committed. Enough free time is one precondition for such a situation. Basic income can provide a material and temporal foundation for the emergence of new spaces for critical reflection.
- *Advancement of alternative economies:* Basic income uncouples wage-labour and existence. Other forms of existence become possible. Hence new forms of economic self-organisation and co-operative production could emerge if people are willing and able to pursue them.
- *Empowerment of employees:* Basic income enables employees to refuse precarious and low-paid jobs. This will

empower unions and employees in demanding higher wages and better working conditions from employers.

- *Minimum wage:* Basic income can be organised with the help of models that allow the definition of minimum wages.
- *Fair taxation:* For financing basic income, tax reforms are needed. This brings up the question of who shall pay for financing the basic income. In many countries the current tax systems favour corporations and the rich, and so income and wealth inequity has been growing. Many global corporations avoid paying taxes and thereby take advantage of society. The introduction of basic income is an opportunity for tackling this problem.

Trade Unions

What is a trade union? Marx gives an answer:

> The *trade unions* aim at nothing less than to prevent the *reduction of wages* below the level that is traditionally maintained in the various branches of industry. That is to say, they wish to prevent the *price* of labour-power from falling below its *value*.[39]

In a trade union, "workers *combine* in order to achieve *equality* of a sort with the capitalist in their *contract concerning the sale of their labour*".[40] Trade unions are "insurance societies formed by the workers themselves".[41]

Late 20th- and 21st-century capitalism has been shaped by many different forms of atypical labour, including, for example, precarious freelancers in the media/cultural/digital industry and other sectors. They do not earn a lot of money, have high individual risks, and tend to work atypical and at times very long hours in order to survive.

The International Trade Union Confederation (ITUC), a large international federation of trade unions, tries to appeal to workers by arguing they are all stressed: "Part-timer, full-timer, trainee, temp, freelancer, student, white collar, blue collar, T-shirt or turtleneck, it doesn't really matter – anyone who's looking for work or trying to keep their job these days likely has one thing in common – they're stressed".[42] But groups of workers and types of labour, such as houseworkers, consumer labour, slave labour, the unemployed, user labour, etc, are missing from this list.

Traditional trade unions have had problems representing and organising atypical labour such as freelancers. Some unions have no intention of representing freelancers because they see them as capitalists. Given that the world of labour has changed, trade unions and their strategies also need to change if they want to advance the interests of the working class. It is of particular importance that unions as well as left-wing, socialist and communist parties/movements come to grips with and represent precarious labour, houseworkers, the unemployed, consumer labour, audience labour, Facebook/user labour, and digital labour, etc.

Given the convergence of production and consumption, some consumer issues have become issues of workers' rights. Trade unions as well as left-wing, socialist and communist parties/movements should therefore consider consumer issues as worker rights issues and should start converging with consumer protection associations.

Surveillance, privacy violations, and data breaches are the issues most frequently criticised about social media corporations such as Facebook and Google. Think of the scandals, such as Cambridge Analytica and Edward Snowden's revelations, that affected Facebook and other capitalist Internet platforms. "Dataveillance" is also users' most pressing concern about these platform corporations.[43] The reason why these platforms collect so much personal data and are reluctant to delete it is because in the targeted-ad businesses, data is a means of achieving profits. And given that the users of targeted-ad-based platforms such as YouTube, Google, Facebook, and Twitter are digital workers who create these companies' profits, then surveillance, privacy violations, and data breaches are workers' rights issues and issues of exploitation and class. It is mainly privacy advocates and human rights organisations that have criticised dataveillance. It is time to create trade unions and trade union branches for digital labour and urge that unions co-operate with privacy advocates, human rights organisations, and consumer protection associations. In the age of digital capitalism, privacy rights, human rights, and consumer rights are workers' rights issues.

In 1893, Clara Zetkin criticised the low level of women workers' trade union membership in light of the growing levels of women's employment as wage workers:

> In view of the increasing use of female labor and the subsequent results, the labor movement will surely commit suicide if, in its effort to enrol the broad masses of the proletariat, it does not pay the same amount of attention to female workers as it does to male ones.[44]

The situation is different, but comparable, today: If the labour movement and trade unions do not manage to engage with and organise on issues such as digital labour, housework, unremunerated labour, freelancing, crowdsourced labour, platform labour, consumption labour, Internet-user labour, privacy, surveillance, consumer protection, and slave labour, etc. and see these issues as key to labour struggles, then it will be committing suicide. In 2015, 43.2 percent of trade union members in OECD countries were women and 56.8 percent were men.[45] In the OECD countries taken as a totality, trade union density was 16.2 percent among women workers and 17.8 percent among male workers.

The role of women in trade unions has certainly improved since Clara Zetkin's time. Table 11.2 presents data on the average trade union density. In 1960, the average trade union density in the OECD countries was 42.0 percent of employees.[46] In 1979, this share had increased to 49.7 percent. With the rise of neoliberalism, it dropped to 40.5 percent in 1995 and 27.1 percent in 2015. The average of trade union density for all countries in the world for which data is available dropped from 32.1 percent in 2000 to 21.9 percent in 2016.[47]

Unions have lost influence and power, which implies that capital's power in class struggles has been strengthened. Part of the problem that unions face is the rapid changes of capitalist society. If unions as well as left-wing, socialist and communist parties/movements want to stop the trend of their loss of power, they have to take into account the changes of capitalism and reflect these changes in their topics, campaigns, strategies, and membership.

Table 11.2 Average trade union density (data sources: OECD – OECD.Stat; global – ILOSTAT)

	1960	*1965*	*1970*	*1975*	*1979*	*1985*	*1990*	*1995*	*2000*	*2005*	*2010*	*2015*	*2016*
Average trade union density in OECD countries	42.0%	38.7%	45.2%	47.1%	49.7%	44.7%	42.5%	40.5%	33.6%	31.4%	28.2%	27.1%	28.5%
Number of countries for which data was available	20	20	23	25	26	25	29	39	36	39	44	37	29
Average trade union density (countries worldwide)									32.1%	28.8%	24.9%	22.9%	21.9%
Number of countries for which data was available									33	40	70	60	42

Neoliberal individualisation of labour, the digitalisation of labour, the blurring of labour-time and leisure-time, and of the factory and society, have resulted in new challenges for unionisation. Many workers are hard to reach. This is especially the case for those who work alone, such as freelancers. Trade unions should therefore be reaching out to these workers to offer special services, such as the organisation of co-working spaces. Another problem is that workers in such new class relations do not always and do not automatically understand themselves as workers, which is why unions as well as left-wing, socialist and communist parties/movements should run campaigns about the changes labour has been undergoing and the associated inequalities.

Capital is global and organises itself in an international division of labour. Global corporations furthermore make use of the international economy in order to avoid paying taxes. Challenging the power of global capital requires the global networking of the working class and the internationalisation of trade unions and trade union membership.

#OccupySiliconValley

Given the globalisation, digitalisation, and informatisation of labour, and the emergence of prosumption, new strike methods are needed. A strike of knowledge workers needs to look different to a strike by transport workers or manufacturing workers. Strike as the mass refusal of labour needs global and digital levels in order to improve the conditions of the soci(et)al worker.

In September 2018, the Canadian campaign group Adbusters, which influenced the creation of the Occupy Wall Street Movement, organised a one-day digital strike against Silicon Valley corporations Facebook, Amazon, Apple, and Google. The campaign call read as follows:

> "Big Tech competes for one thing: our attention. They exploit our basic human instincts in the pursuit of unprecedented financial and cultural control.
>
> What do we give up when we allow four corporations to define our human existence – our socialization, our storytelling, our sharing?

How deep will they go when so far, we've been complicit in letting them dig?

ENOUGH IS ENOUGH

How do we take on the largest and most corrupt corporate Goliaths to ever exist? In 4 steps:

1 Google No Search Day

The ONLY thing we search is: does Google do evil?

We force the megabot to do some soul-searching. We see if it can tell us, the people, what's really going on behind that insidious techno-curtain.

2 Boycott Bezos

We fill our Amazon shopping carts with giant orders, then abandon them before checkout. We flood their servers with imaginary orders never to be fulfilled. We create an uncanny lull on amazon.com.

3 Fine Facebook

We "Report a Problem" and attach an invoice detailing the personal cost of mental health and mutated memory, the hours of time wasted – billed to CEO Mark Zuckerberg. We demand payback for the billions of ad dollars Facebook has made from us over the years.

We create a day of global reckoning!

Starting now, we subvert Facebook from within by changing our profile photos to #OSV (Occupy Silicon Valley) memes ...

4 Accessorize Apple Stores

We go to Apple stores and cover their glossy windows with subversive stickers, slogans, and symbols.

You can turn September 17th into DO NOTHING DAY

Partake in a one-day embargo against tech altogether. Leave your phone at home. Delete your social media accounts. Fuck Google Maps – ask a stranger for directions.

On September 17th, each one of us, in our own sweet way, will participate in a global takedown of Big Tech! We'll expose Silicon Valley's ugly underbelly, thrust its fascist tendencies into the open for the world to see. [...]

Make the Internet ours again".

The point is that such a campaign is not simply a consumer boycott, but a digital labour strike. It shouldn't just be Adbusters that calls for it, but also trade unions, which should also form digital labour branches in addition to their existing branches.

Uber Drivers: Workers or Self-Employed?

Uber became a publicly traded company in May 2019. In December 2018, there were 3.9 million Uber drivers.[48] Uber is a case that well illustrates the problems associated with digital capitalism and the capitalist sharing economy.

Uber explained the imagined advantages for drivers the following way:

> Make great money: You can drive and make as much as you want. And, the more you drive, the more you could make. Plus, your fares get automatically deposited weekly. Set your own schedule: Only drive when it works for you. There's no office and no boss. That means you'll always start and stop on your time – because with Uber, you're in charge.[49]

In 2016, an employment case was brought against Uber on the question whether or not its drivers must from a legal point of view be considered as having the status of workers. James Farrar, one of the two claimants in the Uber employment case, has a view that differs from Uber:

> [M]any of them [private hire drivers] are prepared to accept less money at Uber to get away from the level of discrimination and exploitation they were receiving from corrupt minicab controllers. [...] [At Uber], they don't have to deal with a human controller, it's been replaced by an algorithm. But the model is just as exploitative, if not more so.[50]

The General, Municipal, Boilermakers (GMB) Union argued that some of its members earned as little as £5 per hour in 2015, although the national minimum wage was £6.70 per hour. The GMB filed a case against Uber to the Central London Employment Tribunal, arguing that Uber drivers are bogus self-employees, who are denied the minimum wage, paid holidays, and sick pay. On October 28, the Tribunal reached a verdict.[51]

A first important legal question is whether Uber is a technology company providing an app or a transport company. If it is part of the tech industry, then one can say that Uber just provides a service to both taxi drivers and customers. The point is, however, that Uber does not make money from selling its app, but from charging a rent on taxi rides. The Employment Tribunal ruled that Uber "runs a transportation business and employs the drivers to that end".[52]

A second issue concerns the question of whether Uber drivers are self-employed or company workers. A key aspect here is that workers are in a subordinate and dependent position to employers and management control can be exercised. The Tribunal's verdict was that drivers who have the Uber app switched on are not self-employed, but Uber workers: "The drivers provide the skilled labour through which the organisation delivers its services and earns its profits".[53]

According to the ruling, Uber exerts control by hiring drivers and through its app controls customers, fares, trips, default routes, ratings, and complaints.[54] Uber drivers do not have the same contractual freedoms that self-employed persons have: Drivers "do not and cannot negotiate with passengers (except to agree a reduction of the fare set by Uber). They are offered and accept trips strictly on Uber's terms".[55]

A third matter is how to define the Uber drivers' working time. The Tribunal found that an Uber driver's working time "starts as soon as he is within his territory, has the App switched on, and is ready and willing to accept trips and ends as soon as one or more of those conditions ceases to apply".[56]

Uber's UK general manager Jo Bertram reacted to the verdict:

> Drivers want the freedom to decide where, when and for how long to drive: being classified as workers could deprive them of the personal flexibility they value. Last month, drivers who used our app in the UK made on average over £16 per hour in fares, after our service fee. Even after deducting costs, this is well above the national living wage.[57]

Bertram does not mention the average amount an Uber driver has to pay for deductibles such as fuel, car maintenance and insurance, and bank loans, etc. Bertram creates the impression that the sharing economy is "immaterial". But the reality is that it contains actual physical resources that need to be paid for.

The Uber employment conflict has several implications. First, it debunks the myth that the sharing economy is fair and grassroots. Rather, it shows that class conflicts also persist in digital capitalism. Second, it will have implications for Uber drivers and make them eligible to receive the national minimum wage, sick pay, and holiday entitlement. Third, the ruling shows that although digital capitalism's companies operate globally, local, national, regional and international legislation is a way of trying to hold them accountable and exert legal pressure on them.

The capitalist sharing economy will remain a sphere of conflicts and struggles. It is time that we started transcending digital capitalism with the help of commons-based social production, cultural co-ops, platform co-ops, and a public service Internet. The future will show whether a different type of sharing will not just be possible, but also become actual reality. Trade unions should see the struggle for an alternative Internet as a working-class struggle and should therefore engage in fighting this struggle together with users and digital workers. Uber appealed the verdict and lost the appeal in the autumn of 2018. It then made a second appeal.

The International Workers Union of Great Britain (IWGB) took on the legal representation of Uber drivers in the employment case and has a branch (United Private Hire Drivers, UPHD) that represents such drivers. "The IWGB specializes in representing sections of the workforce which have traditionally been non-unionised and under-represented".[58] The IWGB has organised strikes by gig-economy workers, including Uber drivers. It combines strikes, public information campaigns, and legal actions in it struggle against Uber. It says:

> Analysis by UPHD shows that Uber drivers currently earn on average £5 per hour and work as much as 30 hours per week before breaking even. The drivers are demanding: Fares be increased to £2 per mile.

> Commissions paid by drivers to Uber be reduced from 25% to 15%. An end to unfair dismissals. Uber to respect the rulings of the Employment Tribunal, The Employment Appeal Tribunal and the Court of Appeal confirming 'worker' status for drivers.[59]

11.5 CONCLUSION

Capitalism is based on the class antagonism between capital and labour. Capital exploits the working class in order to yield profits and accumulate capital. The working class does not own means of production and capital and is therefore structurally forced into class relations. The working class's existence constitutes a capitalist dialectic of poverty and wealth. It is poor because it produces wealth that the capitalist class owns and without which the capitalist class cannot exist, which also constitutes the power of the working class.

Marx's notion of the collective worker helps us to theorise the complex structure of the working class as a class that notonly works in factories and offices, but in social spaces all over society. The social working class includes a multitude of workers, such as blue-collar wage workers, white-collar wage workers, the unemployed, workers and the poor in developing countries, freelancers, farm workers, public service workers, pupils, students, preschoolers, kindergarten children, apprentices, consumer and prosumer labour, digital labour, prison labour, slave labour, migrant workers, and racialised workers.

Class struggles are the practical, conscious expression of the working class's desire to weaken capital's power in order to advance a fair, just, and good society. Marxist theory and socialist praxis situate progressive protest movements in the context of capitalism and class.

Given the changes of the working class and the importance of the social worker, the social factory, digitalisation, globalisation, the rise of prosumption, and freelancers in capitalism, then class struggles, communists, socialists, and trade unions require new concepts, new strategies, and new methods of struggle in the age digital capitalism.

Recommended Further Readings About Class Struggles

Colin Barker, Laurence Cox, John Krinksy and Alf Gunvald Nilsen, eds. 2013. *Marxism and Social Movements*. Leiden: Brill.

The chapters in this book point out the foundations of the Marxist analysis of social movements. I recommend that you have a look at the table of contents and read several of the book's chapters.

Rosa Luxemburg, 1899. Reform or Revolution. In *The Essential Rosa Luxemburg*, ed. Helen Scot. Chicago, IL: Haymarket Books. pp.41–104.

Reform or Revolution is a text that Luxemburg wrote in response to the ideas of Eduard Bernstein in the German Social Democratic Party's debate on how to attain a socialist society. The debate is known as the "Revisionism Debate" because Bernstein suggested to revise Marx's theory. Luxemburg engages with the question of the role of reform and revolution on the path to a socialist society.

Jo Freeman. 1972/1973. The Tyranny of Structurelessness. *Berkeley Journal of Sociology* 17: 151–164.

In this paper, Jo Freeman discusses the problem of the lack of structures in grassroots protest movements and its negative consequences. She also discusses alternative organisation methods.

Christian Fuchs. 2014. *OccupyMedia! The Occupy Movement and Social Media in Crisis Capitalism*. Winchester: Zero Books.

This short book presents a dialectical, Marxist analysis of the role of social media communication in the Occupy movements.

Notes

1 Karl Marx and Friedrich Engels. 1845/46. The German Ideology. Critique of Modern German Philosophy According to Its Representatives Feuerbach, B. Bauer and Stirner, and of German Socialism According to Its Various Prophets, 15-539. In *MECW Volume 5*. London: Lawrence & Wishart. pp. 15–539. p. 49.

2 See: Karl Marx and Friedrich Engels. 1848. The Manifesto of the Communist Party. In *MECW Volume 6*, 477-519. London: Lawrence & Wishart. pp. 507-519.

3 Ibid., pp. 52–53.
4 Marx and Engels, The Manifesto of the Communist Party, p. 482.
5 Karl Marx. 1852. The Eighteenth Brumaire of Louis Bonaparte. In *MECW Volume 1*. London: Lawrence & Wishart. pp. 99–197.
6 Georg Lukács. 1971. *History and Class Consciousness*. London: Merlin. p. 196.
7 Ibid., p. 197.
8 Ibid., p. 208.
9 Ibid., p. 208.
10 Ibid., p. 208.
11 Ibid., p. 168.
12 Vladimir I. Lenin. 1920. "Left-Wing" Communism – An Infantile Disorder. In *Lenin Collected Works, Volume 31*. Moscow: Progress. pp. 17–118.
13 Lukács, *History and Class Consciousness*, p. 29.
14 Marx and Engels, The Manifesto of the Communist Party, p. 519.
15 Jo Freeman. 1972/1973. The Tyranny of Structurelessness. *Berkeley Journal of Sociology* 17: 151–164.
16 Friedrich Engels. 1847. Principles of Communism. In *MECW Volume 6*, 341-357. London: Lawrence & Wishart. p. 350.
17 Karl Marx and Friedrich Engels. 1850. Address of the Central Authority to the League. In *MECW Volume 10*. London: Lawrence & Wishart. pp. 277–287.
18 Ibid., p. 287.
19 Ibid., p. 286.
20 Rosa Luxemburg, 1899. Reform or Revolution. In *The Essential Rosa Luxemburg*, ed. Helen Scot. Chicago, IL: Haymarket Books. pp. 41–104.
21 Donatella della Porta and Mario Diani. 1999. *Social Movements. An Introduction*. Malden, MA: Blackwell. p. 16.
22 Mario Diani. 1992. The Concept of Social Movement. *The Sociological Review* 40 (1): 1–25. p. 13.
23 Dieter Rucht. 1996. The Impact of National Contexts on Social Movement Structures. In *Perspectives on Social Movements*, ed. Doug McAdam, John McCarth and Mayer N. Zald. Cambridge: Cambridge University Press. pp. 185–204.
24 Christian Fuchs. 2006. The Self-Organization of Social Movements. *Systemic Practice and Action Research* 19 (1): 101–137.
25 See the contributions in: Colin Barker, Laurence Cox, John Krinksy and Alf Gunvald Nilsen, eds. 2013. *Marxism and Social Movements*. Leiden: Brill.
26 John Bellamy Foster. 2002. *Ecology Against Capitalism*. New York: Monthly Review Press. p. 10.

27 Marx, *Capital Volume One*. London: Penguin. p. 381.
28 Ibid., p.381
29 Ibid., p. 382.
30 Ibid., p. 383.
31 Ibid., p. 390.
32 Ibid., p. 393.
33 Ibid., p. 405.
34 International Working Men's Association. 1868. *Resolutions of the Congress of Geneva, 1866, and the Congress of Brussels, 1868*. London: Westminster Printing Company. P. 5.
35 International Labour Organization (ILO). 1919. Hours of Work (Industry) Convention 1919. www.ilo.org/dyn/normlex/en/f?p=NORMLEXPUB:12100:0::NO::P12100_ILO_CODE:C001 (accessed on 2 October 2019)
36 Silvia Federici. 1975. *Wages Against Housework*. Bristol: Falling Wall Press. p. 3, 5, 6
37 Laurel Ptak, Wages for Facebook, http://wagesforfacebook.com/
38 See: Philippe van Parijs and Yannick Vanderborght. 2017. *Basic Income: A Radical Proposal for a Free Society and a Sane Economy*. Cambridge, MA: Harvard University Press.
39 Karl Marx. *Capital Volume One*, p. 1069.
40 Ibid., p. 1070.
41 Ibid., p. 1070.
42 International Trade Union Confederation (ITUC). 2010. *On the Job for a Better Future: A Best Practice on Organising Young People*. Brussels: ITUC. p. 3.
43 See: Thomas Allmer, Christian Fuchs, Verena Kreilinger and Sebastian Sevignani. 2014. Social Networking Sites in the Surveillance Society: Critical Perspectives and Empirical Findings. In *Media, Surveillance and Identity. Social Perspectives*, ed. André Jansson and Miyase Christensen and André Jansson. New York: Peter Lang. pp. 49–70. Christian Fuchs. 2010. Social Networking Sites and Complex Technology Assessment. *International Journal of E-Politics* 1 (3): 19–38.

Christian Fuchs. 2010. studiVZ: Social Networking Sites in the Surveillance Society. *Ethics and Information Technology* 12 (2): 171–185.

44 Clara Zetkin. 1893/2015. Women's Work and the Organization of Trade Unions. In Clara Zetkin: *Selected Writings*, ed. Philip S. Foner. Chicago, IL: Haymarket Books. pp. 50–59.
45 OECD Employment Outlook 2017, data: Trade union membership by gender in 2015. In *OECD iLibrary*, https://dx.doi.org/10.1787/empl_outlook-2017-graph54-en.

46 Data source: OECD.Stat, own calculations based on trade union density data, available on https://stats.oecd.org/. The averages were calculated based on all available country data for specific years.
47 Data source: ILOSTAT, own calculations based on trade union density data, available on www.ilo.org/ilostat. The averages were calculated based on all available country data for specific years.
48 www.uber.com/en-PK/newsroom/company-info
49 www.uber.com/a/join-new/gb
50 War on Wheels: An Uber Driver and a Black-Cab Driver Debate London's Taxi Trade. *The Guardian Online*, 12 February 2016.
51 www.judiciary.uk/wp-content/uploads/2016/10/aslam-and-farrar-v-uber-reasons-20161028.pdf.
52 Ibid., §88.
53 Ibid., §92.
54 Ibid., §91.
55 Ibid., §90.
56 Ibid., §122.
57 Uber to Appeal against Tribunal Defeat. *ITV News Online*, 29 October 2016.
58 https://iwgb.org.uk/page/about/about.
59 https://iwgb.org.uk/post/5cd28b1260b6f/uber-drivers-in-four-uk.

Index